CONVERGENCE OR CONFLICT IN THE TAIWAN STRAIT

Years of rapprochement between Taiwan and China had convinced many that the Taiwan issue had been resolved, and that it was only a matter of time before the two former opponents would unite under One China. But a reenergized civil society, motivated by civic nationalism and a desire to defend Taiwan's liberal-democratic way of life, has dashed such hopes and contributed to the defeat of the China-friendly Kuomintang in the 2016 presidential elections.

This book draws on years of on-the-ground research and reporting to shed light on the consolidation of identity in Taiwan that will make peaceful unification with China a near impossibility. It traces the causes and evolution of Taiwan's new form of nationalism, which exploded in the form of the Sunflower Movement in 2014, and analyses how recent developments in China and Hong Kong under "one country, two systems" have reinforced a desire among the Taiwanese to maintain their distinct identity and the sovereignty of their nation. It also explores the instruments at China's disposal, from soft power to coercion, as well as the limits of its influence, as it attempts to prevent a permanent breakup between the two sides of the Taiwan Strait. Finally, the book argues against abandonment and suggests that international support for Taiwan as it negotiates its complex relationship with China is not only morally right but also conducive to regional and global stability.

Acting as both a sequel and a rebuttal to earlier publications on Taiwan–China relations, this book takes an intimate and anthropological look at Taiwan's youth and civil society, and applies this to traditional analyses of cross-strait politics. It will appeal to students and scholars of Taiwanese politics, Chinese politics, International Relations and Sociology.

J. Michael Cole is Senior non-resident Fellow at the China Policy Institute, University of Nottingham, UK, Associate Researcher at the French Center for Research on Contemporary China in Taipei, Taiwan, and a former analyst with the Canadian Security Intelligence Service.

Routledge Research on Taiwan

Series Editor: Dafydd Fell, SOAS, UK

For a full list of titles in this series, please visit www.routledge.com

The *Routledge Research on Taiwan Series* seeks to publish quality research on all aspects of Taiwan studies. Taking an interdisciplinary approach, the books will cover topics such as politics, economic development, culture, society, anthropology, and history.

This new book series will include the best possible scholarship from the social sciences and the humanities and welcomes submissions from established authors in the field, as well as from younger authors. In addition to research monographs and edited volumes, general works or textbooks with a broader appeal will be considered.

The series is advised by an international editorial board and edited by Dafydd Fell of the Centre of Taiwan Studies at the School of Oriental and African Studies.

CONVERGENCE OR CONFLICT IN THE TAIWAN STRAIT

The illusion of peace?

J. Michael Cole

LONDON AND NEW YORK

First published 2017
by Routledge
2 Park Square, Milton Park, Abingdon, Oxon OX14 4RN

and by Routledge
711 Third Avenue, New York, NY 10017

Routledge is an imprint of the Taylor & Francis Group, an informa business

© 2017 J. Michael Cole

British Library Cataloguing in Publication Data
A catalogue record for this book is available from the British Library

Library of Congress Cataloging-in-Publication Data
Names: Cole, J. Michael, author.
Title: Convergence or conflict in the Taiwan Strait : the
    illusion of peace? / J. Michael Cole.
Description: Abingdon, Oxon ; New York, NY : Routledge, 2017. | Series:
    Routledge research on Taiwan ; 18 | Includes bibliographical references
    and index.
Identifiers: LCCN 2016013419 | ISBN 9781138696235 (hardback) |
    ISBN 9781315524979 (ebook)
Subjects: LCSH: Taiwan—Foreign relations—China. | China—Foreign
    relations—Taiwan. | Taiwan—Politics and government—21st century. |
    Nationalism—Taiwan. | Civil society—Taiwan.
Classification: LCC DS799.63.C6 C65 2017 | DDC 327.51249051—dc23
LC record available at https://lccn.loc.gov/2016013419

ISBN: 978-1-138-69623-5 (hbk)
ISBN: 978-1-138-69624-2 (pbk)
ISBN: 978-1-315-52497-9 (ebk)

Typeset in Bembo
by Apex CoVantage, LLC

For Ketty

CONTENTS

PART 3
Convergence or conflict? 135

PART 4
Why Taiwan matters 183

INTRODUCTION

This book was nearly a decade in the making. Its central argument – that Taiwan is far more resilient than is normally assumed, which has implications for both its survivability as a nation and the risks of conflict in the Taiwan Strait – was arrived at through a long process of discovery that probably would not have been possible had I not enjoyed the kind of access that is the prerogative of journalists. In the decade that I have written about Taiwanese politics, I have observed my subject from different vantage points: its military, party politics, foreign relations, media, and civil society, among others. In other words, rather than focusing on a single aspect and despite first making my mark writing almost exclusively about military affairs, I chose to engage Taiwan from the perspective of a generalist, doing so both as a journalist and, in more recent years, as an academic. I believe this approach allowed me to develop a more complete understanding of my subject and perhaps to see trends and connections that may have been less obvious to single-issue experts.

Ultimately, what mattered most was that I was on the ground and had gone "native" – and here I use the term without its colonial (and pejorative) connotation. An added advantage was that while mixing with local Taiwanese and often identifying with them, I was nevertheless an "outsider," meaning that I was observing people and developments with the freshness of a different perspective, seeing things that, from too close, may be invisible or seem insignificant.

The more exposed I became to various aspects of Taiwan's society, the more convinced I became that the nation was far more coherent and resilient than is normally thought. Consequently, while many observers either were dispirited by China's seemingly unstoppable rise and indications of flagging U.S. strength or proclaimed that Taiwan's days were numbered, I was becoming *more* optimistic about its prospects for survival as a free and distinct society. This does not mean that I was unaware of the extraordinary challenges Taiwan was facing; in fact, the discussion of those challenges accounts for a large part of this book. But while Taiwan's situation remains precarious, it became clear to me that the Taiwanese would not simply give up to the "inevitable" forces of history. My three years intimately studying Taiwan's civil society, culminating in my book *Black Island: Two Years of Activism in Taiwan*, were instrumental in that process.

This book is an attempt to explain Taiwan's resilience. It seeks to debunk the notion, which has traction in some circles, that Taiwan can simply be ceded to China or that it is on the road to inexorable capitulation. My role is that of an informed and involved observer. I do not pretend to know better than the Taiwanese themselves about who they are or what choices are the most "logical" to ensure their future. I do, however, have strong views on the notion that the 23 million people of Taiwan should be able to determine their own future, a right that far too often is denied them due to Chinese pressure and international complicity.

My aim is to shed light on certain aspects of Taiwan's society that may be misunderstood or simply ignored by people abroad, including many of the Taiwan experts who advise their governments on the subject. It is important that the international community gets Taiwan "right," and this requires having the necessary knowledge. Failure to do so now and continuing to hold on to the old paradigms about Taiwan can only mean serious trouble down the road, for which foreign governments will be ill prepared.

The timing of this book's publication is not accidental. With the return of the Democratic Progressive Party (DPP) to power in the 16 January 2016 elections, many observers have cautioned that there is a real risk of renewed tensions in the Taiwan Strait. This book attempts to dispel some of the myths surrounding the DPP and argues that recent developments in Taiwan will force whoever is in power to adopt a more "centrist" and careful approach when engaging China. In other words, even if the Chinese Nationalist Party (KMT) had been reelected in that election, it is unlikely that its candidate would be in a position to offer the kind of concessions that Beijing hopes to receive after eight years of rapprochement under President Ma Ying-jeou (馬英九).

The implication, therefore, isn't so much that a DPP administration under Tsai Ing-wen (蔡英文), one that now also controls the Legislative Yuan, will be the source of tensions in the Taiwan Strait but rather that the consolidation of an idiosyncratic Taiwanese consciousness, which is spearheaded by the public and which by osmosis is transforming political parties, will. This should put to rest any notion that the KMT is inherently "good for peace and stability" and that tensions between Taiwan and China are solely the result of an "irresponsible" and "proindependence" DPP. In reality – and saying so is often seen as politically incorrect, earning one attacks from both sides – the DPP and KMT have a lot more in common than the fiery rhetoric and occasional fistfights in the legislature, not to mention a polarized media environment, would suggest. That thing in common is a desire to maintain the way of life and political system that define this nation, whether one calls it Taiwan or the Republic of China. Sociohistorical trends will only push the two parties closer together while selecting out the outliers who continue to adhere to ideologies of the past.

Ensuring that decision makers abroad understand that process and its impact on relations across the Taiwan Strait will be essential, if only to avoid having bad choices imposed on the Taiwanese by those who wish to see the problem disappear or to ingratiate themselves with Beijing. Much has been said of the "diplomatic truce" that has occurred under President Ma; much, much less has been said, however, about the attendant consolidation of civic nationalism in Taiwan, which will be just as crucial a variable in future relations with Beijing and the international community.

Additionally, Taiwanese would benefit greatly from a better appreciation of the many biases that militate against their nation in the international system, as this could help them better prepare their future strategies.

This book is divided into four sections. Part 1 (Chapters 1–3) discusses the intellectual, economic, and geopolitical forces that have conspired to limit our understanding of contemporary Taiwan and how this lack of knowledge comports high risks for the future. Part 2 (Chapters 4–8) looks at Taiwan's democracy, both in terms of the protection it confers upon Taiwan and the challenges, both domestic and external, that it faces. This section also covers recent developments in Taiwan's civil society, including the Sunflower Movement and its precursor organizations, and how this reemergent activism has stemmed from and in turn fueled new notions of nationalism and identity within Taiwan. Part 3 (Chapters 9–13) turns to the likelihood of a clash between Taiwan and China resulting from their different societies, political systems, and public expectations, which have become starker thanks to recent developments in Taiwanese politics and the hardening line under Chinese President Xi Jinping (習近平). It also shows how developments in Hong Kong since Retrocession in 1997 can serve as an example and warning of a possible future for Taiwan, should it be annexed by China, and how this could exacerbate opposition to unification among Taiwanese. Finally, Part 4 (Chapters 14–16) turns to the future and argues that the maintenance of a free Taiwan will benefit regional stability and the global community, making the case that appeasement of China would only make matters worse for everybody. The section concludes with a series of recommendations on how Taiwan can improve its chances of survival.

PART 1
The convenient illusion

1

ORPHANED AND FORGOTTEN

It is perhaps no accident that the first work of fiction I read about Taiwan after moving there in 2005 was an English translation of Wu Cho-liu's (吳濁流) novel *Orphan of Asia* (亞細亞的孤兒), a work that has often been described as a formative element of "Taiwanese consciousness." Taiwan was an orphan at the time of the novel's completion in 1945 (first published in Japanese as *Ajia no koji*, アジアの孤児) and is no less a one more than half a century later. Despite its extraordinary successes in modernization and democratization, Taiwan remains a little understood and often ignored member of the international community. Given the size of its economy (ranked twenty-first and an important player in the global supply chain) and the risks that its unresolved status could spark major hostilities in the Asia-Pacific, perhaps leading to armed conflict between the U.S. and China, Taiwan arguably punches well below its weight when it comes to making its voice heard. As Chi Pang-yuan (齊邦媛), the editor of the English translation of Wu's novel, wrote in the foreword, "During the second half of the twentieth century, Taiwan developed into a democratic reality, looking forward to international understanding of our efforts." That understanding, sadly, has yet to materialize.

Why is that?

This chapter looks at some of the variables that have contributed to Taiwan's continued isolation within the international community and how this has undermined Taiwan's ability to counter Beijing's sovereignty claims over it. This isolation stems from a handicap, which itself is the result of a number of persistent factors.

While it is easy to blame China for Taiwan's predicament, to which we will turn in later chapters, there are other reasons why Taiwan's political footprint is that of a fly when it should be that of a fox. There is no doubt that Taiwan harnessed the forces of globalization well before China and that, through its small and medium enterprises (SME), it developed economic ties with every corner of the planet. Therefore in economic terms, Taiwan is without doubt fully globalized. Why is it, then, that when it comes to discussing their politics and culture, the Taiwanese have done so poor a job?

Part of the reason could be a legacy of the authoritarian era, which roughly covers the 40 years between 1947 and 1987. During that period, discussing politics – especially subjects such as Taiwanese identity, independence, and human rights – was a sure ticket to prison on Green Island, or worse. As with any authoritarian regime, the KMT under Chiang Kai-shek (蔣介石) and his son, Chiang Ching-kuo (蔣經國), did not have the means to monitor every single citizen, and instead the party calibrated its repression mechanisms so that the people themselves were incentivized to self-censor. The random application of punitive measures, added to pressures to spy on one's neighbors and even family members, created an atmosphere of uncertainty in which silence and avoidance were the safest strategies. The chilling effects were long lasting. Even today, after liberalization and democratization, people from the generation that came of age during the White Terror (they are now parents and grandparents) remain hesitant to speak up and will often seek to discourage their offspring from engaging in political activism. It is much better, in their view, to focus on getting a solid education and securing a lucrative job. In many ways, this remains a national trait among Taiwanese, and breaking from that mold takes a great deal of courage, as many of the youths who took part in the Sunflower Movement in March and April 2014 will attest. This reluctance to engage in discussions about politics, let alone doing so with a foreign audience, has therefore contributed to Taiwan's invisibility, though there have been encouraging signs in recent years that this may be changing.

A companion to that phenomenon is the fact that Taiwan's democratization in the 1980s was not only highly successful but also overwhelmingly peaceful. In some ways, Taiwan may have been a victim of that success. Although democratization without bloodshed and *coups d'état* might be a fascinating subject for political scientists and historians, the lack of drama means that such developments will receive little attention in the media and among publics abroad that suffer from both attention deficit and compassion fatigue. Without drama, it is unlikely that novels and films will be made to keep the story alive and generate future interest, as the Israelis and, to a certain extent, the Chinese have done so well. And for those who know little about Taiwan – a worldwide phenomenon – the lack of violence or rampant human rights violations means that Taiwan simply doesn't register on their radars.

While peaceful democratization is something that every Taiwanese should be proud of, this comes at the cost of being ignored. Taiwan may have been newsworthy when it was under martial law and one of the many fronts in the Cold War, but it has now been democratized, and with that it would seem that its history "ended." For those who pay attention to Taiwan or live there, it is clear that history did not end in the late 1980s or early 1990s and that democracy is never truly consolidated but rather a *process*, a pendulum that can swing in either direction. But such knowledge is far too granular for ordinary people abroad. As a journalist, I often faced the challenge of selling my articles about human rights violations in Taiwan to foreign newspapers. In most instances, my efforts failed, the response from the editors usually something like, "Interesting, but we'll pass. This is too 'insider baseball'" (Cole 2014).

Of course, when compared with rampant abuses in Myanmar, the locking up of activists in China, the kidnapping of booksellers in Hong Kong, or despots who are developing nuclear weapons, Taiwan's situation is hardly dramatic enough for editors who must prioritize due to limited space and budgets. The same applies to military correspondents, who have had much less to write about in Taiwan than their counterparts who have been covering the rapid modernization of the People's Liberation Army (PLA) on the other side of the Taiwan Strait, thanks in part to more than a decade of double-digit growth in Beijing's annual defense budget.

The same problem has existed on the economic side, even if, to some extent, the economy remains one of the few subjects that foreign media continue to focus on in Taiwan. As with politics and military affairs, Taiwan's economy was no longer one of the major stories in Asia. The booming years, when Taiwan was one of the so-called Asian Tigers, were behind it, and the island was overshadowed by the rapidly expanding economies of China, India, and countries across Southeast Asia. The contrast was stark, and the media wanted to be where the action was. The sense that Taiwan had become a laggard, that it was a thing of the past, was perfectly encapsulated by remarks that Martin Jacques, author of the book *When China Rules the World*, made when I interviewed him in Taipei in October 2009. Jacques, who has made little secret of his admiration for China, told me that the taxi ride from Taiwan Taoyuan International Airport to Taipei had saddened him. "It's so quiet," he lamented, contrasting that with the dazzling construction boom across China in the past decade. "There are so few construction cranes." In Jacques' view, this was a sign that Taiwan wasn't "modern." Many people would, of course, disagree with the notion that we can define modernity by the number of cranes that serrate the horizon. I am one of them. Moreover, Jacques' observation of how "quiet" things were in Taiwan, as well as his contrasting that with the energy that has been unleashed in China, was unfair: China today is where Taiwan was 25 years ago. But as economies mature, they cannot sustain such infrastructure development indefinitely, nor can economic growth remain in the double-digit category in perpetuity. Taiwan's economy has plateaued, much like other previously "hot" economies such as Japan. Yet perceptions that Taiwan was being left behind by the red-hot Chinese economy were prevalent in the media, which no doubt contributed to the view that Taiwan was no longer newsworthy.

As we will see in the next chapter, the nearly eight years of the Ma Ying-jeou administration have also compounded the lack of interest by fostering the notion that peace – a convenient peace – had been achieved in the Taiwan Strait. With the risks of war presumably receding into history, foreign media turned elsewhere (and ashamedly for the human race, they had plenty of places to choose from).

This trend also meant that when international media organizations facing budgetary constraints had to cut resources somewhere, they often did so in Taiwan. Bureaus were closed, staffs trimmed, and top journalists moved elsewhere – usually to China, where there was plenty of drama and action, and where opportunities for career advancement and more competitive salaries were available. Democratized Taiwan had become "boring," of interest only to academics who are captivated by esoteric issues like the *quality* of democracy or obscure surveys on identity.

As a result of this media exodus, knowledge about Taiwan suffered, and reporting often was limited to economics, the stock markets, and business issues – except, of course, brief spasms of global attention during elections, when the politics of the island once again became interesting. The few foreign correspondents who did remain in Taiwan often faced a challenge when they pitched articles about domestic politics to their editors abroad; if they were lucky, they were allowed to write a story, but the allotted word count was usually too restrictive to provide the necessary contextualization. Furthermore, the bylines in articles about Taiwan were increasingly located in Beijing, Shanghai, or Hong Kong. However professional they might be, the China-based correspondents are already busy enough covering China and do not have time to focus on Taiwan, which is also hugely complex and demands exploration *in situ*. Consequently, when called upon to write about developments in Taiwan, the China-based correspondents or staff writers often offered only a cursory relating of events and tended to overrely on official – including Chinese – sources. Many of them have shared their frustrations and lament the closing of their bureaus in Taipei, but that is the economic reality. The Taiwan "blind spot" that results from this phenomenon has seriously hampered Taiwan's ability to make itself heard and understood by the international community. The less it strikes people's imagination abroad, the less Taiwan will succeed in establishing the kind of *emotional* connection that can translate into sympathy for the Taiwanese or into pressure on foreign governments to adopt policies that are more attuned to Taiwan's reality.

It remains to be seen whether the election of a DPP president in January 2016, added to shifting perceptions of China due to its belligerence and crackdown on civil liberties since 2012, will encourage global media to pay more attention to or look more favorably upon democratic Taiwan. The unusually high interest caused by the November 2015 summit in Singapore between presidents Ma and Xi and the 16 January 2016 elections provided a good opportunity for international media to learn more about Taiwan. The extensive coverage and the parachuting of several top journalists there also helped create an emotional connection that hitherto had not existed. Most, if not all foreign correspondents who covered the elections left with an overwhelmingly positive view of the island nation and an awareness of the sharp contrasts that exist between the two societies, Beijing's claims notwithstanding.

As the media exodus was taking place, an increasingly global China was busy launching a major "charm offensive" using its increasingly formidable "soft power." This multibillion-dollar effort included substantial investment in its media operations abroad, with Xinhua alone establishing 117 foreign bureaus. It is claimed that, in 2009, China spent 60 billion RMB (US$8.79 billion) to expand the global media operations of the "big four" outlets – Xinhua News Agency, Central China Television (CCTV), China Radio International, and the *China Daily*. In July that year, Xinhua also launched China Network Corporation (CNC World), an online 24/7 English-language news channel broadcasting via satellite, cable, cell phones, the Internet, and outdoors screens. By January 2011, CNC World had coverage in Asia, Europe, Africa, the Middle East, and North America (Shambaugh). While one of CNC's aims is to make money, it is also part of an effort to tell China's story to the world in a way that, given press censorship and guidance from the CCP (Chinese Communist Party), tends to skip controversial issues such as Taiwan, Tibet, or Xinjiang. Other outlets, such as the English-language *China Daily*, have complemented that campaign, often by signing cooperation agreements with foreign newspapers and wire agencies. Although Taiwan's Central News Agency (CNA) has made efforts to revamp its coverage, with services in Japanese and Spanish, and *Focus Taiwan*, its English-language service, there is no way it can compete dollar-for-dollar with China's state-run media campaigns.

Exacerbating this problem is the tendency among many Taiwanese to look inward and to neglect foreign media, a deficiency that applies not only to ordinary Taiwanese but also to political parties and government agencies. Poor communication and foreign language skills, as well as an inability to package issues in a way that can appeal to distracted foreign audiences, are factors that have also contributed to Taiwan's isolation. Until the Sunflower Movement in 2014, social activists often neglected to have English in their press releases or on their banners and placards, and yet they often complained that international media were not paying attention. The same applies to a number of groups that agitate for Taiwanese independence, whose press conferences are usually in Taiwanese *only*. While most foreign correspondents know enough Mandarin to do their job, very few understand Hoklo, the language that is most closely associated with the independence movement in Taiwan.

Another reason why Taiwanese have struggled to make their voices heard is that for the majority of them, their country – whether it is known as Taiwan or the ROC (Republic of China) – is already *somewhat* independent (the "status quo"), and their situation, though it may not be perfect, isn't untenable. In fact, living in Taiwan is a comfortable experience – high summer temperatures, typhoons, and earthquakes notwithstanding. Despite the dispute with China, contemporary Taiwan is a modern, stable, prosperous, and safe state, something that cannot be said of several countries that are officially recognized by the international community. Moreover, while this will be disputed (usually by foreign observers), Taiwanese generally know *who* and *what* they are; their identity as Taiwanese with a Chinese cultural heritage is already settled and holds no fatal contradictions. Most Taiwanese therefore see little use in explaining this to others, which speaks volumes about their consolidated identity. However, this silence doesn't help educate the rest of the world, which sees things otherwise and regards them as Chinese.

Taiwan's small footprint abroad is also reflected in the book industry and specialized journals. Only a small number of books about Taiwan are published every year in languages other than Chinese, much, much less than is written about China or other countries in the region. While the abundance of books written in Chinese about Taiwanese politics and history is something to be celebrated, it doesn't do much when it comes to helping the rest of the world understand and *care* about Taiwan and its future trajectory as a nation. As is often the case, Taiwan is relegated to brief mentions or footnotes in books that are concerned with the study of China. Many books about nationalism or self-determination published in recent years do not make a single mention of Taiwan, not even a footnote. For example, Allen Buchanan's book *Justice, Legitimacy, and Self-Determination: Moral Foundations for International Law*, described by a reviewer as "exceptional . . . in the breadth of its engagement," contains references to almost every modern nationalist movement, from Quebec to Scotland, Kosovo to the Basques, Kurdistan to Eritrea, but Taiwan is not mentioned once (neither are Tibet and Xinjiang, for that matter). Michael Ignatieff's *Blood and Belonging: Journeys into the New Nationalism*, does not contain a single reference to Taiwan. Meanwhile, a scan of the index of *Nationalism and War*, edited by John A. Hall and Siniša Malešević, shows only two entries about Taiwan, both in the chapter "The state-to-nation balance in power," written by Benjamin Miller. Those two passages refer to *Chinese* nationalism (i.e., "demands for ethno-national unification based on the claim that there are 'too many states' in relation to the number of nations") rather than Taiwanese.

One consequence is that a number of academics, government officials, and ordinary citizens overseas have difficulty seeing the Taiwan "issue" for what it really is: not an unfinished civil war or a mere misunderstanding, but *a bona fide clash of two nationalisms in the Taiwan Strait*. As previously stated, we can only hope that the DPP's resounding victory in the 2016 elections and what it says about public sentiment in Taiwan will encourage analysts to revisit their assumptions about Taiwan's status and create incentives to pay closer attention to the idiosyncratic elements of its nationalism.

Most books written about Taiwan are academic in nature and therefore will not reach a general audience, something that again cannot be said of China. And even those are hard to find, not to mention their usually prohibitive retail price. Consequently, bookstores worldwide rarely carry books about Taiwan in their inventories, as I have discovered to my great regret over the years. I remember paying a visit to an impressively stocked Waterstones bookstore near the University of London's School of Oriental and African Studies (SOAS) in London, which did not have a single book about Taiwan but several about much smaller countries and many about China. Unfortunately, that is the norm rather than the exception. Ordinary shoppers who peruse the Asia section at most bookstores worldwide could be forgiven for not knowing of Taiwan's existence; they will find plenty of books about China, Japan, Vietnam, North Korea, India, Myanmar, Thailand, and Cambodia but few, if any at all, about Taiwan.

What is even more extraordinary (and unforgivable) is the fact that bookstores in Taiwan are just as bad. Though the major chains have good selections of books in Chinese, their English sections on Taiwan are anemic, to say the least, with usually fewer selections than one can count on the fingers of one hand. Whether this is the result of market forces or publishers who are not proactive enough to ensure that their books are stocked in Taiwan is anyone's guess. Surely if there was one place on the planet where one *should* be able to find books about Taiwan, it is in Taiwan.

The lack of basic knowledge about Taiwan (or the acceptance of unverified "truths") also often creeps into semiacademic literature. To give just one example, in an otherwise fine history of China during the War of Resistance against Japan, journalist Richard Bernstein errs when he writes that Taiwan "had belonged to China for centuries," when in reality, as S.C.M. Paine, an associate professor of strategy and policy at the U.S. Naval War College, indicates in her excellent study of the First Sino-Japanese War, prior to the seizing of Taiwan by Japan in 1895, Taiwan "had been a peripheral part of the Chinese empire; it had not become a province until 1885 and remained one for a mere decade before being ceded to Japan." Whether the result of laziness or a misreading of history, such errors contribute to the portrayal of Taiwan as always having been part of China, which has huge implications in terms of the legality of Beijing's claims as well as the consolidation of a distinct Taiwanese identity, not to mention that it perpetuates a false image among the public at large. (Since I maintain that Taiwan currently enjoys status as a state under customary law, I must make accommodations for the same principle applying to Taiwan as a peripheral subject yet still within the boundaries of a historical Chinese empire. That said, what matters is the fact that the majority of Taiwanese *do not* consider themselves to be Chinese, and, a small minority excepted, those who do still do not want to become citizens of the People's Republic of China.)

Another factor that has deprioritized Taiwan as a subject of study is the perception, often encouraged by Chinese propaganda, that its status is either a vestige of unresolved Cold War issues or that Taiwan is merely a spoke in some American neo-imperialist experiment rather than a legitimate issue of self-determination. Anti-American sentiment therefore undermines Taiwan's legitimacy in the eyes of many, especially since the U.S. is the island's sole security guarantor and source of modern weapons under provisions stipulated in the Taiwan Relations Act (TRA) of 1979, implemented in the wake of Washington's decision to cut ties with Taipei and to implement official diplomatic relations with the PRC (People's Republic of China).

The intellectual isolation of Taiwan also applies to university courses and academic conferences, where, rather than being a subject in and of itself, Taiwan is often subsumed into "China studies." There are very few courses on U.S.–Taiwan relations; professors who want to discuss the matter often do so in the context of U.S.–*China* relations, out of their own initiative, and at their own risk.

In academia, Taiwan's visibility is also undermined by institutional self-censorship, which often stems from economics: the financial support by the Chinese government or Chinese corporations for research centers and universities abroad. Consequently, pressure exists on China-funded institutes to avoid "controversial" topics such as Xinjiang, Tibet, or Taiwan in the classroom or peer-reviewed academic journals, which can usually count on at least one anonymous reviewer to "kill" a paper for touching on such controversies. Given that a professor's ability to obtain tenure is contingent on having published a number of peer-reviewed articles in academic journals, the pressure to avoid subjects that risk delaying such prospects can be formidable, especially in the hugely competitive environment that academia has become.

As we saw, university programs that focus specifically on Taiwan are hard to find; even when those exist, some topics are considered off-limits because, should they be discussed, they risk compromising future financial support. For example, talks and articles that address issues such as Taiwanese independence or that argue for the existence of "one China, one Taiwan" or "two Chinas" are discouraged or avoided altogether. As a result, the little presence that Taiwan as a subject of study has on university campuses is often limited to being a component of "greater China," with the implicit understanding that Taiwan does not exist as a sovereign entity and therefore is logically ripe for "reunification." In a growing number of cases, decisions to avoid touching on "controversial" subjects can also stem from Western academic institutions' having remote centers or exchange programs with universities in China and the fear that crossing certain lines could compromise such programs, especially amid signs of a hardening ideological line under President Xi. This is understandable: China has demonstrated it can be retributive and that it has no compunction in punishing its counterparts if the latter touch on core issues as determined by the Chinese government. That is the economic reality and undeniably a handicap for Taiwan.

Self-censorship also occurs online, such as in specialized forums where media professionals, government officials, and academics discuss topics related to China. Members will often choose not to discuss Taiwan publicly or to take a "controversial" (meaning favorable) position regarding it. It is often safer to write "offline," a reluctance to make one's views known by all that may stem from the belief that activities on Web-based platforms are under surveillance by Chinese authorities, which then have the power to deny them the access they need to conduct future research in China.

Also on campus, bullying by nationalistic Chinese has often intimidated Taiwanese students who, rather than seek confrontation, will yield to the pressure and go silent. One result is that Taiwanese student associations are often taken over by the much more vocal (and increasingly large) Chinese student associations. In some instances, Taiwanese students who refused to comply with the demands of their Chinese counterparts (e.g., not showing the ROC flag or not having a "Taiwan" table at campus events) have been threatened. In a few cases, the Chinese students filed a complaint with their university or threatened its staff.

Diaspora Chinese organizations have also taken action worldwide, holding events to oppose Taiwanese independence and the DPP. Historically closely aligned with the KMT, those organizations have gotten closer to the CCP in recent years. Wealthy local tycoons have been instrumental in encouraging that shift.

By narrowing the scope of what is permissible in discussing Taiwan for fear of angering Beijing or the many institutions under its influence, it can be argued that Western universities and think tanks have been complicit in Beijing's efforts to limit the discourse on Taiwan. As a result, the kind of granular knowledge that is necessary to understand where cross-strait relations are heading has been largely absent in academic circles because the necessary information was either ignored or suppressed. It's a little like trying to find one's way around a major capital using a map that shows only a few of its many winding roads, with the roads selected by the editors all leading to a predetermined destination.

While Chinese propagandists, political warfare officers, and United Front workers use every occasion that is given them to saturate their audience with the notion that there is only one China and that Taiwan is an inalienable part of one China, another component of their strategy – one that is just as, if not more effective – is to use China's financial weight to encourage the rest of the world to ignore Taiwan's existence. If nobody knows about Taiwan, then how could there be a problem worthy of our attention? As such, in recent years Taiwan has been mentioned less and less in annual reports and books about China's rise and its impact on regional security. A case in point is the regular omission of Taiwan as one of the claimants in the sovereignty disputes in the East and South China Seas. In June 2012, I attended a two-day conference on the South China Sea dispute at a major think tank in Washington, D.C. Although all the major claimants were represented by speakers (along with some nonclaimants), Taiwan wasn't included; its presence was limited to three staffers from the Taipei Economic and Cultural Representative Office (TECRO), who sat quietly in the back, taking notes, and this author, who during the entire conference was the only one to raise the matter of Taiwan's claims. One of the speakers was from Taiwan, but Fu Kuen-cheng (傅崑成), a former People First Party (PFP) legislator who now teaches at Shanghai Jiaotong University, was there to make *China's* case. In other settings, academics from Taiwan have been invited to speak at conferences on the territorial disputes, but they either had affiliations with Chinese think tanks (the Hainan-based National Institute for South China Sea Studies [中國南海研究院], for example) or argued for Taiwan and China to cooperate in defending their "shared interests," a position that played into Beijing's propaganda efforts by depicting Taiwan and China as two sides of the same coin, though with one side weighing more than the other.

Another problem is the rapidly rising funding of think tanks and centers abroad by the Chinese government, firms, foundations, and private donors, which has been a factor in how they choose to engage (or ignore) the subject of Taiwan. We should also note that China has often very successfully funded and influenced foreign think tanks with the recipients not fully knowing who is behind the money. Writing in the *New Republic*, John B. Judis observes that China and Japan, "two of the main countries that have tried to exercise influence in Washington, have often done so through companies and foundations rather than directly through their governments." Judis shows how the Chinese government may be operating. For example, while the Center for International and Strategic Studies (CSIS) in Washington, does not seem to be receiving any direct funding from the Chinese government, we should note that its new multimillion-dollar headquarters on Rhode Island Avenue houses the Zbigniew Institute on Geostrategy, which, according to Judis, "was seeded by a large grant from Wenliang Wang, who runs Rilin Enterprises, which is headquartered in Dandong, China." As the largest private construction firm in China, Rilin is believed to have extensive Chinese government contracts. Judis rightly asks whether the Institute might not simply have been a shell to facilitate Chinese donations to CSIS.

Several U.S. think tanks, furthermore, are less than clear in their annual reports, with many "anonymous" donors appearing on their lists of contributors. As veteran journalist James Mann writes in *The China Fantasy*, "Many of America's think tanks get sizeable donations from business executives and companies that are doing business in China, and the donors seek to foster policies that will protect or augment their financial interests." Some of those major donors have made little secret of their sympathy for the CCP and objections to U.S. pressuring Beijing on human rights. We can assume that Taiwan's democracy is probably also conveniently disregarded. Mann also points out that many top researchers at U.S. think tanks wear different hats and often fail to mention that they also work on the side as consultants with powerful lobby organizations that also have an interest in encouraging greater trade with China. Many of the large lobby firms that two decades ago had a Taiwan portfolio have furthermore switched sides and are now representing Beijing's interests in world capitals.

Funding by the Taiwanese government under KMT control has also had a profound impact on the ability or willingness of research institutions to study developments such as an increasingly active civil society during President Ma's second term in office. It has also had an impact on which Taiwan scholars have been able to secure visiting scholar status with top research institutions, a phenomenon that admittedly is not limited to Taiwan and China. For example, the Chen-Fu and Cecilia Koo Chair in Taiwan Studies at the Brookings Institution in Washington, launched in 2013 with a substantial donation by the Koo family, links Brookings with the Taipei Forum Foundation, whose chairman is former National Security Council Secretary-General Su Chi (蘇起), a very close aide to President Ma and the KMT. Koo Chen-fu (辜振甫), who died in 2005, was also the founding chairman of the Straits Exchange Foundation (SEF), the semiofficial body that is in charge of conducting the dialogue with China.

Conversely, the proindependence Koo Kwan-ming (辜寬敏) has been a financial supporter of the Project 2049 Institute in Arlington, Virginia, a small think tank that is much more favorable to Taiwan. However, the financial viability of the smaller think tanks is very much in doubt when contrasted with the large sums of money that the Chinese have at their disposal. Consequently, the small ones risk being crowded out by the many more that are willingly echoing Beijing's views.

Given the fact that U.S.–China relations now have the contours of a Cold War, we should note that unlike the standoff with Moscow, where economic relations between the two powers were minimal, think tanks, universities, and corporations today are far more vulnerable to the corrupting influence of Chinese money and markets. Back then, there was no such a thing as Soviet funding of U.S. think tanks, which were all kept afloat financially thanks to donations by the U.S. government and the Ford Foundation, among others.[1] Therefore, whereas supporters of the U.S.S.R. did emerge from within the ranks of Western governments and academia, the majority of them did so out of ideological conviction rather than economic incentives (paid spies being the obvious exception). Few are the academics and Western officials today who go out of their way to avoid offending Beijing or to broadcast its official line out of a conviction of the virtues of authoritarianism. Most of them value democracy and probably agree that it is the "least bad" form of government, but when it comes to their professional career, maintaining their access to China, and securing funding, many tend to put the moral blinders on. Very often, this means shutting up about Taiwan, even if the democratic island is a logical ideological ally.

Other factors contribute to the inability to comprehend and explicate the complexities of Taiwanese society. With a few exceptions, most foreign experts visit Taiwan irregularly and for brief periods of time. Many visit Taiwan only once every few years while traveling to China much more frequently. Furthermore, they usually do so as part of a delegation whose itinerary is organized by Taiwan's Ministry of Foreign Affairs (MOFA). As such, the visits normally consist of meetings with government officials, the president, the KMT, and a few affiliated think tanks. Exchanges with local academics and civil society rarely occur and are furthermore constrained by the fact that a MOFA official is usually present at the meetings, meaning that some people might be reluctant to speak freely.

Compounding the problem is the fact that in recent years MOFA often "forgot" to include the DPP on the foreign visitors' schedule or set the meetings at inconvenient times, such as late afternoon on Friday, hours before a delegation was expected to travel back home. Consequently, the experts often were out of touch with developments in Taiwan or, given their limited interactions, privy only to the official line presented to them by the then-KMT government.

Through its Taiwan Study Camp program (菁英領袖研習班) and direct involvement in bringing foreign academics on six-month to one-year scholarships, MOFA has also sought to expand its so-called soft power. However, interviews with many of the scholars who went through the programs reveal a strong emphasis on aspects of *Chinese* culture during related events (e.g., Peking Opera performances) and very little about Taiwanese culture. For academics who did not know much about Taiwan, such exposure risks leaving the wrong impression and represents a missed opportunity to introduce them to the idiosyncratic aspects of Taiwan.

Furthermore, in recent years visiting scholars were often pressured by MOFA officials to express support for specific government policies in their academic articles and presentations – chief among them President Ma's East China Sea Peace Initiative. On at least one occasion, a foreign academic was made to feel that her being invited to participate at a conference in Taipei (all expenses covered by the government) was contingent on her agreeing to write an article based on information and policy points provided by one of Taiwan's representative offices overseas. Under the Ma administration, many conferences sponsored by MOFA or the Mainland Affairs Council, among others, rarely included speakers whose views differed from those of the administration (e.g., on the East China Sea Peace Initiative or the 1992 consensus), thus undermining pluralism and ensuring that a unified message was broadcast. Academics – both Taiwanese and foreign – who were critical of the administration were simply selected out. As we will see in the next chapter, this kind of selectiveness also served to reinforce positive perceptions about the direction that cross-strait relations had taken under President Ma while silencing dissenting voices.

All of this constituted interference in academic freedom and discouraged criticism of the Ma administration. The very selection of foreign scholars who were invited to come to Taiwan to conduct research was therefore vulnerable to decisions based on the scholar's political and ideological views. It is easy to imagine that under President Ma, very few foreign academics who are strongly pro-Taiwan or who openly advocated for independence were invited to come to Taiwan on MOFA or Chiang Ching Kuo Foundation scholarships, though a few did slip through the cracks. This, however, likely will change after the new DPP administration assumed office in May 2016.

The reaction of many foreign academics to the Sunflower Movement encapsulated the phenomena discussed so far. Many who *should* have known better were caught by surprise and adopted a negative attitude toward the activists' actions, which often reflected the Ma administration's rhetoric. Had they been more attentive to what had been going on in Taiwan, more aware of the "cultural context," it is possible that the occupation of the Legislative Yuan would not have surprised them, nor would they have characterized the act as "illegal," "irrational," and "undemocratic," as a number of them did. The same experts often are the only people foreign media will turn to for commentary on Taiwan. Their ability to provide an accurate portrait of the situation in Taiwan is therefore often limited by the shortcomings discussed in this chapter, though a number of them have begun to adapt their views to the new reality in the wake of the January 2016 elections. As Engerman notes of experts on the Soviet Union, they "focused strictly on policy concerns, receiving less training in cultural context, even language, and they rarely spent significant time in the countries they studied. But the policy credentials provided unprecedented opportunities, producing an ironic result." The same often applies to Taiwan.

Even more revealing, perhaps, are examples of prominent academics who have written articles and sometimes entire books arguing that Taiwan should be ceded to China in return for some commitments by Beijing. In one case, the author admitted he had made his case for abandonment before having ever set foot in Taiwan.[2]

Other think tanks and research centers may be well-intentioned but do not have the resources or access to the information they would need to draw a more complete picture of the situation in Taiwan. In late 2014, I was invited to give a talk about the state of cross-strait relations at the Canadian Defence Association Institute (CDAI) in Ottawa, Canada. In several ways, my 90-minute presentation, attended by retired government officials and university professors, was a condensed version of the book you are currently reading, discussing the challenges facing Taiwan, the rise of Taiwanese civic nationalism, the military balance, the irreconcilability of the social and political systems on both sides of the Taiwan Strait, and the likelihood of renewed tensions in the not so distant future. After my talk, General Ray Henault, then president of the Institute and a former chairman of the NATO Military Committee at NATO headquarters in Brussels, was very explicit in his appreciation for the candid presentation I had just given. "We never hear these things out here," he said. Henault was right – and that is disconcerting, given that Canadian authorities should have a sense of where things are going in the Taiwan Strait, what with the *50,000* Canadian nationals (many of them duals) who live in Taiwan and who would have to be evacuated in case of major hostilities with China.

It is also important to note that while, for those who are based there, Taiwan and the Taiwan Strait tend to be the "center of the universe," the reality is that in major capitals overseas, Taiwan is but a speck in a constellation of pressing issues and must compete with a variety of crises with which officials and the academics who inform their views must constantly deal with. My many visits to Washington, D.C., where I held meetings with and gave briefings to officials there, quickly dispelled the notion that Taiwan is all-important. In reality, there is a limited number of experts on the subject, and most of them tend to be Asia hands or China hands rather than individuals who made Taiwan their principal subject matter. More often than not, Taiwan is pushed aside by more immediate and potentially more dangerous issues like North Korea, Afghanistan, Iran, Iraq, ISIS, al-Qaeda, Israel–Palestine, Lebanon, or Russia. As we will discuss in greater detail in the following chapter, perceptions that the Taiwan issue had been neutralized between 2008 and 2016 and that peace was at hand, thanks to President Ma's cross-strait policies, contributed to further isolating Taiwan as an issue worthy of study and attention.

It goes without saying that Taiwan's inability to join international organizations due to pressure from Beijing (you will not find the word "Taiwan" in a World Bank report) or the prerequisite that it do so under designations like "Chinese Taipei" or "Taiwan, China" exacerbates Taiwan's lack of visibility while fueling perceptions abroad that Taiwan is indeed part of China. Arguably, participation is better than nothing, even if the designations create resentment among many Taiwanese. But that does not change the fact that this pragmatism comes at a cost to Taiwan's brand recognition abroad. And unlike other "nonstates" that strive for recognition (e.g., Palestine), Taiwan has avoided making too much noise and refused to engage in violence or terrorism to make its presence felt internationally. Commendable though such nonviolence may be, it also means that Taiwan faces the extraordinary challenge of finding other, less dramatic ways to position itself globally.

Fundamentally, all of this is the result of the cloud of ignorance that has enshrouded Taiwan since the end of World War II. Two major events, which took place at crucial moments in history, are responsible for the unintended consequences that have generated Taiwan's predicament.

The first one occurred after the conclusion of World War II, when the Allied powers, having dispensed of the threat posed by Imperial Japan, determined Taiwan's fate with an act of obfuscation that continues to reverberate today. The seeds of trouble were sowed then. At the heart of all this is the legal status of Taiwan after the war, which under the standards of international law should have been clearly determined by a peace treaty. Such a treaty was indeed signed – the San Francisco Peace Treaty of 8 September 1951. But even though it was signed by all Allied forces and representatives of Japan, the Treaty, which came into force on 28 April 1952, stipulated (Article 2, item b) only that, "Japan renounces all right, title and claim to Formosa and the Pescadores." But here's where things get rather interesting: The document never explicitly spelled out the territorial rights of the beneficiary. In other words, what the Treaty did *not* say was that Formosa (Taiwan) and the Pescadores were being incorporated into China.[3]

The fuzziness was arrived at not as a result of sagacious policy but rather because the Great Powers at the time could not agree on whether China was the ROC, which had just "lost" China, or the PRC. By 6 January 1950, the U.K., which still could throw its weight around in international politics, had already switched diplomatic recognition to the PRC, while the U.S. would continue to recognize the ROC for another three decades or so. Under U.S. law, Washington could invite only the ROC to participate in San Francisco. And under British law, the U.K. could invite only representatives of the PRC. Unable to agree on whom to invite, Washington and London agreed to disagree. As a result, nobody represented China in San Francisco.

According to Steve Tsang (曾銳生), professor of contemporary Chinese studies at the University of Nottingham, the same thing occurred in the subsequent Taipei peace conference between Japan and the ROC, which had to mirror the agreement reached in San Francisco.[4]

It could very well be, therefore, that the Gordian knot that continues to poison relations in the Taiwan Strait today was first tightened by the inability of the U.S. and the U.K to agree on what China was. Had both recognized the same entity, the problem probably would not be with us today. This also means that a free and democratic Taiwan could also have been an alternative future that never materialized – for example, if both Great Powers had recognized the PRC early on and *prior* to the Treaty of San Francisco. But such what-ifs make for a purely intellectual exercise. What matters is that the disagreement did exist and led to the situation that prevails today.

What made matters worse is that by that time, both the ROC and the KMT were laying claim to the territory of Taiwan as the sole representative of China. The ROC maintained that Taiwan was part of the ROC; the PRC, which denied that the ROC still existed, saw Taiwan as one of its provinces. Taipei returned the favor by regarding the PRC as illegitimate, a preposterous position that it maintains today. Both based their claims on the Treaty, as well as a series of other documents – the Cairo Declaration and the Potsdam Declaration – that in reality did not provide a legal basis for control of Taiwan's sovereignty. Furthermore, by 1949 the KMT had been routed by Mao's CCP and relocated on Taiwan. The defeat raised questions as to whether the ROC still existed in the legal sense of the word. Was the PRC a successor government or merely what is known as a "continuer," and, if so, did the territorial claims of the displaced authority still apply (according to the CCP, they most certainly did). Some people could argue that the ROC will continue to exist only as long as it maintains official relations with diplomatic allies; however, even if that number were to drop to zero, this does not mean that the PRC's claims to Taiwan are any less valid, let alone legal.

So there you have it, the perfect recipe for confusion. Two regimes that do not recognize each other's existence have relied upon various documents to justify their claims of sovereignty over Taiwan, but none of the said documents contains language that would support such claims from a *legal* perspective. Taiwan, for better or worse, was left in a legal limbo. Given the complexity of the matter, the factual and counterfactual arguments that have been made by all sides, and the comprehensive national power of one of the claimants, we can perhaps understand why an already distracted global community has given up trying to figure out what is going on and has conveniently swallowed Beijing's rhetoric on the subject. Legally binding language in the Treaty *might* have provided the necessary clarity; as Beijing has made perfectly clear with its behavior in the South China Sea in recent years, when it comes to claims of sovereignty, the facts are often insufficient. Beijing wants the piece of real estate that keeps it bottled within the "first island chain." The CCP is also desirous of the legitimizing aspects of "reuniting" an idealized (if not mythical) China. And by so doing, Beijing would also benefit from the neutralization of a thorn in its side – the existence of a liberal democracy within "greater China," one that constantly threatens to undermine (some believe) the appeal and legitimacy of its authoritarian governance.

The second historical event is rather a series of decisions that were made by various powers throughout the 1970s, with the U.S. at the center of it all. In sum, this was the decision, based on various calculations (the Vietnam War and the Soviet Union among them) to sever diplomatic ties with the ROC and to establish official relations with the PRC. It is interesting to note that much of the groundwork on the recognition of the PRC occurred before Nixon and Kissinger visited China. As early as 1965, nonprofits such as the National Conference on U.S.–China relations, the American Friends Service Committee, and then the National Committee on U.S.–China Relations held a series of conferences on the subject, funded in large part by the Rockefeller Brothers Fund and the Ford Foundation. The effort convinced academics and then Congress of the virtues of recognizing Beijing.[5]

Even though ceasing to have official diplomatic relations with Taipei was a major development in itself, more important was the conclusion of an ongoing debate that receives little attention today on *how* to implement recognition. Although ultimately Washington and other world capitals chose to recognize the PRC and to do so under variations on the one-China principle, it could very well have occurred under a markedly different framework, one that extended dual recognition of two Chinas, which by granting status to the two sides of the Taiwan Strait would conceivably have had a lasting impact on the nature of the conflict. (As early as December 1963, Roger Hilsman, an assistant secretary of state for Far Eastern Affairs under President Lyndon Johnson, was making the case for two Chinas after it had become clear that the PRC would not collapse as many officials expected.)[6] There is no knowing for sure whether Beijing would have agreed to this formula, but we must nevertheless note that, back then, China was in a much weaker position internationally and may not have had much of a choice. Mao, who had opposed any "two-China" formula, had also died by then. There is good reason to believe that Chiang Kai-shek would have refused, but by April 1975 he had left this world, and successors, C.K. Yen (嚴家淦) and then his son, Chiang Ching-kuo, could have been leaned on to accept, much like U.S. pressure in the 1980s compelled Chiang Jr. to launch Taiwan on the road toward liberalization.[7] As Nancy Bernkopf Tucker, the undisputed authority on such matters, has written, "[B]y the mid-1970s, [Taiwan] leaders understood the inevitability of derecognition, although they refused to discuss it and devised no better response than delay [. . .] Critics would later say that with a willingness to change, Taiwan could have negotiated a better or, at least, less onerous future." But as she notes, the mutual trust that would have been necessary to make that happen simply did not exist.

By 1977, the Presidential Review Memorandum 24 presented four options for the establishment of relations with Beijing. Of the four, two are of interest here: (1) full diplomatic ties with the PRC and ending all formal relations with the ROC; (2) full recognition of the PRC while retaining diplomatic and military links with the ROC. Washington chose the first option, and all official relations with Taiwan ended.

Based on the declassified minutes of the Foreign Relations of the U.S. (FRUS), the option of dual recognition was alive until the summer of 1977. However, instead of the clear status that dual recognition (option 2) would have conferred upon the ROC and the PRC, single recognition (option 1) left us with a one-China principle, or policy that was as vague as it was open to interpretation and abuse by Beijing. In later years, it became difficult to tell the difference between Beijing's one-China policy and other countries' one-China policy, notwithstanding that those countries either "took note of" or "acknowledged" Beijing's argument that there is one China and that Taiwan is part of China. Clarity would perhaps have helped the matter; instead, the Taiwan issue is deeply characterized by differing interpretations and much uncertainty. Even the U.S.'s security "guarantees" to Taiwan could not be completely clear and were instead laid out as "strategic ambiguity."

Of course, it would be unfair to criticize decisions that were made 70 and 36 years ago using the hindsight that we enjoy today. We cannot know for certain that things would have turned out better had different decisions been made then. Be that as it may, the problems that we face today are a direct consequence of the decisions that *were* made back then, no doubt by well-intentioned individuals.

Although Taiwanese can now speak freely about politics at home, they are hesitant to do so overseas, especially when their arguments do not dovetail with those espoused by foreign governments and the financial sector. This is the subject of the next chapter.

Notes

1 For an excellent study of that era, see Engerman, D (2009) *Know Your Enemy: The Rise and Fall of America's Soviet Experts*, New York: Oxford University Press.
2 See White, H (2013) *The China Choice: Why We Should Share Power*, London: Oxford University Press. White eventually made his first visit to Taiwan in 2014 and admitted being impressed by the place. His views on the benefits of abandonment have not changed, however. He made a similar argument in subsequent articles. *The China Choice* was a *Financial Times* Best Book of 2013.
3 For a discussion on this subject, see Lin, C-L, Li, M-J and Lo, C-C, eds (2008) *Unlocking the Secret of Taiwan's Sovereignty*, Taipei: Taiwan Thinktank.
4 E-mail exchange on 5 June 2015.
5 Thanks to Mark Stokes of the Project 2049 Institute for drawing my attention to this issue.
6 The case can in fact be made that a *de facto* two-China policy had been in place starting under the Eisenhower administration.
7 In his book *Democratizing Taiwan* (2012, Leiden: Brill), Bruce Jacobs convincingly makes the case that Chiang Ching-kuo did not launch "democratization" in Taiwan but rather liberalization.

Bibliography

Bernkopf Tucker, N (2009) *United States-Taiwan Relations and the Crisis with China*, Cambridge: Harvard University Press: 89

Bernstein, R (2014) *China 1945: Mao's Revolution and America's Fateful Choice*, New York: Alfred A. Knopf: 51

Buchanan, A (2004) *Justice, Legitimacy, and Self-Determination: Moral Foundations for International Law*, Oxford: Oxford University Press

Cohen, W (2010) *America's Response to China: A History of Sino-American Relations*, 5th ed, New York: Columbia University Press: 211

Cole, M (2014) *Officially Unofficial: Confessions of a Journalist in Taiwan*, CreateSpace

Ignatieff, M (1993) *Blood and Belonging: Journeys into the New Nationalism*, Toronto: Viking

Judis, J (2014) "Foreign Funding of Think Tanks Is Corrupting Our Democracy," *New Republic*, 9 September, http://www.newrepublic.com/article/119371/think-tanks-foreign-contributions

Mann, J (2007) *The China Fantasy: How Our Leaders Explain Away Chinese Repression*, New York: Viking: 61–2

Miller, B (2013) "The State-to-Nation Balance in Power," in *Nationalism and War*, Hall, John A and Malešević, Siniša, eds, New York: Cambridge University Press: 91

Paine, S.C.M. (2003) *The Sino-Japanese War of 1894–1895: Perceptions, Power, and Primacy*, New York: Cambridge University Press: 6

Shambaugh, D (2013) *China Goes Global: The Partial Power*, New York: Oxford University Press: 227–35

Wu, C-L (2006) *Orphan of Asia*, New York: Columbia University Press

2

CHEN THE 'TROUBLEMAKER,' MA THE 'PEACEMAKER'

"Over the years . . . the Taiwan Strait has become an avenue of peace and prosperity, under peaceful and stable cross-strait relations." Thus spoke President Ma Ying-jeou during a meeting in Taipei with a delegation from the U.S. National Bureau of Asian Research in April 2013.

Just a few years earlier, the Taiwan Strait had often been described as a potential flashpoint or "tinderbox." Now the Strait – thanks to President Ma's policies of rapprochement with Beijing, no doubt – was nothing less than an "avenue of peace," a description that must have sounded like music to strategists and officials worldwide who were struggling to cope with a variety of emergencies, from terrorism to global warming, from economic crises to the proliferation of weapons of mass destruction. One year into his second term (in fact, he had begun saying that earlier), President Ma claimed he had succeeded in transforming the dynamics of a relationship that for decades had been on the brink and that at one time, in the early days of the Cold War, had come dangerously close to sparking nuclear war between a nascent PRC and the U.S.

The word peace was often heard following Ma's election in 2008. If we look at it from the angles that the Ma administration (and many foreign governments) wanted us to look at, it is true that the relationship in the Taiwan Strait flourished during that period. As many as 22 agreements touching on a variety of issues from crime fighting to investment, were signed from 2008, including the much publicized Economic Cooperation Framework Agreement (ECFA). Direct flights were implemented, linking several cities in China and Taiwan and obviating the need for inconvenient stopovers in Hong Kong. Tourism flourished: In 2014, as many as 4 million Chinese visitors came to Taiwan. Thousands of Chinese are now studying at universities in Taiwan, which are in dire need of bodies what with the surplus of postsecondary academic institutions in the country. Top officials, first from the semiofficial negotiating bodies and then by representatives of cabinet agencies, have met directly and now do so almost routinely. Above all, trade and economic ties, including the banking sector, have been steadily liberalized.

On the surface, relations between Taiwan and China underwent an extraordinary transformation since 2008, something that would have been inconceivable less than a decade earlier, let alone in the half century that had elapsed since the conclusion of the Chinese civil war, which forced Chiang Kai-shek's Nationalists to flee to Taiwan.

Notwithstanding all those developments, what has developed doesn't even come close to *peace*. As any political scientist will tell you, the absence of war (which Beijing never removed as an option, even when dialogue with Taipei was going smoothly) does not signify an absence of *conflict*. The rapprochement since 2008 occurred at the superficial level and rarely, if ever, touched on the really hard issues of politics. Such liberalization was long overdue and did serve to mitigate tensions at various levels. But the *fundamentals* haven't changed, and in fact recent developments, both in Taiwan and China, suggest that the years of détente were but a brief (albeit not necessarily unwelcome) interregnum.

The tone of the exchanges between Taipei and Beijing had changed, and according to President Ma and officials from both sides, peace was at hand. The fact that President Ma had a receptive audience overseas and a regime in Beijing that benefited from those developments amplified the message. A keynote address at the University of Waterloo as early as in June 2009 by Vivienne Poy (利德蕙), Chancellor Emerita at the University of Toronto and at the time a Toronto senator, epitomizes this phenomenon. In her address titled "Post-Colonial Transformations in China's Hong Kong and Macau: Implications for Cross-Taiwan-Strait and Canada-PRC Links," Poy barely touched on Taiwan. In fact, in her entire speech, Taiwan accounted for only three lines, with references to "China's cross-strait relationship" having "improved dramatically" since Ma's election the previous year. Apparently one year was sufficient for Poy to conclude that more than six decades of bitter hostility had been overturned. Furthermore, the examples that the Hong Kong–born Poy used to support her claims were questionable: China Mobile announcing it would seek to acquire a 12 percent share in FarEastTone, Taiwan's third-largest mobile services provider. The other "significant" development was Beijing "granting" Taiwan observer status at the World Health Assembly under the name "Chinese Taipei." The only other reference to Taiwan in the entire speech occurred toward the end, when Poy stated that Taiwan could serve as a "gateway" into China.

We can wonder why Poy even felt it necessary to include the cross-strait relationship in her speech, except to plug the concept that relations were now much better and therefore unworthy of our attention. The entirety of her speech lamented Ottawa's "harming" good economic relations by focusing on human rights. Not that this should be entirely surprising, given that the coeditor of the volume in which Poy's speech is reproduced wrote in the introduction that a better understanding of China can help Canada "go beyond the foreign policy dead end created by an overemphasis on the social and human rights problems that still pervade Chinese society."

Poy was far from alone in espousing this belief. Foreign media, academics, and intellectuals were quick to embrace the changes that were taking place in the Taiwan Strait and to give it a positive spin. In almost every book and article they wrote, foreign journalists and academics felt compelled to preface their work with variations on the theme of "relations between Taiwan and China have improved 'dramatically' or 'markedly' since 2008." Very few publications cared to qualify those remarks by placing them in their proper context. "Peace" or "markedly" improved relations was the new dogma. It didn't matter that all indicators within Taiwan pointed to a more consolidated nationalism or that China was continuing its military buildup against Taiwan and intensifying its espionage operations against the island – hardly a sign of "dramatically" improved ties.

Better yet, the perception that peace was at hand allowed the KMT and the Chinese authorities, as well as foreign media and officials, to depict the DPP and President Ma's predecessor Chen Shui-bian (陳水扁) as "anti-China" and "troublemakers." Such perceptions were exploited to the hilt during elections in Taiwan, especially in exchanges with officials in Washington and in other foreign capitals who quite welcomed the lowered tensions in the Taiwan Strait.

Although there are valid reasons for criticizing the DPP under Chen, much of the rhetoric about Ma the "peacemaker" and Chen the "troublemaker" rested on myths and false assumptions that can gain traction only if the intended audience suspends disbelief or is too distracted to pay attention to the details of history. Or if the audience benefits financially from stability in the Taiwan Strait, however artificial and temporary that stability might be. Such perceptions have served to game the system in the KMT's favor and have created great difficulties for the DPP, which has been forced into a position of constantly having to explain itself to highly skeptical global interlocutors. An additional effect has been the tendency to put everybody in Taiwan who opposes the KMT and its policies as falling under the DPP umbrella, to which "anti-China," "proindependence," and "irrational" qualifiers are often attached. In this, the KMT, Beijing, and their friends overseas have largely benefited from the lack of granular knowledge about Taiwan that was discussed in the previous chapter. With media focusing almost exclusively on the major political parties in Taiwan, society and the so-called third force rarely had a voice. Consequently, whoever disagreed with the KMT had to be from the DPP or was being "manipulated" by it.

As we just saw, the DPP was not completely blameless. The Chen administration did do things that contributed to tensions in the Taiwan Strait and alienated its principal ally in Washington. Its insistence on symbols affirming Taiwan's statehood, for example, or the tendency of some of its officials to spring surprises on foreign diplomats by publicizing meetings that were being held under expectations of secrecy, caused anger in foreign capitals that radiates to this day, as I discovered during meetings with officials from a Western country in late 2014. President Chen's appeals to more "hardline" elements in Taiwan near the beginning of his second term, along with the exclusivist (ethnic) nationalism that ensued, also poisoned relations both within Taiwan and across the Taiwan Strait.

There is, however, another side to the story. For one thing – and this rarely gets mentioned – President Chen did keep the promises he had made to the U.S. during his first term and didn't declare independence or seek to change the constitution. The small three links were launched, and his administration extended several olive branches to Beijing that, if reciprocated, could have led to the kind of liberalization that occurred under President Ma. But Beijing refused to talk and hardened its stance, compelling President Chen to do just as much.

Another thing that undermined President Chen's image was the international context in which his efforts to solidify Taiwan's global presence occurred – and in this, his advisers seriously failed him. If we look at the actions taken by the DPP at the time from the perspective of self-determination, there isn't much that was done that would come across as illegitimate. After all, self-determination is an accepted principle in many parts of the world, and since the fall of the Berlin Wall a number of states have come into being based on that principle. Unfortunately for President Chen, his efforts coincided with the "rise" of China as an economic powerhouse, which undoubtedly undermined international support for Taiwanese nationalism. Even more consequential, at least initially, was the fact that President Chen decided to make some noise in a time of crisis. For reasons that we can only guess at, Chen's advisers failed to brief the president on the impact that the 11 September 2001 terrorist attacks by al-Qaeda, followed by the U.S. invasion of Afghanistan later that year and the invasion of Iraq in 2003, had on U.S. foreign policy.

Soon after 9/11, President George W. Bush's tone on Taiwan changed dramatically, from "doing whatever it takes to defend Taiwan" in the early days of his administration to publically chastising President Chen during a conversation with Chinese President Hu Jintao (胡錦濤).

Among other things, in August 2002 Chen proposed his own version of former President Lee Teng-hui's (李登輝) two-state theory, reportedly without consulting Washington, and called on the legislature to amend regulations on referendums (Shirk, 2007). These "bombshells," which soured relations with Washington, sealed Chen's fate and have since been regarded as "evidence" of his recklessness. Had it not been for the context, however, there would be little basis for treating such political moves as reckless. After all, the two-state theory very much reflects the reality in the Taiwan Strait, in which Taiwan (or the ROC) has existed as a sovereign entity, and how to regulate the holding of national referendums is very much the remit of national governments. (We must also note the biases that underscore the language of the Taiwan Strait. One China is a *principle* or a *policy*, while two states is merely a *theory*, which serves to delegitimize the notion. At least on the Israeli–Palestinian issue, two states has the more legitimate status of a *proposal*.) But context is everything, and less than a year after al-Qaeda penetrated U.S. defenses, it was deemed inappropriate for President Chen to make those remarks. Washington wanted none of it, and as Taiwan's principal security guarantor with certain "obligations" under the TRA, it did not want to see the situation in the Taiwan Strait further deteriorate. The Bush administration therefore cracked down on President Chen, "sided" with Beijing, and put immense pressure on Taipei not to revise its referendum laws.

President Chen therefore became the "troublemaker." And the sobriquet stuck, so much so that using it became almost a reflex among academics and officials. During an interview with Paul Wolfowitz in 2011, I asked the former deputy secretary of defense in the Bush administration to explain why he thought President Chen was a "troublemaker" after he used that very term to describe the former leader. Wolfowitz, one of the principal architects of the invasion of Iraq in 2003, a quagmire that would make the U.S. even more averse to high tensions in the Taiwan Strait, thought for a few seconds before admitting that the characterization may have been unfair. "We could have shown more understanding," he said, "but we were busy fighting two little wars."

Unfortunately for President Chen and his successors at the DPP, politics isn't very often about fairness. For all his deficiencies, President Chen didn't do anything that other state leaders wouldn't have gotten away with (corruption aside). But where other leaders would have been celebrated as great national leaders, Chen was treated as a dangerous troublemaker who risked sparking a war that could drag in U.S. forces at a time when its military was busy dealing with other contingencies, chief among them the so-called global war on terror.

Of course, the other side of the coin is that the real cause of tensions in the Taiwan Strait, as well as the only country that could decide to launch military operations, was China. But in the strange politics of the Taiwan Strait, a democracy that expresses legitimate desires for nationhood and that sought to bring antiquated legislation on referendums in line with international norms was regarded as a troublemaker; an authoritarian regime that threatened military invasion under legislation of dubious moral foundations (the Anti-Secession Law of 2005) was treated as the reasonable party in the equation, one whose goals were regarded as legitimate. In this La-La Land, the very proposition that Taiwan is an independent state, or the refusal to agree to unification with the PRC under one China, constituted an act of irrationality – a crime in some circles and a career ender in some halls of academia.

So this was the state of affairs in 2008 when Ma Ying-jeou faced off against Frank Hsieh (謝長廷) of the DPP, a party that by then was on the verge of collapse in large part due to the allegations of corruption against the Chen family and other officials. The stage was set for the KMT's return to power, and Ma had his script written already. He would be the anti-Chen, everything that his predecessor was not. He would "repair" relations with the U.S., which had "suffered" under the DPP, put relations with China back on the "right footing" using the disputed 1992 consensus, and "revive" the stagnant economy by liberalizing trade with China. Where President Chen was "irresponsible," Ma would be the voice of "rationality." Chen was a "troublemaker." Ma would be a "peacemaker," the man who, in November 2015, would demonstrate in Singapore that he could even sit down with the Chinese leader, a first since the creation of the PRC in 1949. The vision had great appeal, and President Ma, who was inaugurated on 20 May 2008, rode on that wave.

So did Beijing. Ma opened the door, and Beijing held it wide open rather than close it as it had done when Chen was in office.

Not unlike other presidents over the years, Ma came into office promising to be everything that his predecessor was not. Like George W. Bush after Bill Clinton or Barack Obama after Bush, Ma presented himself as the anti-Chen – "clean," "rational," and willing to work with Beijing. However, unlike his American counterparts, who while campaigning promised to be everything that their predecessor was not, only to embrace continuity rather than a clear break with the past once in office, President Ma significantly altered the direction of politics in Taiwan. The KMT's firm control of both the executive and legislative branches of government gave him the latitude to so do. Ma had the additional advantage of having a willing partner in Beijing, which meant that he was able to implement the kind of changes in bilateral relations that his predecessors Chen and Lee weren't able to, even if they had been willing to do so.

Moreover, Ma's administration correctly interpreted the tea leaves in the international system and understood the desire for stability and predictability in the Taiwan Strait. At the time when Ma was campaigning for election, the U.S. military had just implemented its famous "surge" in Iraq, while in Afghanistan the Taliban, which just a few years ago was believed to have been defeated, was staging a comeback. It would be years still until the U.S. could extricate itself from those two theaters – only to be drawn back in by renewed instability of the rise of new challenges such as the Islamic State in Iraq and Syria or al-Qaeda in the Maghreb. North Korea and then the global financial crisis also put a premium on stability so that decision makers in Washington and elsewhere could deal with the challenges. On the latter issues, Beijing's help was seen as essential; as Pyongyang's principal ally, it was assumed that Beijing could keep the North Korean leadership in line, while Chinese capital could help put the supine global economy back on its feet. Ma therefore promised that Taiwan would not get in the way. To do so, he adopted a strategy that comported two pillars. First, he would play down the sovereignty issue by adopting a "pragmatic" line and thereby defuse tensions on such matters as the name under which Taiwan would participate in global institutions. Second, he would launch a process of rapprochement in the Taiwan Strait that would result in more contact between the two societies and, it was hoped, in greater understanding.

Whether Ma really believed the notion that better understanding would lead to peace in the Taiwan Strait and would resolve the issue, as if the longstanding conflict were the result of a mere misunderstanding, is anyone's guess. Regardless, the international community liked what it was hearing and chose to believe it. That the conflict between Taiwan and China stems from much more fundamental and complex issues – clashing nationalisms resulting from the irreconcilable differences in beliefs and political systems – did not register.

Peace or the illusion of peace was good enough in foreign capitals. To ensure success, Ma also packaged his efforts at rapprochement in terms of Taiwan's economic revival, which had appeal to the majority of Taiwanese.

Ensuring the continuation of that process thus became a priority for governments overseas. Concluding that a second Ma term would be more conducive to stability and the deepening of cross-strait ties than a return by the "proindependence" DPP, the National Security Council in Washington did not hesitate to intervene in Taiwan's democracy, as exemplified by a damaging leak by a top White House official to the *Financial Times* in late 2011 while DPP presidential candidate Tsai Ing-wen was on a visit to the U.S. "She [Tsai] left us with distinct doubts about whether she is both willing and able to continue the stability in cross-Strait relations the region has enjoyed in recent years," the unnamed official was quoted as saying.[1] Academics and former AIT officials also hinted at (some downright telegraphed) their preference for the KMT, which stems also from long standing ties between various U.S. administrations and the KMT since World War II, as well as interest in some political circles in retaining Taiwan's "attachment" to China, which only the KMT can sustain due to its ideology (for better or worse, a DPP government signifies a clean break with China).

As mentioned in the previous chapter, the appearance of peace in the Taiwan Strait – as President Ma liked to say, relations were the most stable and peaceful they had been in 60 years, a refrain that was often repeated abroad – had the effect of obviating the one last aspect about Taiwan (the risk of war) that made it "newsworthy." With the risks of conflict seemingly dropping by the month, foreign bureaus that needed to cut somewhere to save money therefore often thought of Taiwan as the right place to start downsizing. Reporting consequently suffered; the frequency of reports dropped, and less and less did foreign media report about politics in Taiwan, focusing instead on the stock market and financial news. It is no surprise that the only foreign news agency to actually grow during that period was Bloomberg News, which opened a brand-new office, equipped with TV studios, in Xinyi District near Taipei 101. Academic papers, annual reports, and conferences also bought into the idea that peace was flourishing in the Taiwan Strait, and as a result Taiwan received fewer mentions. The Taiwan Strait had been neutralized. It was no longer a potential flashpoint that risked drawing U.S. forces into direct conflict with an emerging China.

The few voices (including this author) that argued that what was occurring in the Taiwan Strait did not remotely constitute peace were often treated with disdain or were regarded as alarmists. Despite the rapprochement and despite President Ma's emphasis on Taiwan's Chinese heritage, the trends in terms of self-identification and support for unification with China were steadily moving in the opposite direction. It was clear that the process that had begun in the Taiwan Strait would not necessarily translate into a blurring of identities in Taiwan of the kind that would lead to unification. In fact, the opposite was occurring, and rather than drop, nationalist sentiment was rising. The fact that it wasn't expressed with the pomp and, in recent years, the fascistic undertones of Chinese nationalism, probably explains why it went unnoticed; it was simply drowned out by the much louder chorus on the other side of the Taiwan Strait.

But by then the bias was well entrenched in the system. Whoever argued that there was no peace to speak of in the Taiwan Strait and that conflict would probably be *likelier* following the interregnum because all that "goodwill" by Beijing would not yield the coveted dividends was immediately accused of all sorts of crimes: warmonger, "China basher," supporter of American imperialism, agent of the CIA, DPP propagandist, or someone who profited materially from U.S. arms sales to Taiwan. In other words, efforts to draw attention to the dynamics within Taiwan society, to demonstrate that rather than a "small group," those who *opposed* unification with China in fact constituted the majority, were immediately discredited with accusations of some nefarious ulterior motives. Those who did so were against peace and therefore "irrational" – despicable, in fact. Another irony is the fact that a large proportion of the platforms in the West where it is still possible to call for the defense of Taiwan are often associated with the right wing of American politics. One good example is *The National Interest*, a prominent U.S. publication that is listed on Right Wing Watch (www.rightwingwatch.org), a website that tracks various institutions that propagate ultraconservative values. By association, those who have published in *The National Interest* have been described as right-wingers, neo-cons and ultraconservatives, a mantle earned not because the authors espouse such values (many of them are what could be called liberal) but rather because they argue for the defense of democracy, support the right to self-determination, and maintain that the 23 million people in Taiwan have the right to decide their own future. Other liberal publications such as *Counterpunch* have also weighed in with articles attacking whoever calls for the defense or arming of Taiwan.

By most yardsticks, the first phase of President Ma's overture to Beijing was the easy part. After all, much of the work that had to be done consisted of liberalizing ties between the two sides that, in the era of globalization, was not only practicable but in fact inevitable. It hardly made sense that in 2008, two interdependent economies remained closed to one another in several areas, especially as more than 1 million Taiwanese, known as *taishang*, already lived in China where they ran factories. The fact that the liberalization of the economic aspects of cross-strait relations made perfect sense also meant that the effort would encounter little resistance, except from those in the "deep-green" camp who early on regarded this exercise as part of Beijing's efforts to maximize Taiwan's dependence on China for political ends. This helps explain why the ECFA signed in June 2010 did not result in the kind of protests that could have derailed the process, as would occur less than four years later with the Cross-Strait Services Trade Agreement (CSSTA, 海峽兩岸服務貿易協議), as will be discussed in Chapter 7.

As such, Taipei and Beijing chose the prudent course, and both signaled their intention to pick the low-lying fruit first before moving on to the more controversial issues of Taiwan's status. For the most part, both governments played it safe and operated within the confines of what was possible – and acceptable to the Taiwanese – at the time. The process may have lacked transparency, and in some instances protocol and proper reviews may have been skipped, but overall as one agreement turned into ten, then into 20, the Taiwanese public did not see anything alarming enough to warrant taking action. Although many critics (mostly foreigners or Taiwanese based overseas) interpreted this lack of resistance as political apathy or "brainwashing" by the KMT, it is important to again point out that much of what was accomplished during President Ma's first term was uncontroversial and probably necessary.

Most Taiwanese undoubtedly understood that Beijing had not relinquished its political motives, but as long as the deals that were being struck between Taipei and Beijing remained within the boundaries of the natural progression *between two states*, they were willing to countenance the process. Moreover, unlike what many critics of Taiwanese "inaction" or "distraction" have said over the years, most Taiwanese today live their lives with a relatively solid understanding of who they are. As such, despite Taiwan's unofficial status in the international community, of which they are keenly aware, in their minds Taiwan (or the ROC) is already an independent state. Therefore, to them, there was nothing unnatural or overly dangerous in signing and implementing the kind of agreements that are normal course between two states. In other words, for them, normalization was, well, *normal*.

The absence of major social unrest in Taiwan as various agreements were signed between Taipei and Beijing further encouraged foreign capitals to celebrate President Ma's efforts. Some observers, including his former mentor, the well respected Jerome Cohen, even started talking of a possible Nobel Peace Prize nomination for Ma. Meanwhile, protestations by the DPP and its smaller ally the Taiwan Solidarity Union (TSU) fell on deaf ears, seen as the spasms of ideological opponents of peace and progress – of the forces of history, even.

But underneath, all was not well. Trade and crime-fighting agreements were one thing; anything that had political symbolism immediately encountered much firmer resistance, as the events surrounding the then Association for Relations Across the Taiwan Strait (ARATS) chairman Chen Yunlin's (陳雲林) groundbreaking visit to Taiwan in November 2008 made clear. The visit sparked days of protests and many examples of direct action, due in part to overreaction by law enforcement authorities, which deployed approximately 10,000 police officers around Taipei alone and mishandled the perfectly legitimate desire to contrast Chen's visit with the brandishing of symbols of Taiwan's sovereignty. By spying on and intimidating activists who were preparing for the visit and by preventing people from displaying ROC or even Tibetan flags (police authorities deny such an order was given), the Ma administration turned the visit into a matter of politics and perhaps even more importantly of civil liberties, and the people took action. The long-term effects of Chen's first visit cannot be ignored. Even if the situation quieted down after his return to China, the seeds of opposition had been sown, and the Ma administration was put on notice. Many of the young individuals who spearheaded the Sunflower Movement in the spring of 2014 first cut their teeth protesting Chen's visit as part of the Wild Strawberries Movement. This includes future Black Island Nation Youth Alliance and Sunflower Movement leader Lin Fei-fan (林飛帆). One female activist whom I interviewed and followed on the day of Chen's arrival, who was subsequently taken to a police station and sustained injuries to a finger after a police officer pried a Tibetan flag from her hands, would years later lead protests by young aborigines in Hualien who had been angered by Chinese encroachment on their traditions. There were many others. Not only did they not forget, but just as significantly they learned important lessons from their first experience in activism, lessons that they would apply with much greater success in 2014. Thus, it is possible to argue that the real roots of the snowballing activism that took over national politics from late 2012 derive from the Wild Strawberries Movement, though it would be nearly four years before most of them would reemerge as political actors.

Just as importantly, the protests that coincided with Chen's first visit to Taiwan put a rising group of young activists in contact with veterans from the prodemocracy Wild Lily Movement from the early 1990s. The former students, now themselves professors and professionals in other fields, would provide much of the intellectual material and strategic thinking for the Sunflower Movement, giving it the legitimacy and depth that bolstered its appeal with the general public.

Another strike against the Ma administration was the fact that in most instances it did little to set the agenda on cross-strait relations. As a result, Taipei's passivity put its negotiators in a position where they often had to react to Chinese demands. Years later, when Beijing was growing impatient with the reelected President Ma, this passivity would cause great trouble for his administration. By then, Ma the "peacemaker" had realized that time was running out. There would not be a third term, and it was clear that he could not deliver the kind of agreement that would earn him the Nobel Peace Prize – agreements such as a peace accord with Beijing. In fact, he would not come anywhere near delivering on that count, unable even to secure the implementation of the CSSTA or the opening of reciprocal representative offices. Forced between democratic accountability and securing his legacy as a peacemaker, Ma chose the latter and paid a heavy price, resulting in social unrest, the occupation of government buildings, and the use of antiriot squads and water cannons. Ma the "peacemaker" had brought the country to the edge of a precipice. It took weeks of drama on the streets of Taiwan to show the world that peace in the Taiwan Strait, hailed as the dawn of a new era just a few years earlier, was illusory.

It had been convenient, and for a while Ma was able to ride on its wave, but in the end the Taiwanese public would not allow him to go beyond the degree of normalization with China that was acceptable to them. The moment he stepped over that line, President Ma broke his contract with the people who had put him in high office, and they were merciless in bringing him down. Ironically, a series of domestic controversies that went largely unnoticed abroad, rather than his China policy, destroyed his administration. Less than two years into his second term, Ma was discredited, his popularity dropping to 9.2 percent, a record for a democratically elected official. From that point on, President Ma would be a lame duck president, stripped of his KMT chairmanship, accused of bungling the 29 November 2014, nine-in-one elections, and counting the days to May 2016 when he stepped down after completing his second consecutive term.

So why, given all this, did the international community so ardently believe that peace was at hand in the Taiwan Strait?

Note

1 It is believed that the NSC official in question was Tom Donilon, President Obama's National Security Adviser.

Bibliography

Cao, H and Poy, V (2011) *The China Challenge: Sino-Canadian Relations in the 21st Century*, Ottawa: University of Ottawa Press: 126–32

Cole, M (2011) "Wolfowitz Praises Taiwan's Democratic Legacy," *Taipei Times*, 24 October

Fifield, A, Kwong, R, and Hille, K (2011) "US Concerned about Taiwan Candidate," *Financial Times*, 15 September

Shirk, S (2007) *China: Fragile Superpower*, New York: Oxford University Press: 203

3

PEACE ON WHOSE TERMS?

Taiwan's democracy – its very existence as a distinct society in the Chinese-speaking world – is highly inconvenient. People all over the world will gladly buy its products, many of them without even knowing that many of the components that run their cell phones, tablets, computers, and other electronic devices are designed or made in Taiwan, but mention its politics – or worse, its predicament – and they will tune out. Some will even go out of their way to be rude. For a country that has never threatened anyone (at least since Chiang Kai-shek let go his illusions of retaking the "Mainland" from Mao Zedong's communists) and that epitomizes success in industrialization, modernization, liberalization, and democratization, that animus is a bit strange.

Some of that can probably be attributed to ignorance. After all, if the idea is that "they're all Chinese," then why should those pesky little Taiwanese make such trouble? Others, echoing the "end of history" theory, will ask why the Taiwanese are complaining. Aren't they a democracy already? And with China's economy booming, others will wonder why the Taiwanese can't shut up and join the bandwagon. The reasons why the Taiwanese do not want to do so, and why they are resisting pressures to unify, are multitudinous and will be discussed in greater detail throughout this book. But for audiences abroad, the differences seem little more than narcissistic.

For those who know better, the inconvenience that is Taiwan is the result of something far more fundamental. Free, democratic Taiwan is a constant reminder of our double standards as we continue to deal with and in fact rapidly accelerate our trade relations with authoritarian China. Nobel Prize winners like Liu Xiaobo (劉曉波) are imprisoned, activists disappear and die in prison, and freedom of expression continues to deteriorate; minority peoples in Xinjiang and Tibet are repressed and forcefully diluted ethnically; the environment is poisoned; Beijing supports a variety of despotic regimes abroad with its no-questions-asked policy of acquiring natural resources wherever it may; and China threatens its smaller neighbors in the South China Sea, but the world chooses to look the other way and continues to do business with it. Even more reprehensibly, we allow Chinese influence in our universities and our media, and we self-censor and bend over backward to avoid "angering" China and hurting the feelings of its 1.4 billion people by cancelling movie showings or denying visas to "enemies" of China. We fear the economic consequences of alienating Beijing. So we pretend we are not sacrificing our morals and values at the altar of our relationship with Beijing, even at a time when under President Xi Jinping the human rights situation across China is getting worse than it has been in several years.

In this context, it is easy to see why Taiwan would be inconvenient. Every particle in our bodies tells us that it would be logical – practicable, in fact – to have normal diplomatic relations with Taiwan and to support its 23 million people as they seek to play their rightful role within the international community. But we don't do it. Instead, we crack down on the aspirations of its people and are thereby complicit in the state-sponsored repression of its people. Taiwan may be democratic, successful, global, and one of the 20 largest world economies, but we treat it like a rogue state – worse, in fact, inasmuch as North Korea, which threatens its neighborhood with weapons of mass destruction and keeps its citizens in a perpetual state of imprisonment, at least enjoys normal diplomatic ties with most countries and has a seat at the United Nations. Even the Palestinians have status as a nonmember observer at the UN. But present a ROC passport at the front gate of any UN institution worldwide, and you will be denied entry inside the building.

What's more, as long as Taiwan continues to exist as an entity that is separate from the People's Republic of China, one with which we must go through all kinds of hoops to entertain unofficial ties, it holds the potential to poison our lucrative relationship with Beijing. As long as it continues to exist and as long as its people refuse to become Chinese and abandon all aspirations to statehood (which they already enjoy in a *de facto* capacity), Taiwan will force us to avert our gaze from the mirror of our conscience lest we realize how unjustly we have been treating it.

We know what we're doing is wrong, but we do it nonetheless. And we blame Taiwan for nagging at our conscience. The West went to war to facilitate the birth of new countries that have far less going for them in terms of their viability than does Taiwan, but when it comes to the latter, we punish it for having similar aspirations. For all these things, Taiwan is the international community's moral blind spot, one that is widened by the greed and cowardice of nations and of those who shape their policies.

For the U.S., Taiwan also presents a bit of a conundrum. Morally speaking, Taiwan encapsulates everything that the American people and its institution like to think they're about – liberalism, democracy, free markets, David versus Goliath, and so on. It also very much appeals to the Manichean views that tend to characterize

much of U.S. foreign policy and American culture. In other words, the good guys
versus the bad guys.

And yet there are those who would just as soon sweep it under the carpet
with the purpose of solidifying ties with China in a time of allegedly dwindling
American influence on the global stage. We need China to ensure a healthy
global economy, to combat global warming and terrorism, to keep North Korea
in check – the list goes on, and it is one that the U.S. State Department, White
House, and National Security Council have been shouting from the rooftops.
It also reflects, with some variations, how other members of the community
of nations have chosen to approach China . . . and by rebound Taiwan. Unfortunately for Taiwan, it stands in the way of the belief (which should have been
discredited by now) that if we integrate China into the international system
and play nice (e.g., maintaining military-to-military ties, inviting its Navy to
participate in annual RIMPAC exercises, and so on), it will become a "responsible stakeholder" and return the favor. Needless to say, no such courtesy will be
extended to Taiwan, one of China's core interests, as doing so would threaten the
entire exercise just described. So not only does the international community go
to great lengths to bring China into the system, we have become hostage to the
process (the "positive atmospherics in the China relationship," as a former U.S.
official called it), something that Beijing has repeatedly exploited. It is therefore
no surprise that as this book was being written, we were in the longest period
since the late 1980s without a U.S. notification to Congress on arms sales to
Taiwan.[1]

The psychological impact of slowing arms sales was captured by Randall Schriver,
a former deputy assistant secretary of state for East Asian and Pacific Affairs under
the George W. Bush administration, in a testimony to the Senate Foreign Relations
Committee in April 2014. "The prolonged absence of a Congressional notification on Taiwan arms sales could be perceived as accommodating Chinese positions
and potential reaction to a formal announcement, as the People's Liberation Army
(PLA) continues to develop and deploy capabilities intended to coerce and/or
facilitate use of force against Taiwan," he said.[2]

Engagement with China at the expense of almost everything else (and certainly Taiwan) also stems from the belief that if we help its middle class become
more prosperous [by granting it MFN (most favored nation) status despite rampant
human rights violations and by subsequently facilitating its accession to the WTO],
China will embark on the road to democratization, which as Jie Chen has made
perfectly clear in *A Middle Class Without Democracy*, is a complete fallacy, a myth
that, I might add, has been kept alive by corporations and individuals who have one
and only one objective in mind: to tap into the large Chinese market in order to
enrich themselves and their shareholders.[3]

Taiwan's continued existence and its potentially detrimental impact on U.S.–
China relations also forces Washington into a corner on the Taiwan Relations Act
and the Six Assurances, whose provisions and responsibilities would simply cease

to exist if Taiwan were to (conveniently) disappear. Among other things, the TRA states that:

> It is the policy of the United States –
>
> 1   to preserve and promote extensive, close, and friendly commercial, cultural, and other relations between the people of the United States and the people on Taiwan;
> 2   to declare that peace and stability in the area are in the political, security, and economic interests of the United States, and are matters of international concern;
> 3   to make clear that the United States decision to establish diplomatic relations with the People's Republic of China rests upon the expectation that the future of Taiwan will be determined by peaceful means;
> 4   to consider any effort to determine the future of Taiwan by other than peaceful means, including by boycotts or embargoes, a threat to the peace and security of the Western Pacific area and of grave concern to the United States;
> 5   to provide Taiwan with arms of a defensive character; and
> 6   to maintain the capacity of the United States to resist any resort to force or other forms of coercion that would jeopardize the security, or the social or economic system, of the people on Taiwan.

It adds:

> Nothing contained in this Act shall contravene the interest of the United States in human rights, especially with respect to the human rights of all the approximately eighteen million inhabitants of Taiwan. The preservation and enhancement of the human rights of all the people on Taiwan are hereby reaffirmed as objectives of the United States.

Many of the provisions contained in the TRA are inconvenient today. Officials in Washington who are keen to see the continuation of cordial relations with China will choose to be liberal in how they interpret some of the language included in the TRA. "The preservation and enhancement of the human rights of all the people on Taiwan" and "peaceful means" can be toyed with to mean just about anything or to justify looking the other way when China uses various means to impose its will on Taiwan. For the drafters of the TRA and to government officials today, the intentions of the act are pretty clear – or should be. And yet many will seek to find ways around the responsibilities contained in the act because meeting them is, well, inconvenient.

It is easy to see, then, how the semblance of peace in the Taiwan Strait between 2008 and 2015 would compel various officials and academics to argue for the annulment of the TRA. "Good riddance," they would say as they celebrate the removal of a key irritant in U.S.–China relations.

The realization that accommodating China has not yielded the expected dividends – it took Chinese belligerence in the East and South China Seas as well as the construction of artificial features in the South China Sea for the international community to find out – may have put a damper on the West's China strategy, but it is unlikely to dramatically alter the manner in which the international community deals with Taiwan. Despite the fact, as Robert Manning, a former undersecretary of state for global affairs pointed out, that the "troubling epiphany that has seized attention from policy-watchers [that the] core assumptions that have guided a bipartisan China policy for eight presidencies, from Nixon to Obama are unraveling" and despite the "pivot" and the strong signaling coming out of capitals like Washington, Tokyo, and Canberra, the principal strategy in dealing with Taiwan is unlikely to change substantially. And that is because the main strategy in how to deal with China will likely continue to center on engagement with a dose of balancing. It is unlikely that the recent tensions between the U.S. and China over the South China Sea or cyber warfare will lead to the kind of bloc containment and confrontation that characterized much of the Cold War between the U.S. and the U.S.S.R., though this is the only scenario in which we could see substantial changes in engagement with Taiwan (as part of the containment strategy) by the U.S. and some members of the international community. Consequently, while recent developments may attune foreign observers to the difficulties of dealing with an emerging and increasingly assertive China, it is unlikely that they will lead to major attitudinal changes on the question of Taiwan, which will continue to be regarded as an irritant and an inconvenience. The reason why is largely a matter of scale. Taiwan has a population of 23 million; China, approximately 1.4 billion, accounting for about one out of every five persons on the planet. Taiwan is one of many members of the Asia-Pacific community; China is its rising hegemon whose actions risk causing great instability and whose annual defense expenditures are second only to that of the U.S., at US$216 billion (officially) in 2014 and rising fast. Lastly, while Taiwan's gross domestic product in 2014 was US$1.022 trillion, China's – by then the world's second largest economy – was US$17.63 trillion and growing rapidly. (That Taiwan's GDP per capita for the same year was US$43,600 versus US$12,900 in China means little to countries who look at trade partners in terms of total size.)

Because of these factors, Taiwan will not only continue to be seen as an irritant but also remain relegated to the status – much as in academia – of a subcomponent of the U.S.–China relationship. And yet, as Schriver said in his testimony, "There are significant opportunity costs to treating Taiwan as a subordinate issue in U.S.–China ties rather than as a legitimate government able and willing to help resolve a broad range of shared challenges faced by the international community." Taiwan, he added, "is not simply an 'issue to manage' in U.S.–China relations."

Whatever "peace" happens in the Taiwan Strait will therefore be deeply influenced by those biases, at least as long as China lays claim to the island. Consequently, as Taiwan is subsumed into the China rubric rather than regarded as an equal entity, it is unlikely that peace will be achieved on its terms.

And this is where things get dangerous, as the outcome will either force the Taiwanese into capitulation (that is, peace on China's terms) or growing tensions with the possibility of resolution at the end of a barrel (in other words, by force of arms). It should therefore not be surprising that for the majority of Taiwanese, the status quo is their preferred (or "least bad") state of existence, as it provides the benefits of actual statehood while delaying the uncomfortable decision that is being forced upon them by China and, increasingly, by the international community.

The fact that Taiwan is for all intents and purposes already a sovereign state, and a democratic one at that, makes the problem all the more complex and is one of the key reasons as to why resolution is of such complexity. Despite Beijing's insistence that Taiwan is merely a "breakaway province," history tells otherwise. For one thing, Taiwan was never part of the People's Republic of China (PRC) and was part of the Japanese empire when the Republic of China (ROC) was founded in China in 1912. Although revisionists tell us otherwise today, even before Taiwan became incorporated into the Japanese empire at the conclusion of the First Sino-Japanese war in 1895, China's control of Taiwan was tenuous at best. Trade and other exchanges occurred routinely, but the island was regarded as peripheral.

However, although history can have some legal implications regarding Taiwan's status, what is of much greater import is the fact that over several decades, the Taiwanese have developed their own way of life, political system, and identity. Moreover, even though its status remains blurred (it has official diplomatic relations with only 21 countries), Taiwan (as the ROC) enjoys *de facto* sovereignty, which should confer upon it the same legal status as items regulated by customary international law. Although the ROC constitution, written in 1947 and imposed upon the Taiwanese after the KMT fled China, still lays claim to most parts of China's territory, contemporary Taiwan has finite and well-defined borders, including Taiwan proper as well as a series of outlying islands. This is what people think of when they think of Taiwan, and this is the piece of real estate that the majority of Taiwanese call their home and country. Among other characteristics that make Taiwan a sovereign state in all but name, it has, as per Article 1 of the Montevideo Convention of 1933, a permanent population, a defined territory, a government, and the capacity to enter into relations with other states. Additionally, it has a recognized currency, a passport that is recognized internationally, a standing army, and regular elections, and it is party to various global institutions (albeit often under creative designations so as not to alienate Beijing). Taiwan therefore has an idiosyncratic identity and functions as a normal state, despite the unconventionality of its status in the community of nations. Those certainly are not the attributes of a mere province; this is statehood, pure and simple.

The language used to describe Taiwan's situation and any future political union with China therefore should reflect this reality. *Reunification*, Beijing's favorite term, evidently misleads, and two objects that were never part of a whole cannot be *reunified*. The same goes for *separatism* and *splittism*, inasmuch as an entity cannot split from something of which it is not a part. *Independence* is the proper term to describe Taiwan's current status, though the designation status quo serves as a convenient euphemism. Any political union involving Taiwan and China should therefore be called *unification* or, if obtained through coercion or force, *annexation*.

What all this means for the appeal of unification with the PRC is often overlooked by the international community, which probably does not know enough to be able to make those distinctions (most people, including media organizations, therefore don't see a problem with referring to "reunification"). But for the Taiwanese, this is the heart of the problem: They are the citizens of a sovereign state, not the residents of a province, no matter how many incentives Beijing throws at them, such as dropping the need for Taiwanese to apply for entry permits to enter China, as it announced recently. Not only that, but Taiwanese have grown accustomed to the benefits of statehood – from the ability of their elected officials to conduct negotiations on their behalf abroad to something as seemingly insignificant as not being treated as an "at-risk" individual (or enjoying visa-free entry) when traveling overseas, something that cannot be said of Chinese citizens.[4]

By now it should be pretty clear why nationhood, that is, the agreement by most Taiwanese that they are the citizens of a nation-state known as Taiwan or the ROC, represents such a stumbling block to eventual unification with China. The question that needs to be asked, but rarely is, is *what could the Taiwanese possibly gain from seeing Taiwan become part of the PRC?* Starting from the assumption that Taiwan *is* a sovereign state, any unification in which Beijing rather than Taipei becomes the center will involve some losses – among those the ability to engage in foreign diplomacy and possibly to have their own armed forces. Even under the most generous offer (a E.U.-type arrangement is presently out of the question, as it regroups a community of *states*), something akin to federalism in the Canadian experiment, Taiwan would lose some of its ability to act independently, and the decisions made at the center would not be made solely in the interests of the Province of Taiwan. Furthermore, as we shall discuss in greater detail in later chapters, political union with an authoritarian state also inevitably leads to an erosion of freedoms and liberties, as is becoming clear with Hong Kong since retrocession in 1997. Additionally, even under the best offer, a political union would be unacceptable to a sizable portion of the Taiwanese population, which would necessitate policing action, if not military pacification, and thus ensure widespread human rights violations and the curtailment of freedoms across Taiwan, even if only temporarily.

The key here is that separatist provinces or territories normally seek a breakup from the center in order to *gain* something and to maximize their ability (often involving a repressed ethnic minority) to chart their own course after the center has proven unwilling or incapable to do so. Kosovo, East Timor, and more recently Ukraine's Crimea and Donbas regions are examples of such separatism (the first two became independent states, while Crimea has "chosen" union with Russia and Donbas has aimed for autonomy within Ukraine).

Taiwan is already what those regions were striving for, though evidently Beijing has often sought to clip Taipei's freedom by limiting what it can actually do within the international community. But we must realize that unification with China would not resolve those issues: Taiwan is currently unable to sign free-trade agreements (FTA) with major economies or to join UN agencies because such efforts are frustrated by Chinese interference; by becoming part of the People's Republic of China, the door to membership in those multilateral organizations would be shut forever. So Taiwan's position might not be ideal, given Beijing's interference, but it nevertheless has all the characteristics of statehood that are coveted by separatist movements worldwide.

The only benefits of unification with China would be the removal of the threat of military invasion by the PLA, as well as the possibility (though, as will be discussed later, this is far from certain) of large financial transfers. Some would argue that a political union would also facilitate trade and the movement of goods, though in the era of globalization, those could still be addressed through the signing of FTAs and other trade pacts between two or more states, as in the E.U., for example.

Rarely have the academics, government officials, and pundits who argue that Taiwan should arrive at some sort of political agreement with China paused to consider the impact that such an agreement – any agreement – would have on Taiwan's way of life and institutions. To them, unification might not seem as such a big deal, but that is because they fail to imagine what it would mean for the Taiwanese to lose some of what is theirs, to see the freedoms and liberties they fought so hard to install whittled away by a foreign regime that would then constitute the center. What's even worse is that many of those academics, people like Hugh White, as well as Charles Glaser and Lyle Goldstein, among others, who have argued that Taiwan should be ceded to China, either because they believe in some inevitable and insurmountable disparity in national power or because doing so would supposedly improve relations between China and the international community (hence the theme of Taiwan as an "irritant"), never asked *what Taiwan's 23 million people want.* It is difficult to believe that this omission is the result of oversight, though in White's case the fact that he had not visited Taiwan prior to airing such ideas may have limited the moral qualms by making an abstraction of the inhabitants of Taiwan; rather, it emanates from a realist view of international politics that tends to treat states and their people as mere commodities. Or it could simply be that these gentlemen already know what the answer would be if they showed the courtesy of asking.

So as we just saw, it is difficult to imagine the conditions under which peace could be achieved in the Taiwan Strait on *Taiwan's* terms. Consequently, whatever peace is struck will be largely based on what Beijing wants and would therefore engender some losses for Taiwan's side. Given that this appears to be unacceptable to the majority of Taiwanese, their best strategy is to buy time and to stick to the status quo until such a time as conditions will have changed sufficiently enough in China that a peace between equals, between two states, is possible. Of course, there is no guarantee that change of this kind will ever occur in China, and in fact even a democratic China – a distant prospect for the time being – might not be much more generous than its authoritarian predecessor when it comes to its territorial ambitions. Taiwan's best hope, therefore, is to hold the line and to do everything it can to delay, preferably indefinitely, the day when its people would be forced to capitulate. Undoubtedly conditions could change so that larger numbers

of Taiwanese become amenable to a political union with China, and if such a decision were arrived at by democratic means, the international community should
respect it. But for the foreseeable future this is highly unlikely to happen given the
trend lines in China under Xi Jinping's leadership and the impact of rising Chinese
nationalism on the treatment of its minorities, of which Taiwan would become one.

Taiwan's greatest asset in its defense against Chinese encroachment also happens
to be what distinguishes it most from its rival: its democracy.

Notes

1 This ended with the 16 December 2015 notification to U.S. Congress of a US$1.83 bil-
lion arms package. An essential resource on U.S. arms sales can be found in Shirley A.
Kan's "Taiwan: Major U.S. Arms Sales Since 1990," Congressional Research Service.
http://www.fas.org/sgp/crs/weapons/RL30957.pdf
2 Testimony of Randall G. Schriver, 3 April 2014. http://www.foreign.senate.gov/imo/
media/doc/Schriver_Testimony.pdf
3 Drawing from extensive interviews and probability sample surveys, Chen writes on pages
27–28, "[T]he low level of democratic support among the middle class tends to cause
this class to act in favor of the current authoritarian state but in opposition to democratic
change."
4 ROC and PRC citizens fall under different categories in the many systems used by law
enforcement, immigration, customs, and intelligence agencies worldwide.

Bibliography

American Institute in Taiwan, Taiwan Relations Act, http://www.ait.org.tw/en/taiwan-
relations-act.html
Bader, J (2012) *Obama and China's Rise: An Insider's Account of America's Asia Strategy*, Washington,
D.C.: Brookings Institution Press
Chen, J (2013) *A Middle Class Without Democracy: Economic Growth and the Prospects for Democ-
ratization in China*, New York: Oxford University Press
Cole, M (2015) "The Question That Is Never Asked: What Do the Taiwanese Want?" *The
Diplomat*, 13 May, http://thediplomat.com/2015/05/the-question-that-is-never-asked-
what-do-the-taiwanese-want/
——— (2015) "What Would Taiwan Actually Gain from Reunification with China?" *The
National Interest*, 19 May, http://nationalinterest.org/feature/what-would-taiwan-actually-
gain-reunification-china-12916
Manning, R (2015) "America's 'China Consensus' Implodes," *The National Interest*, 21 May,
http://nationalinterest.org/feature/americas-china-consensus-implodes-12938

PART 2
Taiwan's democratic firewall

4

THE DEMOCRATIC PENDULUM

It is often said, at least by those who support its continued existence as a free nation, that Taiwan's greatest asset is its democracy. There are several reasons why it may be so. For one, Taiwan's democracy distinguishes it from its neighbor across the Taiwan Strait, where authoritarianism and repression have been the only game in town since the creation of the PRC in 1949. Absent anything else, this contrast leaves no doubt even with those who know next to nothing about Taiwan that a fundamental incompatibility exists between the two societies. Another reason why democracy is an asset for Taiwan is that it has ideological appeal. Not a single speech in favor of Taiwan in, say, U.S. Congress fails to mention Taiwan's democracy as one of the principal reasons why it should be supported politically and militarily. Despite its selective track record on defending (or "exporting") democracy abroad, U.S. support for Taiwan's democracy over the decades is without doubt an instance of inspired and noble policy making, one that transcends the narrow interests of the defense industry that stands to benefit from the relationship. Even for other governments that perhaps aren't as open about their support for Taiwan as the U.S. is, Taiwan's democracy is often a shared value that is referenced with great respect.

Perhaps even more importantly, democracy is the "least bad" form of government known to man. It may be unruly and less "efficient" than the guided economies under the soft authoritarian regimes of Singapore and more restrictive ones like China's, but by giving the people a say in the political decisions of the country, it provides the regular outlets, or pressure valves, that do not exist in autocratic systems. Consequently, democracies can absorb and redirect mounting discontent much more effectively (and peacefully) than authoritarian and totalitarian regimes, where the absence of institutionalized outlets means that discontent cannot be channeled elsewhere and will eventually result in paroxysms of violence – governments overthrown, *coups d'état*, and the usually violent end of the deposed regime. That is why, despite the semblance of stability in China, a collapse of the entire system imposed by the increasingly controlling and paranoid CCP remains a distinct possibility, while such a development in Taiwan, imperfect though its democracy may be, is much less likely. Repression buys time, but it does not fix the problem; it only accumulates pressure. Democracy buys space, enough so that discontent can be expressed through retributive yet peaceful means – that is, regular elections. If a government performs poorly, it will suffer the consequences in the next elections, whether legislative or presidential. And between those elections, democracy allows the space for deliberation and protesting, which also serve the function of dissipating anger.

Moreover, in a society with a history and ethnic composition as convoluted as Taiwan's, democracy means that violent swings in one way or another, in which one minority suffers a sudden and major setback, are nearly impossible. Internal checks and balances exist so that the institutions of governance will tend toward the center. In autocratic regimes, a decision at the top can mean drastic change in one's status almost overnight, with little or any means to turn the situation around – violence excepted. In that same vein, Taiwan's democracy also equips it to deal with the existential threat posed by China because no political leader in Taipei can make unilateral decisions regarding the future of Taiwan's relations with China without paying the price. That is why, for example, the claim by many people in the green camp that President Ma was "selling out" Taiwan to China was a hollow one. However much he may have wanted to do so, Ma simply could not, as the entire government apparatus around him, not to mention civil society, would lean on him and force him to change course. With democracy, checks and balances are institutionalized, first in the form of regular elections and second through the participation of civil society in the political decisions of the country. In most cases, civil society intervenes between elections when the situation is such that society cannot wait until the next scheduled elections to punish wrongdoers.

After nearly three decades of experimentation with democracy, it can be argued that the Taiwanese identity was itself shaped by the adoption of this way of regulating politics and contention. In other words, what it *means* to be a Taiwanese cannot be dissociated from that experience at the state level, and in this respect I disagree with Professor Bruce Jacobs, who argues that, "despite the close association between the development of Taiwan's democracy and the development of Taiwan identity, the two processes remain conceptually distinct." Although Taiwanese identity and consciousness developed and existed well before the era of democratization, since the late 1980s democracy has become intrinsic to self-identification, and there is no doubt that asked to define what makes them distinct, many Taiwanese today would mention their democratic system. It also matters a lot that democracy in Taiwan developed indigenously; it wasn't imposed, even though the case could be made that U.S. pressure on President Chiang Ching-kuo in the early 1980s did force him to take the first steps toward liberalization of the country, which in turn permitted the gradual democratization of the political system.

It can therefore be said that Taiwan's democracy serves as a firewall, a line of defense against external intervention.

But those who argue that this is the case often stop there, which is reminiscent of the many people who concluded that with the fall of the Berlin Wall, the collapse of the Soviet Union, and the emergence of democracy across the globe, history had reached its ultimate stage of refinement. History had "ended." Of course, it took only a few years after the initial celebrations for events to prove otherwise, what with the return to "ethnic" wars in Africa and the Balkans, the rise of al-Qaeda, and the multiple "color revolutions" and "springs" that led to a variety of outcomes, not all of them favorable to democracy. Furthermore, it soon became clear that democracy wasn't a status that, once achieved, would remain in perpetuity. Instead, democracy exists along a spectrum, with an unachievable ideal on one end and failure on the other. Becoming democratic, holding regular elections to choose a leadership, and having opposition parties aren't enough. Just as important is the *quality* of that democracy.

And on that count, Taiwan hasn't fared that well. Not only, as we shall discuss in the next chapter, is China doing whatever it can to discredit and disrupt Taiwan's democracy, but, based on academic research on the subject, Taiwan is entering the make-or-break phase of young democracies – the 25- to 30-year mark where many fledgling democracies have failed and ceased to exist (Mainwaring and Shugart). As Garver notes, "One should not take Taiwan's democracy for granted. It is too easy for people raised and living in stable democracies to forget that history is littered with democracies that proved incapable of meeting the challenges confronting them." Furthermore, Taiwan is arriving at this stage at a time of global democratic malaise, where even "mature" and well established democratic model states like the U.S., the U.K., and Australia are suffering setbacks, which are further contrasted by the emergence of appealing alternatives such as the so-called Beijing consensus, or Chinese "meritocracy," or the late Lee Kuan Yew's (李光耀) "Asian values," which are often used to justify arrested progress on political freedoms.

Several of Taiwan's democratic shortcomings stem from structural problems, many of them legacies of the authoritarian era. Others are the result of an incomplete consolidation and the amplified inherent messiness of the freedoms made possible by democracy. Taiwan's future as a nation and its ability to counter China's influence will be largely contingent on the ability of its politicians and the public whom they represent to fix the many problems that currently haunt its democracy. Simply saying that Taiwan is a democracy isn't enough. In fact, without a proper definition of the term and its implications for the regulation of politics and contestation, it practically means nothing.

Let us first define the term, after which we can attempt to position Taiwan along its spectrum. The *minimalist,* or "narrow," definition of democracy is perhaps best summed up by Schumpeter, who described it as a system "for arriving at political decisions in which individuals acquire the power to decide by means of a competitive struggle for the people's vote." Generally, this is what comes to mind when people think of democracy. Elections are held regularly, there is universal (as opposed to restricted) suffrage, and the system allows for the existence of a plurality of political parties, including an opposition.

But that is insufficient as a definition. In 1953, Dahl introduced the term *polyarchy* ("many" and "rule") to define modern representative democracy with universal suffrage. The "crucial characteristics of polyarchal democracy," Dahl writes, are the right to form political organizations "to influence or oppose the existing government" and the existence of "organized interest groups." As we can see, Dahl's definition already enlarges the field of play by adding organized interest groups, or civil society, meaning that agents who exist outside the institutionalized political system are also a component of democracy with roles to play. All of this, of course, depends on a minimum level of freedom, such as freedom of speech, assembly, and the press, which, as Diamond observes, technically fall under the minimal definition of democracy but are rarely taken into account.

These definitions of democracy all have at their core the assumption that politicians, organizations, and civil society serve a function within the sphere of the holding of regular elections. However, with Dahl's inclusion of organized interest groups and the stipulation of certain freedoms comes the realization that a healthy democracy cannot be considered healthy only in times of election. In other words, the quality of a democracy should be determined not only by adherence to those rules *during* elections but also *between* them. This is where enlarged definitions of democracy, such as Jonathan Schell's "enlarged freedom," which calls for "the capacity to participate in political life, by such acts as voting, demonstrating, even rebelling against the government," enter a contentious zone (Schell). If totalitarianism represents one end of the political spectrum, the extremist definition of "enlarged freedom" can give rise to populism and, beyond that, to anarchy. The quality of democracy between elections and what can be done when institutions fail to play by the rules during those periods are the subject of Chapter 7.

For now, let us concern ourselves with the minimalist definition of democracy and where we can situate Taiwan on that spectrum in terms of popular expectations. Chu and Chang observe that among Taiwanese respondents to an East Asia Barometer survey on the subject, an "overwhelming majority" of views were positive.[1] Responses to questions on the meaning of democracy, moreover, were "generally similar" to those elsewhere in Asia. The largest proportion of respondents, Chu and Chang write, saw democracy as "either (or both) 'freedom and liberty' and 'political rights, institutions, and processes,'" which is consistent with the "standard Western understanding of liberal democracy" – in other words, the *minimalist* definition discussed earlier. The second highest definition of democracy among Taiwanese (24.1 percent) saw it as "popular sovereignty," "people's power," or "a government that cares what people think." "By and for the people" came in third, at 17.1 percent. According to his survey, the proportion of Taiwanese who ranked populist views was higher than anywhere else in Asia, while the proportion who defined democracy along the lines of liberal democracy (minimalist) was lower than in most of the new democracies. In other words, based on those findings, Taiwanese are generally more favorable to a somewhat "enlarged" definition of democracy than elsewhere in the region.

For anyone who has observed Taiwanese politics firsthand, it is rather clear that Taiwan's democracy is highly imperfect and not quite consolidated (no democracy will ever be fully consolidated, as democratization is a gradual process of advances and retreats). The flaws are rife and include various imbalances stemming from the authoritarian era, as well as high polarization along two main "ethnic" groups, political paralysis, hasty and incomplete constitutional reform, arrested transitional justice, corruption, "black gold" politics, irresponsible media, and the role of big business, all of which is exacerbated by the China factor, as we shall see in the next chapter. Taiwan has chugged along, but it is uncertain that it can continue to do so indefinitely, especially in light of the existential challenge posed by China. Moreover, the problems that plague Taiwan's democracy have contributed to growing disillusionment with the system, which has both undermined public confidence and encouraged recourse to more "extreme" measures.

In many ways, Taiwan's democracy today is reminiscent of the new democracies described by Diamond in the early 1990s, many of which he regarded as "quite 'illiberal.'" "Yes," he wrote (Diamond 2003), "they had competitive elections, even real uncertainty about which party would win power, and even alternation in power, but for much of the population, democracy was a shallow or even invisible phenomenon." He continues:

> What many (or most) citizens actually experienced was a mix of distressed governance: abusive police forces, domineering oligarchies, incompetent and indifferent state bureaucracies, corrupt and inaccessible judiciaries, and venal, ruling elites contemptuous of the rule of law and accountable to no one but themselves [. . .] There were elections, but they were contests between corrupt, clientelistic parties that served popular interests only in name. There were parliaments and local governments, but they did not represent or respond to broad constituencies.

Taiwan's democracy certainly isn't as dire, but many of the problems described in that paragraph should be familiar to those of us who closely observe its politics. Given its Leninist roots, the KMT never was intended to operate as a political party in a pluralistic environment. Though survival compelled it to adapt and eventually to democratize the system over which it had ruled as an authoritarian regime for 40 years (or nearly 80 if we include its time in China), the KMT has yet to divest itself of all the advantages it accumulated under authoritarianism. This includes immense wealth, deep and far-reaching connections within the business community, indirect control of or substantial influence over the media, privileged relationships with the military and security branches, and a tendency to treat internal dissent undemocratically. The money connection remains a major impediment to the party's reform, as its existence and competitiveness as a political entity are directly linked to a business community that both depends on it for the advancement of its interests and can cause the party severe harm if it fails to meet their expectations, which increasingly means the ability to conduct business in and with

China. As such, the KMT is very much the kind of "clientelistic" party Diamond writes about, which became all too evident when KMT legislators and negotiators who were very close to major business interests became involved in the signing of various economic pacts with China, including the CSSTA, which sparked the Sunflower occupation in March 2014. Moreover, while it reluctantly embraced democracy, the KMT transformed into a machine meant to perpetuate its existence by developing a huge network at the grassroots, recruiting "native" Taiwanese and using its wealth and connections with the business community to create dependencies. This helps explain why a much reviled party that ruled Taiwan with an iron fist for four decades was still able, after democratization, to win free and fair elections – and to stage a comeback after it was briefly displaced by the DPP between 2000 and 2008. The KMT adapted, and it adapted well, but by joining the democratic game it also warped the ideal.

It is not surprising, therefore, that when Chen Shui-bian won the presidency in 2000, the DPP, which originated in the streets and had no experience in governance, ended up adopting many of the practices of its predecessor (including the retention of a central standing committee). Consequently, while there is no doubt that the founders of the party intended to gain power so that they could transform Taiwanese politics, in the end the DPP eventually turned into the same kind of electoral machine that the KMT had become: dedicated to its self-perpetuation and having to develop a good relationship with the business sector, even though the DPP could never dream of securing the kind of relationships that the KMT had built over decades. It also meant developing ties with influential and often wealthy religious organizations such as Tzu Chi (慈濟), the prounification Fo Guang Shan (佛光山), and even conservative Christian churches like Bread of Life (靈糧堂).

Governance meant that, little by little, the DPP lost its essence as a progressive party and its original ideology as a force for democratic change in Taiwan. Its members became politicians, and in that process they severed their connection with the people, a transformation that is certainly not unique to the DPP in the history of politics. Many members continued to espouse the party's progressive ideology, but over time their ability to redirect the party toward its foundational ideals diminished.

As a result, by the time civil society decided to take action in the spring of 2014, many disillusioned activists placed the KMT and the DPP on an equal footing. Indicatively, when the civic organization Citizen 1985 (公民1985) held a rally by the Legislative Yuan on National Day in October 2013, it symbolically raised both the KMT and DPP flags. The major parties, the only two that truly had a shot at running government under the current system, were undistinguishable symbols of public resentment. Whether that was a fair assessment of the two parties is debatable, but there is no doubt that this sentiment was shared by a large number of people in Taiwan. During the two years that I closely monitored social movements across Taiwan, I had often asked young activists whom they intended to vote for in 2016. The majority of them – some resignedly, others angrily – told me they would simply cancel their vote as both parties "sucked." Others said they would vote for independent candidates or a "third force."

The fact that young and educated activists, conceivably the most politically aware people from that generation, had become so disillusioned with party politics in Taiwan was certainly a bad omen for Taiwan's democracy. Among many young people, this state of affairs led to resignation and the belief that politics were beyond their control and that their destiny and that of their nation were subject to unstoppable forces. Such perceptions, of course, played right into the Chinese propaganda on "historical inevitability."

As Chu and Chang argue, poor performance by a newly installed democratic regime "may foster doubts about democracy as a whole." Unfortunately, the East Asian Barometer survey used by the authors is not only the only survey that, to my knowledge, looks at perceptions of democracy in Taiwan, but it also ends with the Chen Shui-bian era and therefore does not take into account the impact that a highly unfavorable assessment of the Ma Ying-jeou administration, especially during its second term, is likely to have had on perceptions of democracy. Although recent events may have undermined the reputation and appeal of democracy (and the CCP has used this to disparage democracy as a workable system), it is possible that the belief that governance under President Ma had become more authoritarian than under his predecessor – a view that was prevalent among many of the activists who took to the streets from 2012 onward – may have encouraged Taiwanese to pay more attention to the quality of democracy and to take necessary (and, according to some, drastic) action.[2]

Moreover, in their section discussing survey results on the meaning of democracy, the authors observe that only 6.3 percent of respondents stated that "social equality and justice" were an apt way to describe democracy. In light of the mass rallies, sustained activism, and escalating social tensions that emerged under President Ma over controversies such as the death of Army conscript Hung Chung-chiu (洪仲丘) in July 2013 or the forced evictions and home demolitions in Miaoli County, there is a distinct possibility either that Chu and Chang's findings wrongly reflected underlying beliefs in "social equality and justice" as being part of the definition of democracy among Taiwanese or that such factors as human rights violations took on renewed precedence under the Ma Ying-jeou administration.

While there were warning signs of a possible "democratic breakdown" in Taiwan in the spring of 2014, the outcome of the nine-in-one elections on 29 November that year, in which the KMT was severely punished for its perceived bad governance and lost control of most municipalities around the nation, has served as a respite and may have renewed faith in the ability of retributive democracy to keep government in check. The election of Ko Wen-je (柯文哲), a trauma surgeon who ran as an independent candidate and who was closely affiliated with civic movements, as Taipei mayor against the KMT's Sean Lien (連勝文), who to many embodied everything that was wrong with the existing system, also contributed to the cooling of tempers. Moreover, immediately after coming into office, Mayor Ko launched a frontal attack on the corrupt or at a minimum opaque practices of government bidding that had become common practice under his predecessors – a formula that one wishes could be applied at the national level. Ko's election and the setback suffered by the KMT in the municipal elections partly explain why civil society, which had acted with such unity during the Sunflower Movement occupation of the legislature, seemed to come undone only months later: President Ma, stripped of his party chairmanship, was a lame duck president and in no position to impose policies that did not have public support. With nothing to focus on, civil society returned to its previous state of heterogeneity and infighting (more on this in Chapter 7).

In the lead-up to the presidential and legislative elections in January 2016, it appeared that many Taiwanese were amenable to waiting 2015 out. For many, the upcoming elections – and DPP presidential candidate Tsai Ing-wen's embrace of and willingness to work with elements of the "third force" – were a cause for optimism; the last chance, perhaps, for democracy to prove itself. But doubts persisted, and while Tsai seemed genuinely committed to turning her party around after two arguably disastrous years under her predecessor Su Tseng-chang (蘇貞昌), who was widely accused of "missing the boat" on social activism, party reform is proving difficult, in part because of the need to compromise with different internal factions, vested interests, and the refusal of party elders and conservatives to retire and give space to a new generation of leaders.

It goes without saying that healthy political parties are indispensable components of a healthy democracy.

As Huang Kuo-chang (黃國昌), an outspoken activist and researcher at Academia Sinica, said before he became chairman of and ran for office on the New Power Party (NPP, 時代力量黨) ticket, "several heads would need to roll" before the public could trust the DPP again. To a large extent, Tsai succeeded in rebuilding that trust ahead of the 2016 elections by fielding many new candidates and forming alliances with smaller parties, such as the NPP, that had emerged from civil society in the wake of the Sunflower Movement. A true test of the party's ability to govern and to convince the public that it can do so will be the performance of the DPP mayors who won by a landslide in late November 2014 and whether they deal more effectively and justly than their predecessors with issues of accountability, development, urban renewal, and corruption. And, of course, in the wake of the 2016 elections, how well it can run the entire country.

The controversy over the 25 December 2014 Tainan city council speaker election, in which four DPP city councilors voted for Lee Chuan-chiao (李全教), the KMT candidate, after receiving substantial sums of money, also hurt the party's image, though Tsai's decision to immediately expel the four from the party likely mitigated the long-term impact. The keen interest of a number of DPP councilors who were elected in late 2014 to run in 2016 also smacked of careerism and created a bad impression with the public, which had every right to expect that the people they elected would complete their full terms.

The DPP also continues to be haunted by the accusations of corruption that surrounded the Chen Shui-bian family toward the end of his second term. A party that had come to power promising a clean break with the past had ended up doing no better than its predecessor. The long-term impact that this has had on public trust in the DPP cannot be underestimated and seriously contributed to the public's cynical view of politicians.

These problems continue to haunt the KMT, which has more than its share of dinosaurs and conservatives, not to mention those who continue to actively oppose the further "Taiwanization" of the party, which is necessary if the party is to remain relevant and *electable* in Taiwan. However, all things being equal, if both camps fail to reform, the wealth disparity and resources in favor of the KMT will continue to give it an advantage over any of its opponents. The DPP therefore has every advantage in being the better party, to be seen to be serious about reform, and to reform to the extent that its appeal will be regarded as threatening enough to the KMT that it sees no option but to reform itself, much as it did in the early 1980s when it faced the prospect of international isolation.

No doubt there are forces clamoring for moderation and change within the KMT, even more so following its poor performance in the 2016 elections; whether they can have the upper hand against the more conservative elements within the party will be largely contingent on the outcome of the upcoming internal battles. Of course, this assumes that rational forces (rational in the sense that they seek to reflect public expectations) are guiding the party.

Another factor that contributes to the rising cynicism about the main political parties is the high degree of polarization that exists in Taiwanese politics. The scorched-earth politics that the KMT and the DPP, as well as their allied smaller parties, have engaged in over the years has been detrimental to Taiwan's democracy. Not only has it poisoned the political environment, it has made cooperation nearly impossible and ensured that Taiwan remains a house divided – "blue" versus "green," "Mainlander" versus "Taiwanese." This schism, which has been irresponsibly reinforced by an equally dualistic media environment, with talk shows, newspapers, and TV stations clearly aligning with one or the other side, has made reconciliation and transitional justice incomplete at best. And it has led to paralysis, as seen in the legislature during the Chen era, where the KMT repeatedly blocked the budgets necessary for national defense and the acquisition of foreign arms to help defend the nation. Politics – party politics – took precedence over ensuring that Taiwan had the ability to defend itself against external aggression, a folly that continues to hurt Taiwan to this day by costing it nearly a decade of force modernization. Similar blocking tactics have been used by the DPP camp to prevent the implementation of policies favored by the KMT. Far too often, real negotiations were replaced by fistfights in the legislature and a travesty of the legislative process. There was little will, let alone space, for cooperation. So the nation stalled, and this paralysis was a contributing factor in the loss of faith in Taiwan's democracy, which was increasingly associated in the public mind with "chaos" in the legislative chambers or the assumption of ulterior motives in everything that politicians did.

This division also helped Beijing, which in its efforts to drag Taiwan into its embrace never had to deal with a United Front in Taiwan; instead, the Taiwanese did the work of dividing China's opponent all by themselves. As we will discuss in Chapter 7, mounting discontent with the longstanding "ethnic" and political polarization was a key contributor to the reemergence of civil society and the rise of a new form of civic nationalism that dispensed with the follies of a dying era.

A few words need to be said about Taiwan's media and their impact on the nation's democracy. As previously discussed, the existence of a free press is one of the criteria for the minimalist definition of democracy. To a large extent, the media in Taiwan is considered to be free, and according to annual surveys by organizations such as the U.S.-based Freedom House, it is one of the freest in Asia. Although Taiwan has followed the global trend whereby major traditional media outlets are taken over by large corporations, there is no major problem of censorship of the press in Taiwan, at least not to the extent seen in China, Singapore, and, increasingly, Hong Kong. The media outlets that fall under the Want China Times Group (旺旺中時集團) are the exception, which explains why Group chairman Tsai Eng-meng's (蔡衍明) attempt to acquire Next Media's operations in Taiwan in 2012 sparked mass protests and why a large number of its editors and journalists have resigned in recent years.

The main issue with Taiwan's media is that they tend to be highly sensationalistic and often fail to fulfill several of the principal roles of the press, which are to hold government accountable and to speak the truth in the face of power. There is very little investigative journalism in Taiwan; instead, readers are bombarded with trivialities – the juicier the better. Gossip about the sexual misdemeanor of members of the artistic community, food scandals, and looped footage of car accidents consume a lot of airtime on TV news. There is surprisingly very little coverage of major global political developments, which includes China, where crises can send ripples across the Taiwan Strait.

Taiwanese journalists are overworked, often very young (and female) and therefore unable to stand up to their editors when unreasonable requests are made of them. Moreover, the high output that is expected of beat reporters encourages cutting corners, with the result that information often goes unverified. Far too often sources are anonymous, and sometimes they are invented altogether. Overstretched journalists often have no option but to "pool" information with others, relying on accounts by other reporters – including their competitors – to produce their own articles. As the premium is on covering everything, everything is diluted. The result is a regurgitation of press conferences by government officials or company representatives, and little else. Moreover, if a media outlet reports something, all the other outlets must also report it. This is usually done by rewriting an initial article without giving proper attribution, creating a feedback loop: As even minor events are covered by all the media, it becomes difficult to tell the difference between news that matters from all the noise that is generated. Moreover, this race to cover everything means that a false news item, or downright fabrication, will also become its own reality through replication and false corroboration.

Such is the frequency of disinformation going through the system that it has become difficult to trust traditional Taiwanese media as a reliable source of information about developments in Taiwan. Telling real news from what isn't is an onerous task, and consequently responsible journalism is often drowned out.

Politicians have also exacerbated this problem by constantly spreading disinformation to undermine their political opponents. Such tactics reached a new low during the 2012 presidential campaign when the KMT, aided by cabinet officials, falsified documents pertaining to DPP candidate Tsai Ing-wen's role in Yu Chang Biologics Co (宇昌生技). The campaign director for Sean Lien, the KMT's mayoral candidate for Taipei in the nine-in-one elections in November 2014, continued the tradition with various attacks against independent Ko Wen-je, arguably turning the campaign into one of the nastiest in Taiwan's recent history. Similar tactics were again used in the 2016 presidential election.

In return, a complicit media report every single allegation by politicians, however disreputable they may be. The fact that a legislator who would have been forced out of office by the Appendectomy Project in early 2015 if referendum thresholds were not so high in Taiwan (the KMT has opposed efforts to lower them as part of constitutional reform) continues to receive airtime in the media is a symptom of Taiwan's ailing industry. Whenever those individuals say something or post a comment on their Facebook page, their arguments, however wild, take over the airwaves and become the subject of TV talk shows and thus cannot be ignored by the people against whom the allegations are made. Consequently, politicians are compelled to defend themselves and to "prove a negative." In the end, rather than discuss their policy platforms, politicians and the talking heads who appear in the media on their behalf engage in cycles of claim and counterclaims, until the next cycle begins.

The situation with the media has become such that at least one major U.S. defense firm with a presence in Taiwan now refuses to talk to journalists. They have been burned too often. Even more troubling is the fact that some foreign wire agencies, which do not have enough resources in Taiwan, often translate news articles from Chinese-language media. In several instances, those translated articles have little grounding in fact, which nevertheless become "reality" overseas.

The sensationalism and fabrication that are characteristic of Taiwanese media have in turn exacerbated the polarization of society, both in terms of the zero-sum battle between the DPP and the KMT and on such matters as national defense, where journalists and their audiences delight in exploiting every accident, every espionage case, to discredit the armed forces. Nobody seems to care that this risks undermining morale in the ranks and hurts the military's ability to recruit soldiers.

The media, which tend to be "positioned" according to their ideology and political camp, therefore amplify the political schism, turning news into entertainment or propaganda. Rather than act as a check on government, they take sides and rarely provide the middle ground where real debate and new ideas could emerge. The positioning of media outlets also affects every individual in the industry. Consequently, a journalist or editorial writer for the *Ziyou Shibao* (自由時報) will always be assumed to be supporting the DPP no matter what. Those who strive for neutrality are discredited by association, the assumption being that they have no free will and are therefore merely automatons regurgitating propaganda that is fed them by their employers.

The many problems with journalism in Taiwan have turned off young journalism students, who are aware that the ideals of the profession will be compromised the moment they start on the job. The good ones are overtaken by the rotten apples and by a system that cannot tell the difference between the two. Pressure for advertisement revenue in an oversaturated media environment is only making matters worse and ensuring that the smaller, new online media that have appeared in recent years, in large part due to disillusionment with the traditional media, will struggle to survive.

As a result, the media in Taiwan have been failing in the task to inform the population so that it can make enlightened decisions. Taiwan's dysfunctional media sector has a detrimental impact on the quality of Taiwan's democracy. State intervention, which would raise all kinds of questions about censorship, will not work. Not until the public starts demanding true media reforms by taking action through boycotts or activism, as with the attempted acquisition of Next Media in 2012, will the necessary change occur. Until that time, traditional media will continue to undermine rather than bolster Taiwan's democracy. It is little wonder that Taiwanese youth have increasingly relied on social and new, online-based media for their information, although those can also suffer from problems related to reliability and quality control.

Other, more structural, problems are associated with stalled reform, a process that has often fallen victim to the high polarization and that is also held hostage by the fact that Taiwan cannot write a new constitution to better reflect its current needs and reality. As President Chen told the opening ceremony of the International Conference on Constitutional Reengineering in New Democracies in September 2005, "[N]ot only the design of the current constitution is laden with contradictions and incompatibilities, its actual implementation is also morbidly inefficient." But doing so would likely be regarded by Beijing as *casus belli*.

So reforms have been incremental at best and often politicized. As a result, the current system is a Frankenstein monster, which limits government efficiency and serves to undermine trust in democracy, even though democracy has nothing to do with the problems with governance that have been encountered. According to Chu and Chang, the attendant "underdevelopment of constitutionalism" meant that among the third-wave democracies, "Taiwan's democratic transition was often cited as a unique case where a quasi-Leninist party not only survived an authoritarian breakdown but also capitalized on the crisis to its advantage."

Among other things, the constitutional revisions that were implemented between 1990 and 1997 were marred by "unilateral imposition," with President Lee designing a semipresidential system that gave substantial autonomy to the cabinet and the legislature but also ensured that the president could control the two branches as head of the party. Furthermore, as Chu and Chang observe, the constitutional revisions were "poorly designed for the unanticipated scenario of a divided government," which is exactly what Taiwan ended up with in 2000, with the DPP securing the presidency with a mere 39.3 percent of the popular vote but severely handicapped by its minority in the Legislative Yuan.

The lack of a level playing field also ensures that, besides the KMT and the DPP, smaller parties – including the new "third force" that emerged in the wake of the Sunflower Movement in 2014 – face extremely high thresholds that limit their ability to play an institutionalized role in governance. There has been talk of transitioning from a mixed-member majoritarian (MMM) system in the legislature to mixed-member proportional representation (MMP), as exists in Germany, but so far there has been little movement toward implementation, in part because doing so would benefit smaller parties and threaten the KMT's uninterrupted control of the legislature. Additionally, the strong links that have developed between powerful corporate interests and Taiwan's main political parties over the years (as stated earlier, the DPP had to mimic the KMT in order to survive) means that the smaller parties will be at a disadvantage in that they will not have the resources necessary to compete.

Commenting on electoral politics in Taiwan during a conference call in April 2014, Diamond was unsparing, calling it "a really bad electoral system."[3]

Largely contributing to this, he said, was that "Taiwan stuck itself with extremely unfortunate institutional arrangements that got worse rather than better in the last round of constitutional revision" in 2004, when the number of seats in the legislature were halved from 225 to 113 and a single-member district, two-vote system was enacted for legislative elections. The "incremental reforms," which received high popular support and also led to the abolition of the Assembly, were in response to what Rigger describes as plummeting support for an "overreaching" and "obstructionist" legislature.

But in Diamond's view, this was a mistake. "The single non-transferrable vote system [used by Taiwan in the past] was such a disaster, almost anything would have been an improvement," he said. But the new system that was adopted in 2004 failed to improve the situation.

"Taiwan adopted a highly majoritarian electoral system in which the vast majority of the seats are single-member-district, winner-take-all seats," Diamond said. "Why the DPP agreed to this I still can't figure it out, because it was utterly predictable that it was not going to be to their advantage initially."

"And the KMT won most of the seats – surprise, surprise," he said, adding that political scientists had all along predicted that this was going to happen.

According to him, the decision to halve the size of the legislature was a "really bad idea." Taiwan is now "stuck with very sub-optimal political institutions that contribute to political polarization."

"You've got a situation where the DPP is underrepresented in parliament relative to its natural relative base of support in society." Consequently, "there's an excessively large majority, and a large number of DPP legislators, frankly, have resorted to pretty dramatic obstructionist tactics."

One of Diamond's recommendations would be for Taiwan to bring back the number of seats to its original number, which would create the necessary "maneuvering room for alternative political voices [and] more fluid coalitions."

Many of the problems that were identified with Taiwan's democracy exist elsewhere, even among much more "mature" and stable democracies. For example, the stranglehold that the two major parties in Taiwan have over the body politic, which leaves very little room for the emergence of new political forces, has long existed in the U.S. and elsewhere, and for the most part, this has been detrimental to the quality of the democracy in those countries as well. But one thing sets Taiwan apart from those other ailing democracies: It faces an existential threat from a giant authoritarian neighbor that is fully committed to annexation, by force if necessary. As such, while democratic crisis can cause all kinds of trouble in countries like Canada, Australia, or the U.S., such breakdowns are unlikely to put the survival of those nations at risk. For Taiwan, however, breakdown has ramifications for its survivability as a sovereign state, and as such every improvement to the system, every reform that fosters cooperation and unity, strengthens the island's ability to stand on its own against external meddling.

As mentioned at the beginning of this chapter, Taiwan's democracy acts as a firewall against China. The healthier it is, the more credible its defenses will be. Conversely, weaknesses risks being exploited by China, which in times of hostility and rapprochement alike never stopped in its attempt to corrupt, thwart, and undermine Taiwan's democratic institutions. In fact, the rapprochement that has occurred during the eight years of the Ma Ying-jeou administration has largely facilitated Beijing's job by opening up almost every sector of Taiwan's society to China – its money, its influence, and its intelligence officers who operate under many guises.

Notes

1 Surveys should always be regarded as scientifically imperfect instruments to assess public opinion, where methodology, sampling, and the framing of the questions are all subject to the authors' biases. I would also add that Chu and Chang's categories of democracy have been disputed by other academics. Nevertheless, the *East Asia Barometer* is one of the most cited surveys on the subject among Asian respondents. Readers are also encouraged to consult the Academia Sinica-based Taiwan Social Change Survey, which tracks a variety of long-term trends within Taiwanese society.
2 Asked to contrast the past regime with the Ma regime (Chen Shui-bian), 12.6 percent of respondents saw the past regime as "very dictatorial" and 49.4 percent as "somewhat dictatorial," versus 1.3 percent and 13.0 percent, respectively, for the CSB regime. To my knowledge, no such survey has been held comparing the Ma Ying-jeou regime with that of his predecessor.
3 https://www.youtube.com/watch?v=2FGxKzgC8VQ

Bibliography

Chu, Y-H and Chang, Y-T (2008) "How Citizens View Taiwan's New Democracy," in *How East Asians View Democracy*, Chu, Y-H, Diamond, L, Nathan, A and Shin, D-C, eds, New York: Columbia University Press: 91–2
Dahl, R (1998) *On Democracy*, New Haven: Yale University Press: 90
Diamond, L (2003) "Defining and Developing Democracy," in *The Democratic Sourcebook*, Dahl, R, Shapiro, I and Cheibub, J, eds, Cambridge: MIT Press: 32

——— (2008) *The Spirit of Democracy: The Struggle to Build Free Societies Throughout the World*, New York: Henry Holt: 292

Garver, J (2011) *Taiwan's Democracy: Economic and Political Challenges*, Garver, J, Ash, Robert and Prime, Penelope B, eds, London: Routledge: 5

Jacobs, B (2012) *Democratizing Taiwan,* Leiden: Brill: 6

Mainwaring, S and Shugart, M (1993) "Juan Linz, Presidentialism, and Democracy: A Critical Appraisal," Working Paper #200, Notre Dame, IN: Kellogg Institute, July 1993

Rigger, S (2011) "The Politics of Constitutional Reform in Taiwan," in *Taiwan's Democracy* London: Routledge: 45

Schell, J (2003) *The Unconquerable World: Power, Nonviolence, and the Will of the People*, New York: Henry Holt: 238

Schumpeter, J (1947) *Capitalism, Socialism, and Democracy*, 2nd ed, New York: Harper: 269

5

CHINA'S ASSAULT ON TAIWAN'S DEMOCRACY

It is often said that Taiwan's democracy, which has been described as the first "Chinese" democracy, is a thorn in the side of the CCP, whose ability to remain in power in China depends on the continuation of single-party authoritarianism. Although it is true that the existence of a democratic alternative within such geographical and cultural proximity to China is seen as a threat to Beijing, the CCP's efforts to discredit and thwart it are not primarily in response to a perceived threat.

The reason is simple: The Chinese do not need foreign examples of democracy to appreciate its advantages, nor do they need Taiwan to experience liberal democracy at work. Between 1978 and 2003, a total of 700,200 Chinese students and academics studied in 108 countries and regions all over the world (Tao, Berci, and He). According to statistics from China's Ministry of Education, 459,800 Chinese were studying abroad in 2014 alone. Since 1978, a total of 3.5 million Chinese have received an education abroad. And those numbers will only continue to rise as the Chinese become wealthier and increasingly mobile. Furthermore, given the long standing trends, the great majority of Chinese who head overseas to receive an education end up in Western democracies, with the U.S. as the most favored destination. Consequently, even if Taiwan no longer existed or if its political system reverted to authoritarianism, the ability of ordinary Chinese to experience democratic systems firsthand would not be undermined. As will be discussed later, it should also be said that Taiwan is not a means to an end, such that its existence as a democracy is not necessary for the future democratization of China. If the Chinese want democracy, they can develop it on their own; they have enough intelligent people to achieve that. The notion that Chinese need to be "taught" democracy, either by the West or their Taiwanese counterparts, is an insult to the Chinese people.

Of course, a large enough number of Chinese must want democracy for themselves. Various studies suggest that exposure to democracy among Chinese students abroad has not translated into a greater desire for democracy in China; in fact, depending on how one defines democracy, the reverse seems to be the case. "Living overseas had a negative effect on respondents' support for Chinese democratization, as the longer they had lived in the United States, the better they understood Western democracy and were suspicious about whether China should pursue immediate democratization," Han and Chen observe in the abstract of a recent study on the subject. We should keep in mind, however, that for a variety of reasons, a number of Chinese academics have been complicit in the CCP's efforts to invalidate or undermine the appeal of democratization in China. For example, the University of Macau, where one of the authors of the study teaches, has become notorious in recent years for muzzling and firing professors who refused to toe Beijing's line (Chou).

Discussing another survey on Chinese attitudes toward democracy, Shi writes that while "many of the same democratic values that undergird the old and new democracies in Asia are also widespread in China," they tend to function to "engender citizen support for the nondemocratic regime." Moreover, most Chinese respondents associated democracy with "the people are masters of the country" and "the authorities listen to people's opinions." Both of these responses, Shi writes, are "compatible not only with the doctrine of socialist democracy but also with classic Confucian ideas of benevolent dictatorship, since they do not require competitive political pluralism to be put into effect."[1] In other words, as long as what the people define as "democracy" does not threaten the CCP's authoritarian grip on political institutions in China, it will tolerate it, although it will not be democracy as it is understood and practiced in Taiwan, let alone in the West.

If the CCP truly abhorred and feared the "pollution" of Western-style liberal democracy, it would have done a lot more to prevent young Chinese from going abroad and being exposed to those ideas – including Taiwan, where a growing number of Chinese have come to study in recent years. Assuming that the attitudinal surveys just discussed are right, if exposure to Western-style democracy is not leading to a desire for such a system in China and may in fact harden "anti-Western" sentiment, then we could argue that, like many of his Western counterparts who believed that engaging China would help create a middle class and spark democratization in China, President Ma was either naïve or had ulterior motives and used the promise of democratization in China as cover for other, perhaps less noble objectives.

China's problem with Taiwan's democracy is not, therefore, primarily ideological. Instead, it is *technical*. And that is why the term "firewall" is the perfect word to describe Taiwan's democracy. The CCP resents Taiwan's democracy because this system of regulating policy decisions and contention, with competitive political pluralism at its core, makes it substantially more difficult for China to get what it wants from Taiwan – unification. Used to a consensus style of decision making and top-down implementation with only marginal input from society, the CCP has hit a wall with Taiwan, as its counterparts in negotiations must be directly answerable to the public. Besides electoral retribution (and fear thereof), which can set back policy or impose correctives (as occurred in the 2016 elections), Taiwan's democratic system leaves space for civil society to take action between elections when a government is seen to have overreached, as the Sunflower Movement made clear in 2014 over the CSSTA.

A sign of the maturity of Taiwan's democracy is that it goes beyond merely allowing society to play a role in policy making; when civil society feels compelled to protest or even take dramatic measures, the boundaries of the response that is permissible by law enforcement agencies impose constraints that simply do not exist in authoritarian societies like China. In other words, to echo Schell, the manner in which Taiwanese define their democracy includes permission to take action against the government without the armed forces or antiriot police taking extreme measures to reinstate public order, such as what occurred around Tiananmen Square in June 1989, not to mention the actions taken on a regular basis by quasi occupation forces in Tibet and Xinjiang. The fact that society reacted with such horror to the overuse of police powers during the eviction of the Executive Yuan on the night of 23–24 March 2014, in which several dozen protesters were injured, speaks volumes about what Taiwanese regard as permissive use of force to counter dissent, a threshold that tends to be much lower than in many mature Western democracies.

As a result, governments in Taiwan cannot simply impose their will on society, even when they have control over the Executive and enjoy a majority of seats in the legislature. When governments show contempt for that aspect of Taiwan's democracy, as the Ma administration quickly realized, they pay a heavy price, both at the polls, as occurred on 29 November 2014, and as a result of internal pressures to bring government more in line with public expectations. That the KMT came close to a mutiny during the Sunflower occupation, followed by Ma's ouster as party chairman and complete discrediting as a national leader, should be sufficient to remind autocratically inclined politicians of the risks of alienating the public. The split that has widened within the KMT in the past year was in my opinion directly related to the Sunflower occupation, no matter how hard President Ma has tried to downplay the movement's long-term impact on domestic politics. Democracy tends to push parties toward the middle and weeds out more extremist forces. In a Taiwan context, this means that hardline, or deep green, parties that advocate for immediate independence and "anti-China" policies are nonviable as political forces and will remain on the margins; the same applies to hardline, or deep blue, parties that support immediate unification with the PRC and with which the CCP has cooperated over the years. The "moderate" zone in between, where the light greens and light blues interact, is where the real action takes place.

A healthy democracy therefore imposes checks and balances and consequently prevents the sudden shifts that can occur in authoritarian societies. Policy change is therefore gradual and can end if it is seen to have gone too far. That is why a Taiwanese leader could not suddenly announce the unification of Taiwan and China or even the signing of a "peace agreement." That is also the reason why a leader could not unilaterally declare *de jure* independence – Beijing's nightmare scenario.

The second reason why Taiwan's democracy is problematic for the CCP is that the healthier it is, the greater the contradiction that exists between the two societies. Thus, as long as democracy continues to function in Taiwan, it will be very difficult to achieve the ultimate goal of unification on China's terms (and those are the *only* terms on the table). Moreover, the healthier Taiwan's democracy is, the further China will be from achieving its goals, as this has direct ramifications for the terms under which Taiwanese *could* agree to unification. In other words, how a democracy performs – from the good functioning of government institutions to the ability of society to take direct action when institutions are seen to be failing – influences perceptions of the *legitimacy* of democracy. And the more legitimate a democracy is regarded, the harder it will be to convince the population that an alternative system, especially one in which rights and freedoms are curtailed, is worthy of embrace.

This, above all, is why Beijing has worked so hard over the years to discredit and corrupt Taiwan's democracy. While progress in cross-strait relations has occurred, in China's assessment it has been too slow, especially after Xi Jinping assumed the leadership in 2012. Supported by rising nationalist sentiment in China and the view that China needs to move on to bigger things (i.e., becoming a regional or global superpower), President Xi has stated that the Taiwan "problem" cannot continually be passed down to future generations. And although other leaders before him have used similar wording, there is reason to believe that President Xi, who is conceivably the most powerful Chinese leader since Deng Xiaoping (鄧小平) if not Mao Zedong (毛澤東), is much less patient than his predecessors, something that has become apparent with China's recent activity in the South China Sea. Hence, since 2012, the acceleration of China's efforts to undermine Taiwan's democratic institutions and the increasingly active relationship between CCP officials and the prounification forces that exist outside government, including crime syndicates, businessmen, and local persons of influence in Taiwan. This is the kind of "underground front" that Loh describes in her book of the same title about CCP activities in Hong Kong before and after Retrocession in 1997.

This has also meant grooming, co-opting, and empowering Taiwanese politicians who favor unification and whose views have tended to be out of step with those of contemporary Taiwan, particularly its youth.

After eight years of rapprochement and "goodwill," Beijing has realized that it didn't get as much as it had hoped for from Taiwan. Political talks remain off the table and are unlikely to occur for the rest of the Ma administration. What's worse, whoever comes after President Ma will probably be even less amenable to, or able to deliver on, the kind of agreements that the CCP would regard as real "progress."

President Xi's impatience has also led to a tightening of the CCP's grip on every aspect of Chinese society, which the new National Security Law (國安法) promises to make even tighter (including, presumably, for the Taiwanese). Press freedoms, already in a deplorable state, have further eroded. Law enforcement agencies have clamped down on civil society, and the education system faces tremendous pressure to conform. A xenophobic and anti-West sentiment has risen and in fact has been encouraged, and the pacification of Tibet and Xinjiang has intensified, so much so that Xinjiang SAR could very well be a Palestine or South-ern Lebanon in the making. Recent disturbances in Hong Kong have also led to a hardening of Beijing's stance there, and across China President Xi has rid himself of his political opponents under the guise of a nationwide campaign against corruption.

All of this has occurred at a time when Beijing was trying to win the hearts and minds of the Taiwanese. Aware of the stark contrast between developments in China and Taiwanese society, the CCP had no choice but to accelerate its efforts to present a friendly façade. Consequently, censorship, propaganda, political warfare, and United Front activities accelerated, and Beijing worked even harder to co-opt influential members of the business community in Taiwan. Beholden to the belief in economic determinism, despite its proving to be a failure in Tibet, the CCP also tried to sell ordinary Taiwanese on the material benefits of closer economic inte-gration with China.

What this tells us is that Beijing's ability to win the hearts and minds of the Tai-wanese people hinges on two principal variables: the quality of Taiwan's democracy, and the situation in China. At the moment, the situation in China, which is char-acterized by an increasingly repressive system, serves to intensify the contrast with Taiwan and therefore undermines the appeal of unification. Meanwhile, although it remains fragile, the "rise" of civil society and its impact on political parties have given new breath to Taiwan's democracy, which also undermines support for uni-fication with China. In other words, the current trends in both societies are dia-metrically opposed to the "peaceful" unification coveted by Beijing. Given what is at stake, it is surprising how little ordinary Taiwanese seem to know about develop-ments in China and Hong Kong (see Chapter 6). It would be in their interest to pay much closer attention to what is going on there and for Taiwanese media to provide better coverage (the challenges posed by greater censorship there notwithstanding).

What with all the contradictions, economic disparity, and crises that exist across China, as well as the brewing trouble on its "peripheries" (e.g., Hong Kong, Xinjiang, and Tibet), it is unlikely that the CCP will loosen state controls anytime soon. Since more repression risks further diminishing the already low appeal of unification, the CCP can only hope to dim the contrast between the two societies by whittling away at Taiwan's democracy to make it less efficient and to discredit it in the eyes of the Taiwanese. In other words, one of China's strategies against Taiwan is to make its society more closely resemble that of China (see Chapter 12).

The CCP has taken several approaches to erode Taiwan's democracy and thereby undermine the performance of its institutions, with the twin aims of (1) accelerating the process of unification ("quick results" such as agreements, concessions, etc.) and (2) discrediting democracy as it is practiced in Taiwan and blowing holes in its fire-wall ("long-term results" with more durable impact).

Political warfare, propaganda, and United Front Work

In the more traditional sense of the word, China's efforts to penetrate Taiwanese soci-ety have revolved around conventional espionage. Key military installations such as radar sites, naval and air bases, arms procurement deals with the U.S., and the communications systems used by the Taiwanese government have long been in the Chinese espionage apparatus's crosshairs. Through various means of collection, the recruitment of sources and cyber warfare, the PLA and Chinese state apparatus have sought to gain an advantage over their ideological opponent by accessing its secrets.

Less well understood are China's multifaceted political warfare efforts, which rather than stealing secrets, are geared toward persuasion by means both covert and overt. Loosely defined, propaganda and United Front Work are also part of that sustained campaign, involving dozens of agencies, CCP departments, and hundreds, if not thousands, of businesses, organizations, groups, charities, foundations, and individuals.

The PLA's General Political Department's Liaison Department (GPD/LD),[2] "an interlocking directorate that operates at the nexus of politics, finance, military operations, and intelligence," has spearheaded those efforts. Needless to say, Taiwan has been one of its principal targets, and as the PLA, its activities have intensified rather than atrophy in the midst of warming relations between Taipei and Beijing. Much of the propaganda and political warfare operations launched against Taiwan in recent years has involved individuals or front organizations that are linked to the GPD, under what is known as the Three Warfares (三戰): psychological operations (心理戰), public opinion/media warfare (輿論戰), and legal warfare (法律戰). Making sense of it all is a substantial challenge, as China's political warfare apparatus consists of layer upon layer of associations and organizations, many of which are also engaged in legitimate business. And many are registered in Hong Kong, which has facilitated entry into the Taiwanese market by bypassing strict regulations (albeit gradually loosened under President Ma) regarding "Mainland" operations.

A constellation of organizations, such as the China Association for International Friendly Contacts (CAIFC, 中國國際友好聯絡會), are actively involved in fostering exchanges with similar organizations in Taiwan. With ostensible connections to connected and extremely wealthy organizations such as China Energy Fund Committee (CEFC, 中華能源基金委員會), a subsidiary of the energy giant the CEFC China Energy Co., Ltd. (Huaxin, 中國華信), these groups organize conferences, forums, and various "cultural" events where academics and younger people are exposed to China-centric propaganda. The China Institute of Culture Limited (CIOC, 中國文化院), another CEFC subsidiary, has organized a number of cross-strait forums over the years. These endeavors, which come with free travel and sponsorship, create their own incentives for participation and therefore encourage self-censorship among those on the Taiwan side who are keen to participate or to receive funding for future activities. Culture, tea, literature, graphic arts, cinema, and Buddhism have all provided a façade that could facilitate political warfare and a convenient means to penetrate Taiwanese society.

Revealingly, CEFC (中國華信) has an office in the Taipei 101 building, where it operates under the name China Ocean Fuel Oil Co. Ltd. Many art galleries are believed to serve as fronts for the GPD/LD, as well as local temples and a variety of businesses. Some of those organizations have also cooperated with universities in Taiwan, sometimes with the participation of the Taiwan Provincial Government (臺灣省政府). Individuals who are believed to be associated with the GPD/LD have also played roles organizing visits to China by Taiwanese officials, including figures from the opposition DPP, such as Frank Hsieh, whose itinerary was reportedly prepared for maximum propaganda effect. Whether Hsieh, a former presidential candidate and chairman of the DPP, and his entourage were even aware of this is very much in doubt.

Many of the individuals involved in those operations are also current or former intelligence officers. One example is Wang Shu (汪澍), chief executive officer of China Huayi Broadcasting Corp (CHBC, 中國華藝廣播公司), which in October 2014 co-organized a salon titled Promoting Cultural Integration and Increasing Cultural Identity in Fuzhou, Fujian Province. Wang is also the commander of GPD 311 Base (61716 Unit), which is reported to be at the "forefront" of "applied psychological operations and propaganda directed against Taiwan." According to Stokes, as a deputy-corps-level organization, 311 Base "carries roughly as much status as all those six conventional missile brigades [from the Second Artillery Corps' Base 52] that target Taiwan *combined*." The Base is located in the same building as the Huaxin Training Center (華信培訓中心), which itself is funded by the Fujian Huaxin (CEFC) Holding Company, a subsidiary of the US$30 billion CEFC China Energy Co. CEFC denies any knowledge of 311 Base's operations.

The same investigation demonstrates the complexity and range of the networks involved in such activities. Wang has also been seen in the company of Xu Jialu (許嘉璐), who is associated with CAIFC, CEFC, and Confucius Institutes and is the president of the Nishan Forum on World Civilizations (尼山世界文明論壇), which overlaps with several GPD/LD organizations, including CEFC. Xu is also chairman of the China Association for the Promotion of Culture (CAPCC, 中華文化發展促進會), an organization that is actively involved in the promotion of a cross-strait "peace accord" and reunification. It is claimed that Xu "orchestrates" China's overall political-warfare strategy.

The CAPCC also has close associations with the Hong Kong–based *China Review News* (中國評論新聞), which is suspected of serving as an instrument for the GPD/LD to conduct political warfare and propaganda work on Taiwan. The publication has journalists in Taiwan.

Another interesting figure who is often seen in the company of Taiwanese negotiators, academics, and former officials at cross-strait conferences is Xin Qi (辛旗), a deputy director of the GPD/LD since at least 2011, who is also vice president of the CAIFC and a senior director of the CAPCC. Xin has been a leading figure promoting the early initiation of peace accord negotiations and unification talks with Taiwan. According to Stokes and Hsiao, he has also proposed the notion of Taiwan and China forming Cross-Strait Peace and Development Committees to augment the unofficial SEF-ARATS channel and has been a strong proponent of joint efforts to defend China's maritime interests. Xin Qi also reportedly played a crucial role in the drafting of the so-called Anti-Secession Law in 2005 (Kamphausen, Lai, and Scobell).

Other seemingly benign institutions, such as the Peace and Development Research Center (四川國際和平與發展研究中心), the National Society of Taiwan Studies (全國台灣研究會), the China Painting Academy for Friendly Contact (中國友聯畫院), the China Unification Promotion Party (中華統一促進黨), the Concentric Patriotism Association (中華愛國同心會), the Alliance for Unification of China (中國統一聯盟 (統盟)), the Chinese Democratic Progressive Party (中國民主進步黨), the Cross-Strait Integration Society (兩岸統合學), the Chinese Huangpu Four Seas Alliance Association (中華黃埔四海同心會), the China People's Democratic Unification Association (中國全民民主統一會), the Cross Strait Unification Association (海峽兩岸統一促進會), the Taiwan Cross Strait Peaceful Development Association (台海兩岸和平發展研究會), the Taiwan One Country Two Systems Studies Association (台灣一國兩制研究協會), the China Federation for Defending the Diaoyu Islands (中國民間保衛釣魚台聯合會), and the Chinese Association for Political Party Liaison (中華政黨聯誼會) are also involved, one way or another, in such efforts. A good number of those organizations were created in 2008 or 2009.

In Taiwan, the Fo Guang Shan Foundation for Buddhist Culture and Education (佛光山文教基金會), Tsai Eng-meng's Want China Times Group, and the Chinese New Immigrants Party (中華新住民黨), among others, have cooperated with some of the abovementioned organizations to organize a variety of events promoting Chinese culture, with a strong emphasis on the position that Taiwan is part of China, and may have played liaison roles.

These are just a few of the many companies and organizations that play a role in the Three Warfares against Taiwan. Identifying all of them and countering their activities are insurmountable tasks, given how much the CCP has invested in those programs and the billionaires on both sides of the Taiwan Strait who have lent their resources to such projects. In May 2015, Taiwan's National Security Bureau (NSB, 國家安全局) revealed that its agents had discovered more than 100 Chinese offices that were operating illegally in Taiwan, with some reportedly engaging in activities that threaten national security. We can assume that some of those were engaged in "underground work," conducting espionage or political warfare, recruitment or acting as channels to move money around. Those are only the ones that were discovered or that failed to maintain a good cover of legitimacy. There likely are many, many others.

Track Two diplomacy, often involving academics and universities focusing on issues such as the territorial dispute over the Diaoyutai islets in the East China Sea (known as the Senkakus by Japan), also appears to have been infiltrated by the CCP propaganda department and the GPD/LD. In some instances, this has resulted in calls for and pressure on the Ma administration to cooperate with Beijing in defending "shared interests" in the East and South China Seas against "external aggression." Students have also reportedly been targeted by political warfare and United Front Work bodies.

According to recent reports, the Bank of China (中國銀行) and the Industrial & Commercial Bank of China (ICBC, 中國工商銀行), which has been trying to acquire a 20 percent stake in the banking arm of Taiwan's Sinopac (永豐金融控股), may also be used to move money around to facilitate criminal activities. A case in Italy, in which the bank has been drawn into a "massive money-laundering investigation,"[3] highlights the risks that such legal institutions could be called upon to conduct similar work in Taiwan, such as providing underground Chinese organizations with the funds that they need to sustain their operations, recruit and pay sources, and so on. The banking sector is among those that have been liberalized in recent years under President Ma. The Bank of China is active in Taiwan and its headquarters, which opened on 27 June 2012, is located in Xinyi District.

Even though they are not overtly belligerent, those activities nevertheless serve to undermine Taiwan's democracy by creating dependencies, cultivating sources, encouraging self-censorship, and using their formidable resources to elbow out other voices and thereby narrow the discourse on culture and identity in the Taiwan Strait. The involvement by PLA intelligence officers in this whole enterprise should leave little doubt as to the ultimate intentions of such endeavors.

As the recent controversies over Dio Wang (王振亞), an Australian senator, and Michael Chan (陳國治), Ontario's Minister of Citizenship, Immigration and International Trade, have made amply clear, the Chinese government may also insert its migrants as agents in positions of influence in foreign governments. Both Wang, who emigrated to Australia in 2003, and Chan, who did so in 1969, have expressed strong support for the manner in which the CCP handled the Tiananmen Square protests in June 1989 (Nylander), with Chan, for example, referring to China in a CCP-run publication as "my motherland." Chan is also believed to have developed a network of pro-Beijing officials, some of whom are known to have engaged in efforts to censor criticism of Beijing in Chinese-language newspapers (Offman). Chan's dual allegiances arguably constitute a conflict of interest, as he is in a position to influence Canadian trade and immigration policy in a way that favors China and that may be detrimental to Canada's democracy. Moreover, this means that pro-Beijing agents are in a position to influence Canberra and Ottawa's policies on Taiwan. The parallels with developments in Taiwan are hard to miss.

Big business

Pressure by high-profile Taiwanese tycoons on the government (and society) to adopt policies that favor the further loosening of trade and economic regulations across the Taiwan Strait did not begin with the arrival of President Ma, nor, for that matter, did cross-strait business exchanges commence after 2008. But the ability of the Chinese government to manipulate and use Taiwanese tycoons to influence policy and warp Taiwan's democracy has increased by leaps and bounds under Ma.

Months after his election, President Chen Shui-bian was already under pressure by China-based tycoons to liberalize his economic policies, which many in the business community regarded as too restrictive. For example, Wang Yung-ching (王永慶), the founder of Formosa Plastics Group (台塑集團), lambasted

President Chen in December 2000 for his adherence to the Go Slow, Be Patient policy of engagement with China and failing to do what was necessary to improve the cross-strait economic environment. One of the things that Wang wanted Chen to do, among others, was to recognize the one-China principle – a no-go for the DPP. Taiwan Semiconductor (TSMC, 台灣積體電路製造股份有限公司) Chairman Morris Chang (張忠謀) and Quanta Computer (廣達電腦) Chairman Barry Lam (林百里) (Taiwan's sixth wealthiest man in 2015), who attended the meeting between Chen and Wang, echoed the sentiment and called for relaxed restrictions (Kastner).

During the same period, Taiwanese companies like Chi Mei Corp (奇美實業), whose owners were vocal supporters of President Chen and the DPP, were treated as green, and Chinese officials warned other companies across China not to buy their products, resulting in millions of dollars in losses. In 2005, just as Chi Mei was preparing major additional investments in China, company founder Hsu Wen-long (許文龍) gave in to Chinese pressure and announced in a retirement statement that, "Taiwan and the Mainland belong to one China."

Several Taiwanese entrepreneurs who own businesses and factories in China have learned over the years to hide their political colors to avoid getting into trouble with the Chinese authorities. Those who failed often encountered additional red tape, harassment, and difficulties with local law enforcement. Consequently, to ensure business continuity, they have often felt compelled to spread CCP propaganda, even if they do not believe a word of it, which nevertheless contributes to the chorus of voices that call for closer ties across the Taiwan Strait. *Taishang* organizations have also joined the effort and helped promote the KMT's China and economic policies. Although most of them are legitimate, some elements have been co-opted by the CCP, as the Tung Shu-chen (董淑貞) incident made clear during then-KMT Chairman Eric Chu's (朱立倫) visit to China in May 2015.[4]

Following Ma's election in 2008 and as Taiwanese firms became increasingly dependent on the China market for growth or their survival, China-based tycoons applied even more pressure on the government in Taipei to lift restrictions on investment. They needed access to China's booming market in order to sell their goods, to the supply chain in which China had become the "world's manufacturer," and in order to remain competitive, to the large reserves of low-cost labor there. Looser environmental restrictions and rules on work conditions were also appealing attributes. The Economic Cooperation Framework Agreement (ECFA), signed in June 2010, was the first major article of economic liberalization between the two sides and was followed by several other agreements and relaxed rules on targeted industries.

Over time, several sectors, such as the tourism industry, became utterly dependent on the Chinese market and turned into powerful lobbies to pressure the government to further relax regulations on the number of tourists who are allowed into Taiwan on a daily basis and eventually to permit the entry of free independent travelers (FIT). Many of the companies and sectors that benefited from the loosened regulations had ties with local officials or with the KMT, which served as a way to reward supporters of President Ma's China policies and to punish those who opposed them. This created "winners" and "losers" and furthermore explains why the GDP growth engendered by the ECFA and subsequent agreements only had a marginal impact on overall wealth generation. A few made fortunes; many didn't benefit; others were forced out of the market.

The KMT–CCP nexus and the dynamics that cross-strait liberalization generated created major incentives for the business community to bandwagon. Compounding this was the fact that the DPP was perceived as "weak" on the economy and, because of its ideology, unable or unwilling to expand cross-strait ties to the extent that was beneficial to the corporate world.

Consequently, in the 2008 and 2012 presidential elections, many high-profile business leaders came out and clearly stated their support for the KMT candidate while threatening economic catastrophe if the DPP were elected. Although the DPP has indeed tended to be more conservative when it comes to opening up Taiwan's markets to China, the fears were overblown but were nevertheless repeated ad nauseam within the business community, in the media, and in capitals abroad.

It didn't help the DPP that some of the top negotiators on Taiwan's side had business interests in China or had family members who did, a conflict of interest that seems to have been lost on many observers. The family of Straits Exchange Foundation (SEF) Chairman Chiang Pin-kung (江丙坤), Taiwan's chief negotiator on cross-strait issues during most of the Ma administration, had business interests in China, a fact that, according to the opposition, should have discredited him and prevented him from having the job (Chiang called those "irresponsible slanderous remarks.")

Sensing a way in, Beijing began using those tycoons, upon whom the KMT relied to discredit the DPP on the economic front, for propaganda purposes. More of them began advocating pro-Beijing positions, including the so-called 1992 consensus, the recognition of which Beijing has made the inevitable basis for continued cross-strait relations. Many have made about-faces or what critics would call Faustian deals, including the previously mentioned Tsai Eng-meng, Hon Hai Precision (鴻海科技集團) Chairman Terry Gou (郭台銘), Evergreen Marine (長榮海運) Chairman Chang Yung-fa (張榮發), Cathay Financial Holdings (國泰金融控股股份有限公司) Chairman Tsai Hong-tu (蔡宏圖), and Far Eastern Group (遠東集團) Chairman Douglas Hsu (徐旭東), among many others.

Gou, Taiwan's second wealthiest individual in 2015 with a personal wealth of US$6.7 billion, has involved himself directly in Taiwan's electoral politics, often appearing with KMT candidates at local rallies and promising investment if local voters make the "right" choice. The outspoken Gou also attempted to intervene during the Sunflower Movement's occupation of the legislature, a bizarre move that raised questions about the intentions of a businessman who has cozied with the regime in Beijing. Gou has occasionally expressed displeasure with democracy in a way that was oddly reminiscent of the CCP's views on the subject. In May 2014, he lamented that, "social movements have let talent go to waste and wasted the nation's resources," adding that democracy "does not put food on the table."

That same month, Gou also threatened to stop paying his taxes if the National Communications Commission (NCC, 國家通訊傳播委員會) did not rule in favor of his 4G venture, which would have brought in transmission towers by China's Huawei Technologies (華為), a company with presumed ties with the PLA and that many Western countries – as well as Taiwan's NSB – have regarded with suspicion.

In 2015, Gou once again used his status and fortune to meddle with politics, this time at the municipal level, by buying a half-front-page advertisement in six Chinese-language newspapers to pressure the Taipei City Government on construction projects, a move that Taipei City Mayor Ko Wen-je likened to "corporate threats." Then, in June that year, Gou offered high-paying jobs to the former Xinyi police chief, whom Ko had publically berated for failing to take action against a prounification group that had repeatedly assaulted Falun Gong practitioners outside Taipei 101 and his wife. It was difficult not to interpret the job offer as a slap in Ko's face.

Another wealthy entrepreneur who has affected Taiwan's democratic institutions is Farglory Land Development Co. (遠雄建設) Chairman Chao Teng-hsiung (趙藤雄), who in 2013 bemoaned that "social justice" and activism had arrested Taiwan's economic development in the past decade. In other words, a healthy democracy was, in his view, detrimental to the pursuit of money – by the rich and the powerful. Chao himself soon became a victim of "social justice" when activists began protesting at the site of the Taipei Dome (大巨蛋), an already unpopular project that became even more controversial after Farglory began cutting down old trees on two major roads. As with other controversial construction projects elsewhere, the construction company resorted to physical violence and hiring individuals likely tied to organized crime to intimidate civil society. Chao, who subsequently faced corruption charges, also became the target of Taipei Mayor Ko's scrutiny of the bidding process for the Taipei Dome process, which showed indications of impropriety and perhaps outright corruption.

The list of Taiwanese business leaders who have adopted a pro-Beijing stance also includes HTC Corp. (宏達電) Chairwoman Cher Wang (王雪紅), the daughter of the aforementioned Wang Yung-ching. Hoping to tap into the gigantic cell phone market in China and facing growing competition from other handset makers, Wang, a once proud Taiwanese entrepreneur, started referring to herself as Chinese (中國人). Wang has also been accused of allowing Chinese authorities to monitor dissidents using HTC handsets. Those allegations remain unproven.

Additionally, Wang's strong Christian beliefs may also have played a role in her desire to ingratiate herself with the Chinese government, whose permission she presumably needs for her Faith-Hope-Love Foundation to continue its work in Guizhou, one of the poorest areas of China. The Forerunner College, started with a US$28.1 million donation by Wang, provides three years of free or low-cost education to students from low-income families. Wang's husband, Chen Wen-chi (陳文琦),

is a born-again Christian and CEO of VIA Technologies, which runs the college. In a 2001 interview, Wang described VIA as "god's company."

Besides providing homes and education, one of the main goals of the foundation is to spread the gospel. The website ChristianVolunteering.org lists volunteering opportunities at the Guizhou Forerunner College, which it describes as "great for Christians." There is no doubt that proselytizing is a major endeavor of the college. Given the CCP's very strict controls of religion and severe assault on "underground churches," it is not inconceivable that Wang's ability to sponsor such schools in China is contingent on her willingness to reciprocate in some manner.

The negative effects of big business on Taiwan's democracy can be serious, as high-profile tycoons use their immense resources and influence to maximize their interests, which sometimes can come at the expense of the national interest and impose serious costs in terms of the freedoms enjoyed by the Taiwanese and the nation's sovereignty. Knowing that money is one of the tools used by the CCP to bring Taiwan ever closer to its embrace, trade agreements, investments, and other deals cannot be regarded solely as business deals; when it comes to relations in the Taiwan Strait, *everything* is political. Consequently, even if they might not agree with Beijing's ideology or support unification (most do not), business tycoons can often make decisions – or influence decisions by the Taiwanese government – that play right into Beijing's strategy. In the end, their actions can narrow Taiwan's maneuvering room and limit the ability of its people to determine their future.

Media

Given its ability to keep the public informed and to serve as a check on the authorities, the media has also become a battlefield for the CCP. Its crackdown on journalism (and "rumors") in China, with closures, fines, and arrests, has been successful and stands as one of the most glaring broken promises on Beijing's part following the 2008 Beijing Olympic Games. Investigative journalism has been forced underground, and the number of foreign journalists who were expelled or who were unable to renew their work visas has risen considerably in recent years. Beijing has also not hesitated to block foreign news services in China to punish those who did not comply, thus creating strong incentives for self-censorship. Bloomberg, Reuters, and the *New York Times* are among the major foreign news outlets to have faced such a dilemma recently. Hong Kong media have also encountered difficulties due to business dependencies and takeovers, leading to self-censorship and, at the *South China Morning Post* (*SCMP*), the firing of reputed journalists and editors.

The State Council Information Office (SCIO) acts as regulator and uses its vast powers to ensure that media outlets do not depart from the "correct" line. Working in tandem with the CCP Propaganda Department, the State Press and Publishing Administration, the State Administration for Film, Radio and Television, and the State Council's Ministry of Industry and Information Technology, the SCIO enforces censorship across print, the airwaves, and the Internet and ensures that sensitive subjects such as government corruption, environmental disasters, public health, separatism, and of course national defense are covered in accordance with the guidance provided by the official state media (when a media outlet publishes or airs something sensitive, expect that it has either been vetted by the authorities for reasons known only to the leadership or that the journalists and editors responsible will soon be punished). According to Shambaugh, there are ten major media conglomerates in China, whose political connections and need to remain in the good graces of the CCP to ensure their financial well-being also ensure a modicum of compliance with Beijing's censorship rules and avoidance of "dangerous" subjects.

Of course, such state controls of information are in stark contrast with the "out-of-control" media environment in Taiwan, where almost anything – including fabrication – goes. Although investigative journalism is not strongly encouraged, when it occurs and when political scandals are exposed, the journalists, editors, and media outlets responsible will not be threatened with imprisonment, fines, or closure for their actions. Nor, thankfully, will they risk being physically attacked by pro-Beijing gangsters, as happened to a number of media tycoons and editors in Hong Kong in the past few years. In other words, Taiwan's media is "free," even though the existence of conglomerates gives rise to the conflicts of interest that exist in even the most "mature" democracies.

As part of its strategy to undermine Taiwan's democratic institutions, China has also sought to erode press freedoms on the island in order to control the message and create an environment that is more favorable to China and more conducive to the ultimate goal of unification. Indirectly, the CCP has benefited from media conglomerates with substantial business interests in China. Chief among them is Tsai Eng-meng's Want China Times Group, which controls a plethora of print, radio, and television outlets, as well as cable distribution systems, in Taiwan. One of the wealthiest individuals in Greater China and the number one billionaire in Taiwan, with a personal wealth estimated at US$8.3 billion, Chairman Tsai has made his fortune selling food and beverages in China, where he now operates hotels and hospitals and has real estate investments. Stridently probusiness and pro-China, outlets under Mr. Tsai's control, such as the *China Times* (中時電子報), *Shibao Zhoukan* (時報周刊), and CtiTV (中天電視), have heavily self-censored and very much toe Beijing's line on matters pertaining to cross-strait relations.

Moreover, one will not find criticism of Beijing's human rights record or repressive policies in Tibet and Xinjiang in the pages of the *China Times* or in CtiTV news broadcasts. Mr. Tsai's acquisition of the China Times Group in 2008 has led to a marked deterioration in the quality of its news coverage and heavy politicization in favor of the KMT and Beijing. Some analysts also point out that Mr. Tsai started receiving VIP treatment in Beijing after his acquisition of the China Times Group.

Senior Chinese officials have visited studios under the Group, and Mr. Tsai has also cooperated with the CCP-controlled Fujian Daily Group in launching *Media Plus* (兩岸傳媒), a magazine focusing on "cross-strait media and cultural affairs."

In a media environment that is already notorious for loose fact-checking and fabrication, media outlets under Mr. Tsai's control are in a league of their own. Several editors and journalists in recent years have resigned in anger or taken early retirement after being forced to write false news articles targeting critics of the Ma administration, including activists like Huang Kuo-chang and Chen Wei-ting (陳為廷), under their byline. Such activities became normal practice amid the escalating protests over Mr. Tsai's attempted acquisition of Next Media Ltd.'s (壹傳媒) Taiwan operations in 2012 and 2013, which critics said would have created a "media monster" controlled by China's "black hand," and during the Sunflower Movement occupation of the Legislative Yuan in 2014. Some individuals associated with Mr. Tsai also put immense pressure on and assassinated the character of officers at the NCC charged with evaluating Mr. Tsai's attempted acquisition of cable TV services owned by China Network Systems (中嘉網路) and Next Media, seriously undermining democratic processes.

It goes without saying that had Mr. Tsai's bid to acquire Next Media succeeded, the *Apple Daily,* a thorn in the side of the CCP, would probably have suffered the same fate as the *China Times* or the *South China Morning Post* in Hong Kong. One of the few media outlets that remain critical of Beijing (and the KMT) would have been neutralized (which explains why some senior persons at the Liberty Times Group seemed to hope that the takeover would proceed, as this would very likely have had a positive impact on sales of the *Liberty Times*).

Besides providing "coverage" and editorials that were highly critical of the young activists during the Sunflower occupation, an investigation has shown that firms affiliated with the group may have engaged in "electronic warfare." For example, attempts to post articles on Wikipedia that described the actions of overzealous riot police during the eviction of the Executive Yuan on the night of 23–24 March 2014 were systematically blocked by a user whose IP address was eventually traced back to a communications company that is believed to belong to the Want China Times Group and that has operations in Taiwan and China.

Mr. Tsai has also been accused of allowing what is known as "placement marketing" – advertisement prepared by various levels of the Chinese government that passes off as news. In most cases, placement marketing operations have proceeded as follows: A regional government in China pays money to a media outlet and in Taiwan requesting "positive coverage" that is timed to coincide with a visit to Taiwan by a Chinese provincial governor, mayor, or delegation.

Needless to say, the temptation to resort to such methods to support various trade or other agreements with China is very strong, and the mechanisms by which this is accomplished may have become more refined since the use of placement marketing was exposed a few years ago. Media companies that draw advertising revenue from China, which has risen steadily following the lifting of restrictions on Chinese investment in Taiwan, may also be tempted to shape their reports and editorials accordingly, without the need for direct placement marketing.

Besides Mr. Tsai, other Taiwanese billionaires have sought to acquire media outlets in Taiwan. HTC Chairwoman Cher Wang was part of an investor group that took over Hong Kong's TVB in 2011. When, in January 2015, TVB sold its majority (53 percent) stake in its Taiwan business, TVBS (無線衛星電視台), three Taiwanese investment firms – Li Mao (利茂投資有限公司), Te En (德恩投資股份有限公司),

and Lien Hsin (連信投資股份有限公司) – scooped it up. All three are allegedly related to Wang. In January the next year, it was announced that the three share-holders would acquire the remainder of the shares in TVBS.

Like Wang, Gou and Daniel Tsai (蔡明忠), chairman of the Fubon Group (富邦集團) and one of the nation's richest individuals, have also long expressed interest in acquiring media in Taiwan. The acquisition of media outlets by big conglomer-ates with business operations in China could have a substantial impact on press freedoms in Taiwan and the public's ability to access the information they need to make informed decisions.

Additionally, the need to secure advertising revenue and the inherent incen-tives for self-censorship mean that media engaging in investigative journalism and critical of China or pro-Beijing authorities in Taiwan will be unable to touch that money and will therefore remain in a permanent state of financial uncertainty, a problem that big conglomerates do not face. Comparisons of the front pages of the major dailies in Taiwan following major political developments on the island under the Ma administration are usually revealing: The pro-KMT and pro-Beijing newspapers have half- or full-page ads by major companies, while the pro-DPP or Taiwan-centric newspapers splash the entire page with photos and coverage. For example, the 19 August 2013 front pages of the *Liberty Times* and *Apple Daily* were entirely dedicated to the events of the previous night, when protesters marched from Ketagalan Boulevard in front of the Presidential Office and occupied the Ministry of the Interior (內政部) building to protest a series of forced evictions and demolitions; conversely, the *China Times* and *United Daily News* (聯合報) had full-page advertisements by Chanel. It soon becomes evident that major corpora-tions (Chinese or with large stakes in the Chinese market) can use the denial of advertisement revenue as a weapon to punish media outlets that cause trouble by providing coverage on controversial issues.

The sword of censorship also hangs heavily above the film industry, with copro-ductions between Taiwanese film companies and their counterparts in China and Hong Kong having a negative impact on the subjects that can be treated in the pro-ductions. As with the news media, producers and directors whose work is regarded as proindependence or that touches on subjects that are frowned upon by Beijing risk being increasingly marginalized, with direct repercussions on their ability to secure funding and to distribute their films to a wider market.

The desire to access the huge China market also creates incentives that are det-rimental to a free press in Taiwan. For example, both Formosa Television (民間全民電視公司) and SET TV have allegedly stopped featuring news coverage that is critical of China or, in SET TV's case, have cancelled a talk show whose host was openly critical of the CCP, in return for the ability to broadcast entertainment programs in China (the host of the program has never confirmed that his fate was related to his employer's desire to tap into the Chinese market).

The situation with the Want China Times Group is a huge missed opportunity for Taiwan, as the empire enjoys the kind of access in China that other media companies in Taiwan can only dream of. But instead of encouraging its journalists to do real journalism, they merely asked them to engage in "safe news" (e.g., business, travel, human interest, and so on) and propaganda. More than ever, Taiwanese need to know about political and social developments in China. The one media company that could provide such a service will not do so.

According to Freedom House's 2015 *Freedom of the Press* report, cyber attacks originating in China also pose a serious threat to press freedoms in Taiwan. For example, the Hong Kong and Taiwan websites of the *Apple Daily* and its parent company, Next Media, were the targets of repeated distributed denial-of-service (DDoS) attacks in 2014, leading to the "total collapse" of its websites on 18 June. In times of high tensions in the Taiwan Strait, similar attacks would likely be launched against other media outlets in Taiwan and overseas.

Another worrying development that could have a negative impact on the already limited ability of Taiwanese journalists to report on developments in China is related to the passing of the new National Security Law in China in June 2015. The new law, which contains obligations for "all Chinese people" in China, Hong Kong, Macau, and Taiwan, could cause serious legal problems for Taiwanese journalists and columnists, namely for reporting on a variety of topics that fall under the purposefully ill defined category of "national security." Article 81 of the law, for example, states, "Violations of this law and other relevant laws, by failing to perform national security obligations or engaging in activities endangering national security, shall be investigated for legal responsibility according to law."

As the Hong Kong Journalists Association (HKJA) recently observed, the new law "covers an overly broad range of areas, not in alignment with The Johannesburg Principles on National Security, Freedom of Expression and Access to Information which have been stipulated by international experts and widely adopted globally, thus rendering it easily subject to abuse, and infringement of human rights."[5]

The Association of Taiwan Journalists (ATJ, 台灣新聞記者協會) has also weighed in, observing that the law's extraterritoriality ignores the fact that "Taiwan, whose constitutional name is the Republic of China, is a democratic sovereign and independent state whose sovereignty does not overlap with the PRC." If implemented and enforced, China's new National Security Law could force any Taiwanese who travels frequently to China for work to avoid writing about subjects that may fall under the "violations" stipulated. Of course, any reference to Taiwan existing as an independent state or any work that supports Taiwan independence would likely fall in that category, as this constitutes "splittism," one of the so-called three evils (the other two being "terrorism" and "extremism").

Local proxies

President Ma had four good years of engagement with China, during which his government was able to deliver most, if not all, of the low-lying fruits coveted by Beijing. However, it soon became evident after his second inauguration that the CCP was losing patience with him. The clock was ticking, and Ma had been unable to initiate political talks with China, which all along was the ultimate goal of engagement – at least that's how the CCP saw it.

Late in his reelection campaign, Ma had floated the idea of signing a "peace accord" with China, a *faux pas* that backfired and reminded Ma and Beijing that such matters remained highly controversial and that attempting to tackle them was premature. Needing to win the presidential and legislative elections, Ma and his KMT had no choice but to burst that trial balloon, and the peace accord was duly shelved. Once again, democratic pressures had forced a corrective on the government. Back in China, some academics were beginning to express their frustrations with the Ma government, accusing it of "foot dragging" and of being a closet proindependence president – a claim that would sound outlandish to many of Ma's critics back in Taiwan, who saw him as little more than a puppet of Beijing (in my opinion, he was neither).

Looking ahead to his final four years in office, President Ma must also have known that he had little time left to accomplish what he wanted and thereby secure his legacy as the politician who engineered peace in the Taiwan Strait, to be rewarded in the form of a summit with Chinese President Xi Jinping and perhaps even a Nobel Peace Prize. In reality, President Ma probably knew that he had even less than four years, as 2015 would likely be overtaken by the campaigning ahead of the January 2016 presidential election, during which time political adventurism and drastic departures from the middle ground would risk damaging his party's chances at the poll. In other words, a major breakthrough in Taiwan-China relations was unlikely to occur in 2015, as electoral pressure would force KMT candidates to adhere to the safe status quo and perhaps even to sound somewhat more "Taiwan-centric" than they usually do (Ma himself did that, emphasizing Taiwan ahead of elections only to return to the ROC and focus on its Chinese origins once in office).

Ma, who presumably was aware that his Chinese counterparts were becoming impatient, nevertheless overshot. As a result, his second administration became much less accountable to the public and made a travesty of democratic procedure. Elements from civil society that began coalescing over domestic matters (e.g., media monopoly, forced evictions, laid-off factory workers, deaths in the military) eventually joined forces with those who were agitating against Ma's cross-strait policies (chief among them the "black box" Cross-Strait Services Trade Agreement).

By early 2014, this potent mix caused the government serious headaches and annihilated Ma's chances of delivering what Beijing (and the businesses that stood to benefit) wanted. In its wake, the Sunflower Movement left the CSSTA dead in the water and unlikely to be implemented before Ma steps down in 2016. Furthermore, the events nixed the possibility of implementing a follow-on trade in goods agreement and likely caused substantial delays to plans of opening reciprocal representative offices in Taiwan and China. The Sunflower occupation severely weakened Ma by isolating him within his own party, which would eventually force him to step down following the KMT's disastrous performance in the nine-in-one elections in November that year.

If Beijing was paying any attention to what was happening in Taiwan and to President Ma's ability to survive mounting discontent – single-digit approval ratings, shoe campaigns, daily protests hounding cabinet officials, occupation of the Ministry of the Interior – it probably realized by 2013 that Ma was no longer their man and that future gains on the political front would depend on the CCP's ability to cooperate with forces that existed outside the administration.

And that is exactly what it did. It is no surprise, therefore, that the intensification of the political warfare efforts and increasing usage of the instruments described in this chapter coincided with Ma's fall from grace. Beijing never abandoned interactions with the government in Taiwan altogether. That is not how it operates. But there is no doubt that it felt compelled to intensify its activities outside official channels.

Beijing already had a list of individuals on whom it could count for help. The principal and most public figure was Lien Chan (連戰), an extremely wealthy, opportunistic, and conservative former KMT chairman who had already made repeated visits to Beijing and had met both Hu Jintao and Xi Jinping. Lien served a number of purposes. When President Ma was still regarded as a partner for Beijing, the CCP used Lien, who was now "honorary chairman," to pressure the Ma administration by advocating for overwhelmingly pro-Beijing policies. In so doing, Lien, who had a chilly relationship with Ma, appealed to the more conservative wing of the KMT that also tended to identify more with China. Ma was thereby able to present his policies as "moderate."

Other hardliners, including Hau Pei-tsun (郝柏村) and Wu Poh-hsiung (吳伯雄), have played a similar role by visiting China and participating in cross-strait forums where Beijing's position on the Taiwan issue was the only voice. More peripheral figures like New Party (新黨) Chairman Yok Mu-ming (郁慕明) and Taiwan New Alliance Association Chairman Hsu Li-nung (許歷農) (a former director of the General Political Warfare Department), as well as lesser prounification figures, have also become involved and have met with Chinese officials in Beijing.

When Ma fell into disfavor, allies like Lien became the means by which Beijing could bypass the state authorities in Taiwan and reach out directly to the grassroots. According to research by Wu Jieh-min (吳介民), an associate research fellow at Academia Sinica's Institute of Sociology, individuals with such connections may be acting as go-betweens for Chinese officials, conduits for the transfer of Chinese money, and an unofficial means of getting into contact with Taiwan's grassroots.

Community leaders and *lizhang* (里張) have been the primary targets of the CCP's strategy, which involves bribes and all-expenses-paid trips to China. In return, those individuals are expected to influence elections through "bloc voting" or vote buying (funded by China) or to pressure legislators on policies regarding Chinese investment, among other things. Significantly, when the Taiwan Affairs Office (國務院台灣事務辦公室) Minister Zhang Zhijun (張志軍) visited Taiwan in June 2014, the Mainland Affairs Council, the government body in charge of cross-strait exchanges, was excluded in favor of grassroots contacts.

At some point during his tour, Zhang requested that he not be accompanied by Taiwanese officials, saying he had organized his own meetings with locals. The request was granted. Among others, Zhang reportedly met with Kuo Yun-hui (郭雲輝), chairman of the Taiwan Borough and Village Warden Association (台灣村里長聯誼會), during a visit to Taoyuan. Kuo was part of a delegation to Beijing in February 2014 led by Lien Chan, during which the subject of future interactions with the grassroots in Taiwan was discussed. During Zhang's visit to Taiwan, Kuo also reportedly acted as a go-between to facilitate contact between the Chinese official and even more local representatives, down to the borough level.

There have been several reports of CCP officials making inroads with locals in Hualien County, where they have bought influence using similar means. There, the CCP has been helped by County Commissioner Fu Kun-chi (傅崑萁) (known locally as the King of Hualien), who in recent years has made no effort to mask his intention to ingratiate himself with Chinese officials and investors. Such activities came to a head in August 2014 when Fu pressured aboriginal leaders from Fata'an and Tafalong, the oldest *niyaro'* (villages) of the Amis tribe in Hualien, to break their traditions by allowing minority groups from China's Guangxi Province (and presumably officials) to attend the *Ilisin*, or "yearly offering," a sacred ceremony. A source within the Amis community there (I had first met her during the protests surrounding Chen Yunlin's initial visit to Taiwan) said the whole thing had been arranged by Fu himself.

Among other things, members of the tribe were asked to perform a dance during the first evening of the *Ilisin* for the Chinese visitors. The *Ilisin* is the most important ritual (*lisin* means "ritual"; *Ilisin* means to be "at ritual"), in which only members of the specific *niyaro'* can participate (the ceremonies pay homage to Malataw, the highest god, and their ancestors). On rare occasions, allied *niyaro'* will pay a visit on the first day of the *Ilisin* (known as *palafang*), where they will be treated as guests. However, no other people are allowed in.

The Fata'an and Tafalong communities were divided and unsure of how to deal with the visit. Although community elders "do not really know what these people represent and want to treat them well because they, with a kind of naiveté, regard such performances as 'cultural exchanges,'" younger tribe members wanted to chase the Chinese away and threatened direct action if necessary. A small group, known as the Fa-Ta Alliance for Attack and Defense (馬太攻守聯盟), came into being to deal with the crisis. In the end, Fu gave in to the pressure, and a compromise was reached. No Chinese were allowed to attend the ceremony.

Like elsewhere across Taiwan, communities are increasingly pressured by China's charm offensive and the local officials who make it possible. Poorer and more vulnerable communities, including aborigines, are likely a primary target of the CCP, which has the ability to dispense with large sums of money to buy influence. Such activities are expected to continue and could accelerate following the DPP victory in the January 2016 presidential and legislative elections.

One important takeaway is that the less of a partner Beijing has in Taiwan's government institutions and traditional political parties, the more tempted it will be to cooperate directly at the local level. Taiwan's opening up to Chinese investment and tourism and the ease with which Chinese can now travel throughout Taiwan have facilitated such interactions.

Organized crime

Criminal organizations, or so-called triads, have served as an instrument for Chinese authorities to get things done since time immemorial. In their long battle with the Communists, Chiang Kai-shek and his son Chiang Ching-kuo often relied on secret societies, like Shanghai's Green Gang, to penetrate, harass, and eliminate their political opponents. After it fled to Taiwan, the KMT continued the tradition, as demonstrated by the October 1984 assassination in Daly City, California, of Henry Liu (劉宜良, aka 江南), a journalist who was writing an unauthorized biography of Chiang Jr. (Kaplan). An investigation into the murder drew direct links between the KMT, the military, and triads such as the Bamboo Union (竹聯幫).

Once it had displaced the KMT in Beijing, the CCP also harnessed the powers of crime syndicates. Over the years, many of them began playing a role within the CCP's United Front Work efforts and made good use of the historical ties between the secret societies in China and those that had fled across the Taiwan Strait with the KMT. After establishing their turfs in Taiwan – which often meant fighting pitched battles with native crime syndicates, known as *jiaotou*, that had emerged in response to the Mainland gangsters – Chinese triads engaged in the kind of activities that are normally associated with organized crime: gunrunning, underground gambling, debt collection, prostitution, drug trafficking, kidnap for ransom (usually using taxi companies), and so on.

As Chin observes, little by little, the major triads diversified their portfolios and also developed more "legitimate" operations such as construction and garbage collection. This transformation was also accompanied by the participation of gangsters in politics; a number of them became legislators, which gave them legitimacy, certain protections, and most assuredly influence over government policy. Throughout that period, crime organizations became part of the grassroots, a situation that is still true today, where men in black shirts often intimidate political candidates and their supporters, remove political flags and banners, and play a role in vote buying – and that's when they are not running for office themselves.

Nationwide crackdowns on organized crime in the 1990s accelerated the process of legitimization; not only were the traditional, street corner operations threatening the entire criminal organization, they were increasingly bad for business. Moreover, selling drugs and firearms had become much less lucrative than major construction deals, which were often secured through threats and blackmail.

As the twenty-first century opened, the main triads in Taiwan had followed in the footsteps of their counterparts in Hong Kong and Italy; they had become businesses and were run as such. More and more, the scions of the first-generation gangsters were going to business school abroad and learning the skills necessary to run major moneymaking operations in construction, hotels, entertainment, and other sectors. They were also less ideological than they had been in the past. In fact, if they had an ideology, it was moneymaking.

Gangsters also slowly receded into the background of politics. Less and less would people like Lo Fu-chu (羅福助), a leader of the Celestial Alliance (天道盟), double as legislators. But they were never far from the surface and continued to have substantial influence on top politicians, thus ensuring that corruption remained a major factor in Taiwanese politics.

One triad in particular has played a role in politics across the Taiwan Strait and served as an agent of the CCP: the Bamboo Union. One man, above all, has ensured that this relationship continued to exercise influence on politics in Taiwan: Chang An-le (張安樂), also known as White Wolf (白狼). A self-described politician who is stridently prounification, Chang served a decade at the U.S. federal penitentiary at Fort Leavenworth, Kansas, on heroin-trafficking charges and was indirectly involved in the Henry Liu murder case. Six other members of the Bamboo Union were arrested in New York, Texas, and California during the sweep by U.S. law enforcement. After serving his sentence, in the course of which he obtained a number of university degrees, Chang returned to Taiwan. He fled to China in 1996 after being accused of involvement in a bid-rigging case.

It likely was during his exile in China that Chang was first cultivated by the CCP, a relationship that has become symbiotic. By his own admission, Chang met several of the CCP "princelings" and individuals who are involved in United Front Work, though he said that the latter were "powerless." Chang was reportedly introduced into princelings circles through a cousin who had stayed behind in 1949 (Garnaut 2014a). That cousin's father, Hou Weiyu, was a former executive vice president of the Communist Party School. During that time, Chang also developed a close friendship with Hu Shiying (胡石英), the son of Hu Qiaomu (胡喬木), a CCP propaganda chief, and an old associate of President Xi (Hu Qiaomu died in 2002). While in China, Chang formed the China Unification Promotion Party (中華統一促進黨), which promotes the unification of Taiwan and China under "one country, two systems." Remotely, Chang reportedly mobilized protests against the Tibetan spiritual leader the Dalai Lama during a visit to Taiwan in 2009 and is believed to have provided security for KMT candidates during political rallies. Using a taxi company with ties to the underworld, Chang may also have been behind the bizarre "exfiltration" operation in 2009 at Taiwan Taoyuan International Airport after the return of Kuo Kuan-ying (郭冠英), an acting director of the information division at Taiwan's representative office in Toronto, who was fired and subsequently relieved of his civil servant status, after it was discovered that he had authored a series of hateful articles against the Taiwanese under the pen name Fan Lan-chin (范蘭欽). Since then, Kuo has been actively involved with the prounification New Party and is often seen at rallies organized by the China Unification Promotion Party or other underworld figures.

Even before his return to Taiwan in 2013, Chang had also developed ties with the family of President Ma Ying-jeou. Ma Yi-nan (馬以南), President Ma's elder sister, is believed to have attended a fund-raiser organized by Chang in Shenzhen, and years later she would show up alongside Chang at a New May Fourth rally organized by prounification elements in Taipei. Chang's number two is Lee Kuo-yung (李國榮), a retired general who at one time headed the Ministry of National Defense's Chung Cheng Armed Forces Preparatory School.

The State Council's Taiwan Affairs Office (TAO) is the agency from which Chang appears to be receiving his directions (Lee and Hung), with the princelings presumably providing the financing.

Chang ended his self-imposed exile in June 2013 and returned to Taiwan after a 17-year absence. On Taiwan's most-wanted list, he was immediately arrested after landing at Taipei (Songshan) International Airport. Hours prior to his return, hundreds of supporters, many of them ostensibly members of criminal organizations, gathered outside the airport to welcome him. Flanked by police, Chang displayed the little blue booklet he had authored making his case for uni-fication. Hours after his detention, he was released on NT$1 million bail. Chang told a journalist from the *Sydney Morning Herald* that some members of the DPP were reportedly involved in securing his return to Taiwan. If true, his claim sug-gests that the web of influence woven by Chang, the TAO, and the princelings has already extended well beyond the nominally prounification party (Garnaut 2014b).

A free man, Chang didn't wait long before entering politics. Denying he had any ties with the Bamboo Union, Chang presented himself as a politician, open-ing campaign offices across Taiwan (including in Tainan, the "heartland" of Taiwan independence), and appearing on various TV talk shows.

With Chang's return to Taiwan, gangster politics have also returned with a venge-ance. Chang and his followers have threatened proindependence activists, Tainan Mayor William Lai (賴清德), intimidated and attempted to buy off an NGO that was spearheading a "shoe throwing" protest against President Ma, attacked protest-ers outside a campaign rally for the KMT's Sean Lien in November 2014, and twice showed up during the Sunflower Movement occupation of the legislature in March and April 2014. In the first 2014 incident, young gangsters threatened activists outside the Legislative Yuan with knives and homemade explosives, while in the second, on 1 April, Chang and hundreds of his followers "passed through" on Zhongxiao West Road near the legislature, during which a number of people were physically assaulted despite a large police deployment.

Gangsters have also shown up wherever Chinese officials like TAO Minister Zhang Zhijun have visited Taiwan, intimidating protesters and sometimes attacking them, resulting in a number of minor injuries among TSU (台灣團結聯盟) legisla-tors and young members of the Black Island Nation Youth Alliance (黑色島國青年陣線), which organized protests against Zhang. Similar incidents occurred dur-ing a meeting between the TAO's Zhang and Mainland Affairs Council Minister Andrew Hsia (夏立言) in Kinmen in late May 2015. Whether the counterprotest-ers were associates of Chang and the Bamboo Union remains to be determined. However, there was no doubt as to their affiliations with organized crime and their prounification ideology.

Figures from the underworld also took part in a protest against Tsai Ing-wen and her delegation as they were embarking on a visit to the U.S. in late May 2015. Using two taxi associations, the protesters gathered at Taiwan Taoyuan International Airport and waved banners calling on Tsai to recognize the 1992 consensus.

Calling her a "very courageous woman," Chang announced his full support for Hung Hsiu-chu (洪秀柱), the KMT's first presidential candidate in the 2016 elections, before she was replaced by Eric Chu. Chang and his followers participated in a protest outside KMT headquarters in Taipei before her replacement.

In Taiwan, Chang is also close to Zhang Xiuye (張秀葉), a founding member of the pro-CCP Concentric Patriotism Association (中華愛國同心會), which since its creation in 1993 has been the object of repeated public complaints over harassment and physical assault, earning its members the sobriquet "Communist thugs in Taiwan." Zhang was born in Shanghai and moved to Taiwan sometime around 1993 after marrying a Taiwanese. Prior to moving to Taiwan, she reportedly worked for an "unnamed NGO." She and her husband divorced soon afterward.

Zhang's "boss," Zhou Qinjun (周慶峻), was a regular presence at pro-Beijing rallies in front of Taipei 101 and has led other activities against the Falun Gong at other venues in Taipei, including Sun Yat-Sen Memorial Hall. Zhou, who fled China in 1961, is the head of the aforementioned Alliance and chairman of the prounification Chinese Democratic Progressive Party (CDPP, 中國民主進步黨), of which Chang An-le is "honorary chairman." Zhou has been involved in various forums and meetings with prounification elements within the CCP, including the China Council for the Promotion of Peaceful National Reunification (CCPPR, 中國和平統一促進會). Zhou was reportedly invited to participate in a large cross-strait forum organized in 2012 or 2013. Former KMT chairman Wu Poh-hsiung believed to have been instrumental in securing Zhou's participation at those events. Zhou has been in contact with Zhu Zhengming (朱正明), vice president of the World Guang Gong Culture (世界關公文化) organization and director of the Hubei Provincial Committee United Front Work Department.

As with the "onion layers" of CCP political warfare against Taiwan, pro-Beijing criminal organizations also form a constellation of interlocking and overlapping interests that is difficult to draw a complete picture of, which serves to confuse counterintelligence agencies, law enforcement, and investigative journalists. As Lee Kuo-yung's role in Chang's party demonstrates, former generals in the ROC military are also prime targets for recruitment by the GPD/LD and other political warfare organizations.

Although the Chang "network" may be the most prominent, several others are operating in different areas. Many of the brothels that are located near military bases across Taiwan are run by organized crime with links to China, which undoubtedly has national security implications.

Moreover, many of the massage parlors and "hair salons" around Taiwan are believed to be operated by gangsters. In many of them, masseuses are young Chinese women from Fujian who were smuggled into Taiwan by crime syndicates, some of which likely have ties to the CCP. Most of those women live at the site of or next to their workplace, and their freedoms are limited. While many of those are probably purely moneymaking operations, we can surmise that some of those women may also be used for "extracurricular" activities such as "honey baits" to ensnare political and military officials. The line between criminality and political work can be very thin, and such activities take place right before our eyes on a daily basis.

Military

The most direct assault on Taiwan's democracy comes in the form of coercion. Through the buildup and deployment of the People's Liberation Army and the Second Artillery Corps (第二炮兵部隊), regular exercises simulating attacks on Taiwan, and the passage of state laws such as the Anti-Secession Law in 2005, the Chinese leadership has sought to narrow the democratic options that otherwise would be available to the Taiwanese and that *should* be available to any people with a legitimate case for self-determination. The threat of war, which will be discussed in Chapter 12, has direct ramifications on support for *de jure* independence, which would conceivably be much higher if the threat of invasion by the PLA were not a variable. By minimizing *overt* support for independence among the Taiwanese, Beijing succeeds in creating a false impression abroad that has left many observers to conclude that desire for independence is limited to "a small group of people."

The threat of force has also been used during elections to sow fear among voters to give an advantage to the party that is seen as less likely to spark hostilities with Beijing. Even though the 1995–1996 Missile Crisis backfired and ended up helping Lee Teng-hui, the candidate that Beijing did not want to see elected, fears that Beijing would again make good on its threat – with PLA capabilities being much more impressive today than they were 20 years ago – are undoubtedly a factor. In any other situation, this would be regarded as external intervention in the democratic processes of a sovereign state and therefore illegal. However, in the context of the Taiwan Strait, such pressures have become part of the narrative.

The entire "underground network" that has been described in this chapter serves as a quasi parallel government upon which the CCP can depend to achieve its political goals. Efforts to cultivate those elements seemed to intensify beginning with President Ma's second term and when it had become clear to Beijing that democratic pressures would make it impossible for Ma and his KMT to give Beijing what it wanted. In light of the outcome of the 2016 elections, Beijing will conceivably rely even more on those forces to make progress on the Taiwan "question" by eroding Taiwan's democratic institutions. The central government will have a limited ability to counter growing Chinese influence in Taiwan – unless the new leadership dramatically increases the resources allocated for national security and overturns eight years of engagement between the two sides, an unlikely prospect at this point. Therefore, while the genie of Taiwan's democracy is out of the bottle, so is the demon of China's Three Warfares.

As will be discussed in further detail in Chapter 12, China is assaulting Taiwan's democracy not primarily for ideological reasons but because it needs to make it more like itself to make unification possible. By eroding Taiwan's democracy to force unification on Beijing's terms, China also hopes to avoid having to resort to force to resolve the Taiwan issue, a last-resort course of action that, as we shall see, comports extraordinary risks for China.

Notes

1 As subjects of a repressive regime that is paranoid about the existence of any potential competitor, Chinese respondents may avoid providing responses that support political pluralism, as this could get them into trouble.
2 The GPD was disbanded in January 2016 and was replaced by the Political Work Department of the Central Military Commission.
3 "Italian Prosecutors Seek to Indict Bank of China, 297 People," The Associated Press, 20 June 2015. http://www.scmp.com/news/world/article/1824491/italian-prosecutors-seek-indict-bank-china-297-people
4 Tung, a China-based businesswoman and consulting committee member of the Overseas Community Affairs Council (OCAC), was an overseas delegate of the Jiangxi Provincial Chinese People's Political Consultative Conference and director of an overseas division of China's United Front Work Department. During Chu's China visit, Tung made remarks to the effect that the KMT should ignore the voice of the Taiwanese people and focus on accelerating unification. She later stepped down from her position with the OCAC.
5 See submission on new National Security Law of PRC in Relation to Human Rights Protection「三會就新國安法中的人權保障問題提交的聯合意見書」, June 2015. http://www.hkja.org.hk/site/portal/Site.aspx?id=A1-1354&lang=en-US

Bibliography

Association of Taiwan Journalists (2015) "Statement on China's National Security Law,"「台灣新聞記者協會反中國《國安法》聲明」, 3 June, http://www.smh.com.au/world/hungry-like-the-wolf-20140706-3bh7j.html (in Chinese)

Chin, K-L (2003) *Heijin: Organized Crime, Business, and Politics in Taiwan*, New York: M. E. Sharpe

Chou, B (2015) "Patriotic Generation – Political Mission for Tertiary Institutions in Macau." http://hkcolumn.blogspot.tw/2015/01/bill-chou-patriotic-generation.html

Cole, M (2015) "Unstoppable: China's Secret Plan to Subvert Taiwan," *The National Interest*, 23 March, http://nationalinterest.org/feature/unstoppable-chinas-secret-plan-subvert-taiwan-12463

Freedom House, Freedom of the Press Report 2015, https://freedomhouse.org/report/freedom-press/2015/taiwan#.VX_AxhZD_zI

Garnaut, J (2014a) "China's Rulers Team Up with Notorious 'White Wolf' of Taiwan," *Sydney Morning Herald*, 11 July, http://www.smh.com.au/world/chinas-rulers-team-up-with-notorious-white-wolf-of-taiwan-20140711-zt488.html

——— (2014b) "Hungry Like the Wolf," *Sydney Morning Herald*, 12 July, http://www.smh.com.au/world/hungry-like-the-wolf-20140706-3bh7j.html

Han, D and Chen, D (2015) "Who Supports Democracy? Evidence from a Survey of Chinese Students and Scholars in the United States," *Democratization*, June (Taylor & Francis)

Kamphausen, R, Lai, D and Scobell, A, eds (2010) *The PLA at Home and Abroad: Assessing the Operational Capabilities of China's Military*, Carlisle: Strategic Studies Institute, U.S. Army War College

Kaplan, D (1992) *Fires of the Dragon: Politics, Murder, and the Kuomintang*, New York: Scribner

Kastner, S (2009) *Political Conflict and Economic Interdependence across the Taiwan Strait and Beyond*, Stanford: Stanford University Press: 68–97

Lee, Y and Hung, F (2014) "Special Report – How China's Shadowy Agency Is Working to Absorb Taiwan," *Reuters*, 27 November, http://uk.reuters.com/article/uk-taiwan-china-special-report-idUKKCN0JB01F20141127

Loh, C (2010) *Underground Front: The Chinese Communist Party in Hong Kong*, Hong Kong: Hong Kong University Press

Neumann, J (2016) "China's ICBC Offices in Spain Raided in Money-Laundering Probe," *Wall Street Journal*, 7 February, http://www.wsj.com/articles/spanish-authorities-raid-office-of-industrial-commercial-bank-of-china-1455711371

Nylander, J (2015) "Outrage in Australia After Senator Defends Tiananmen Massacre," *Forbes*, 10 June, http://www.forbes.com/sites/jnylander/2015/06/10/outrage-in-australia-after-senator-defends-tiananmen-massacre/

Offman, C (2015) "The Making of Michael Chan," *The Globe and Mail*, 17 June, http://www.theglobeandmail.com/news/national/the-making-of-michael-chan/article24994796/

Poon, A and Hsu, J (2013) "China's ICBC to Buy Stake in Taiwan Bank," *Wall Street Journal*, 2 April, http://www.wsj.com/articles/SB100014241278873232965045783982328 50992560

Shi, T (2008) "Democratic Values Supporting an Authoritarian System," in *How East Asians View Democracy*, Chu, Y-H, Diamond, L, Nathan, A and Shin, D-C, eds, New York: Columbia University Press: 209–15

Stokes, M and Hsiao, R (2013) *The People's Liberation Army General Political Department: Political Warfare with Chinese Characteristics*, Project 2014 Institute, 14 October, http://www.project2049.net/documents/PLA_General_Political_Department_Liaison_Stokes_Hsiao.pdf

Tao, L, Berci, M and He, W (n.d.) "Study Abroad," *New York Times China Rises Companion*. http://www.nytimes.com/ref/college/coll-china-education-003.html

6

HONG KONG

The canary in the mineshaft

In many ways, the Taiwanese who worry about Taiwan's future as a liberal democracy enjoying *de facto* sovereign status have the advantage of knowing not only the kind of tried and tested tactics that the CCP will likely use to undermine Taiwan but also what it would be like for Taiwan to become a special administrative region (SAR) of China.

For those who have been paying attention, it is clear that Hong Kong (HKSAR), which was reincorporated into China in 1997 after a little more than 150 years of British colonial rule (and four years under the Japanese), stands as a possible future for Taiwan under the "one country, two systems" model proposed by Beijing. Increasing signs that the formula in HKSAR is coming apart at the seams and that Beijing's meddling in the local affairs of the territory is engendering conflict and tensions have served as a warning for Taiwan. If Beijing cannot get Hong Kong right by respecting the wishes of the local population, it is even less likely that it would perform well after annexing Taiwan, whose history, political system (we must remember that, unlike Taiwan, Hong Kong has never been a democracy), and detached geography from the "Mainland" are even less amenable to a workable unification with authoritarian China.

As early as 1981, Beijing had outlined a proposal for the reunification of Taiwan and China. Under the nine-point proposal, Taiwan SAR would enjoy a high degree of autonomy, retaining its armed forces, its socioeconomic system, and its way of life, and Beijing would not interfere with Taiwan's local affairs. However, Beijing soon realized that the proposal had little chance of success in Taiwan, and the CCP instead focused its attention on Hong Kong, under the premise that a successful process there would facilitate reunification with Taiwan in the future.

Recent developments in Hong Kong, including the political crises stemming from the forced Sinicization of school curricula, the imposition of Mandarin over the local Cantonese language, growing discontent over the social impact of large

Chinese tour groups, suffering press freedoms, rising wealth inequality, capital flight, and the denial of universal suffrage by the central government are all clear indications that the process, despite getting off to relatively a good start, is unlikely to remain smooth. It also points to the tremendous challenges that China would face in administering Taiwan SAR and how such a political union would erode the freedoms that the Taiwanese now take for granted. Moreover, Beijing's rigidity in dealing with the situation in Hong Kong should dispel any notion that it would be more flexible when it comes to addressing the desires of the Taiwanese. After all, despite signs that the "one country, two systems" model may have outlived its utility in HKSAR, President Xi reaffirmed in 2014 that the same model would be imposed on Taiwan following unification.

Anyone who still believes that retrocession did not adversely affect Hong Kong's society either lives on a different planet or receives his information directly only from the CCP propaganda department or its proxies in the former British enclave. The building discontent with the state of affairs finally found its expression during the Umbrella Movement, which paralyzed parts of the city in late 2014. Much as with the Sunflower Movement in Taiwan, which took action earlier that year, the Umbrella Movement was largely led by young students, who refused to accept that their future would continue to be determined by forces that are largely unaccountable and highly corrupt and that espouse an ideology that has little traction with youth.

Given all this and what can be learned from the HKSAR experience, it is shocking how little attention ordinary Taiwanese seem to be paying to developments in that society. While part of this can be attributed to an irresponsible media that, as we saw, prefers to report on car accidents and sex scandals instead of things that matter, this lack of interest runs deeper. For the majority of Taiwanese, what happens in Hong Kong is of little relevance to them as it is clear in their minds – despite Beijing's claims to the contrary – that the SAR is part of a different country. This reality is made very clear every 4 June. Only a few hundred people gather at Liberty Square in Taipei for a series of speeches and concerts, which is in stark contrast with the tens of thousands of people who participate in the vigil in Hong Kong.

According to Wu'er Kaixi (吾爾開希), one of the Tiananmen protesters who was forced to flee China and now lives in Taiwan, the disappointing turnout in Taiwan can be explained not by political apathy but rather because, for ordinary Taiwanese, those events took place in a foreign country, as clear a signal as we could get that in the minds of the Taiwanese, the identity issue is no doubt settled. However, while it is hard to argue against this logic, the Taiwanese should nevertheless keep in mind that this is not how Beijing sees things, which by default means that developments in China have direct ramifications for Taiwan. This failure of imagination on Taiwan's part therefore can be a dangerous blind spot.

Essentially, Hong Kong's experience as a subunit of the PRC provides two hugely important lessons for Taiwan. The first is the "underground" that the CCP relied on prior to and has relied on since retrocession to tighten its grip on every aspect of HKSAR and thereby manipulate the system to the advantage of the central government in Beijing. Identifying those techniques can shed light on the underground that, as we saw in the previous chapter, Beijing has been actively building across Taiwan. The second lesson is that of a possible future that awaits Taiwan should it be annexed by China. If the HKSAR is any indication (and there is every reason to believe that it is), Beijing's promises that Taiwan's way of life and the integrity of its political system would be ensured under the "one country, two systems" formula are not worth the paper that they are written on, as often is the case with any promise made by Beijing.

In many ways, Taiwan today is in a period similar to Hong Kong between 1977 and 1989, described by Loh as when the CCP was focusing on "taking back" and "shaping" the colony. During negotiations with the British government and aware that a large segment of the population of Hong Kong looked with apprehension to a future under Chinese control, the CCP did what it could to avoid drawing undue attention to its activities in the territory. As such, prior to 1997, CCP activities there were instead funded via a series of China-controlled organizations, including the Hong Kong branch of the Bank of China, with Xinhua Hong Kong, for all intents and purposes the liaison office under the State Council's Hong Kong and Macau Affairs Office, serving as the receiver and local disburser. Presumably, the reciprocal exchange offices between Taiwan and China, first proposed in 2013 but still unrealized at this writing, would play a similar role, with the Chinese office officially falling under the semiofficial Association for Relations Across the Taiwan Strait (ARATS) but in reality likely under Taiwan Affairs Office control. In the absence of the office, whose implementation appears to have been stalled alongside the CSSTA after the Sunflower Movement's occupation of the legislature, the TAO is ostensibly relying on other Chinese offices to fulfill such functions.

Around the same time, Deng Xiaoping stated that United Front Work should focus on making the residents of Hong Kong "love the motherland." In some ways this was similar to Beijing's recent efforts to "win the hearts and minds" of the Taiwanese through propaganda, United Front Work, and political warfare operations in Taiwan. During that period, the CCP also began grooming future pro-Beijing leaders to rule Hong Kong. This generally involved financial sweeteners, as is believed to have been the case with Tung Chee Hwa (董建華), whose struggling shipping company was reportedly saved from bankruptcy by Beijing, in part thanks to a credit loan provided by the Bank of China.

Xu Jiatun (許家屯), the head of the Xinhua Hong Kong office between 1983 and 1989 who was eventually expelled from the CCP after fleeing to Los Angeles and sympathizing with the protesters at Tiananmen Square, also organized a series of trips to Beijing for Hong Kong individuals it hoped to groom as future leaders of the SAR. Both practices have striking echoes today, with the delegations of Taiwanese politicians and business leaders doing a similar journey to meet with Presidents Hu and Xi.

Then and now, Beijing sought to form a political alliance with the capitalists, or what has been described as the "political absorption of economics." This process of co-optation, which Lo has called "patron-client" pluralism, was meant to create winners and losers: those who cooperated with the CCP were promised riches or a future role in decision-making or consultative processes (e.g., membership in the Chinese People's Political Consultative Conference, or CPPCC, 中國人民政治協商會議). As Loh writes, United Front Work was deeply involved in the matter and "enabled the targeted groups to grow accustomed to the fruits of their membership in the post-reunification establishment so that they have a stake in maintaining it."

Those who refused to cooperate with the CCP, meanwhile, were marginalized and as a result suffered materially. United Front Work therefore also engaged in exclusion and attacked those individuals as "unpatriotic."

As we have seen, an almost identical process has been initiated to co-opt members of the Taiwanese elite and business community, the only difference being that for the time being Taiwanese cannot, by law, become members of the CPPCC (some defectors have done just that, however).

China's propaganda arm used a variety of techniques to achieve its goals in Hong Kong prior to and after retrocession. This included repetition of consistent messages meant to reassure the local population that their freedom, way of life, and standard of living would not be compromised after retrocession, along with intentional vagueness, personal attacks, labeling and demonization of critics (e.g., "anti-China"), and the "some/few people" argument (e.g., "only a small group of people oppose . . ."). Much of those techniques will be familiar to those who follow cross-strait politics.

As with Taiwan today, prior to retrocession the CCP had to deal with Hong Kong "as if it was enemy territory," as Loh writes, which meant using "old-time revolutionary tactics" and "a fifth column operation" with the aim of infiltrating Hong Kong society. Starting in 1983, the Organization Department of the CCP Central Committee took charge of a program to send highly educated and skilled cadres to Hong Kong on one-way permits. Loh has identified five sponsoring bodies that played a role in the vetting and selection of those cadres: the Hong Kong and Macau Office, the Ministry of State Security, the United Front Department, the Overseas Chinese Office, and the Taiwan Affairs Office. Once they arrived in Hong Kong, the cadres, most of whom were in their thirties and forties, were expected to remain in contact with the Xinhua Hong Kong office and the "relevant sponsoring bodies." For the CCP, it was useful to have people in place as insurance against trouble, such as occurred following the Tiananmen crackdown, which for good reasons heightened fears of Chinese rule among the residents of Hong Kong.

There are, of course, differences between what the cadres dispatched to Hong Kong and similar agents dispatched to Taiwan could do. For example, the cadres had the ability to engage in bloc voting to influence Hong Kong's Legislative Council elections, something that is not possible in Taiwan under current regulations – unless, of course, the cadres obtain ROC citizenship, which currently takes six years. There are about 350,000 Chinese spouses in Taiwan. In addition to not having to renounce their PRC citizenship in order to become ROC citizens (an exception that does not apply to other foreign nationals), there is no guarantee that spouses who, say, are dispatched to Taiwan by Chinese intelligence agencies will not engage in activities in support of the CCP's goals in Taiwan.

The same applies to the cadres that are sent to Taiwan for work, which has become much easier following a series of amendments to regulations. Though most of them are probably in Taiwan to perform legitimate work, we can assume that a percentage of them are controlled by the TAO or the Chinese intelligence apparatus and are performing a variety of functions such as intelligence gathering or facilitating the movement of money needed to sustain the underground – gangsters, prostitutes, businessmen, journalists, spouses, and so on. As with the situation in Hong Kong prior to 1997, the cells can be dormant when relations between Taipei and Beijing are good and only activated ahead of major elections or when the relationship sours. While a CCP underground has existed in Taiwan for decades, the liberalized exchanges that have taken place under President Ma had greatly facilitated the CCP's ability to penetrate Taiwanese society in a way that is quite reminiscent of Hong Kong in the 1980s and early 1990s.

Another mission of the Xinhua Hong Kong office (and later the Liaison Office) was to influence the media. This was largely accomplished through changes in media ownership and by binding media owners using their business interests in China or by appointing them to political bodies. Taiwan's pro-Beijing billionaire Tsai Eng-meng himself made a bid in 2009 for 47.58 percent of Asia Television (ATV), prompting Loh to ask whether "united front is now hard at work across the Taiwan Strait."

Already by 2007, a survey by the Hong Kong Journalists' Association revealed that 30 percent of media workers had exercised self-censorship in the past year, and 40 percent said they knew someone who had done so. A press freedom survey by the Association in 2014 showed that self-censorship was common and that owners or management at media operations regularly exerted editorial pressure on journalists and editors. On a scale of 0 to 10 (with 10 indicating that it is "very common"), media personnel rated pressure from owners or management at 6.5. Alibaba Group (阿里巴巴) Chairman Jack Ma's (馬雲) acquisition of the *SCMP* in December 2015 caused additional fears of eroded journalistic freedoms. Meanwhile, there are also indications that business pressure and self-censorship are having an impact in bookstores in the SAR, where works that are critical of CCP policies or that touch on "controversial" subjects such as Taiwan, Tibet, and Xinjiang, are increasingly hard to find or are simply not carried on the shelves. The apparent kidnapping in late 2015 of five Hong Kong booksellers, who resurfaced in China and made highly publicized "confessions," has also caused fears over the future of the publishing industry there.

What can be said of the CCP's United Front, propaganda, and political warfare efforts in the period prior to retrocession and in the years afterward is that it was, on the whole, rather successful. By 1997, many of the people who apprehended reunification – fears that were exacerbated by the events of 4 June 1989 – had moved overseas and no longer constituted a direct threat to CCP rule in the former British colony. As for the millions who stayed behind, they did not see a fundamental change in their way of life, at least not initially, and the CCP appeared willing to abide by the stipulations of the Joint Declaration, a weak international document that was meant to protect Hong Kong's way of life and that technically will expire in 2047.

And yet the seeds of future discontent and the reason why Beijing would not respect its commitment to not interfere in the affairs of HKSAR were sown when Beijing was still negotiating the conditions with the British government for the handover. That it should be so should not be a surprise. After all, the CCP has always been confident in the superiority of its political system and would never brook anything that could threaten the foundations of the political system that have existed in the PRC since 1949.

Thus, the "one country, two systems" formula was flawed from the very beginning, mostly as a result of the CCP Leninist and highly interventionist ideology and *modus operandi*. As Tsang observes, however "ingenious" the "one country, two systems" formula may have been, allowing the PRC to "have its cake (reclaim sovereignty) and eat it too (retain Hong Kong's economic utility)," the guiding principle was to "further the interests of the PRC as defined by the Communist Party." Hong Kong therefore had to have a "positive value" for the PRC.

Deng Xiaoping was confident enough that the PRC could absorb the inherent contradiction of absorbing what essentially was a capitalist society to supplement a socialist system. However, as Tsang observes, the contradiction would be allowed to exist for a limited time only. "Deng never intended to let Hong Kong be the catalyst to set off a chain reaction to change, let alone subvert or supplant, the socialist system in the PRC." As such, "if Hong Kong were to be deemed the source of such a menace, it would be dealt with accordingly."

Anyone who believes that the CCP would take a different approach with Taiwan, which outside observers often regard as a possible "catalyst" for change and democratization in China, needs a reality check.

Furthermore, despite his high confidence in the superiority of the CCP, Deng did not take any chances with Hong Kong. For one thing, he told the drafters of the Basic Law (中華人民共和國香港特別行政區基本法), the HKSAR's "mini constitution," that "they should not think that Hong Kong affairs should all be handled by Hong Kong people." So even though Deng "instructed his party to go against its tradition and make an exception of Hong Kong," this wasn't meant to last. Moreover, party ideology soon took over the process.

The negotiation process to chart the future of HKSAR under Chinese rule therefore was never one between equals, and there was never any doubt as to who, at the end of the day, would be in charge. This was made perfectly clear by Article 17 of the Basic Law, which stipulates that the Standing Committee of the National People's Congress (SCNPC, 全國人民代表大會常務委員會) has the power to invalidate a local Hong Kong law if it determines that the law does not conform with the Basic Law regarding Beijing's responsibilities or those of the Central Government and the SAR.

Furthermore, Article 14 of the Basic Law stipulates that while the 6,000 or so PLA soldiers who are garrisoned in HKSAR "shall not interfere in the local affairs of Hong Kong," the vague language concerning instances in which the PLA *can* be called into action is troubling, to say the least. The Hong Kong government, it says:

> may, when necessary, ask the Central Government (Beijing) for assistance from the garrison in the maintenance of public order and disaster relief . . . the garrison shall perform its duties in accordance with the provisions of the national laws that the Central Government decides to apply in Hong Kong *in the event that the Standing Committee of the National People's Congress decides to declare a state of war or, by reason of turmoil within Hong Kong which endangers national unity or security and is beyond the control of the HKSAR Government, decides that Hong Kong is in a state of emergency.* [My italics]

The invisible hand of the CCP was all over the Basic Law Consultative Committee (BLCC) and the Basic Law Drafting Committee (BLDC), whose members were often secretly handpicked or approved by Beijing. Although the BLDC, which consisted of 59 members (36 from China and 23 from Hong Kong), sought to "balance the opinions and interests of different people," its key members were either Beijing officials or people that Beijing trusted – in other words, good Chinese patriots. Formed one month later (July 1985), the BLCC was immediately mired in controversy after some of the individuals proposed for membership were turned down because some influential Hong Kong tycoons did not like them. Furthermore, a new organization made up primarily of business elite, known as the Group of 89, eventually assumed primacy over the BLCC and elbowed out more liberal-minded voices in the consultative body.

As Xu Jiatun, whom we met earlier, later admitted, the committees ignored due process because "those concerned, including himself, lacked any appreciation of the democratic procedure."

It didn't help either that the CCP was convinced that the British government was conspiring to undermine Beijing's efforts, a belief that conceivably exacerbated the CCP's nondemocratic tendencies. Given the party's high paranoia, there is no doubt that similar means would be employed during the negotiations preceding unification with Taiwan and that many of the individuals who are invited to participate in consultative committees would either be handpicked beforehand and used for co-optation or to provide a façade of legitimacy.

Beijing's approach to rule in Hong Kong therefore was never one that would allow for full autonomy under "one country, two systems." While, as per Deng's direction, CCP officials were initially encouraged to adopt a hands-off strategy and to avoid displays of overt CCP rule in the SAR, it never hesitated to intervene whenever the situation called for it. As long as things were going smoothly, Beijing was happy to govern Hong Kong remotely by relying on local officials.

The situation soon deteriorated, however. According to data by Civic Exchange, in June 1997, 66 percent of respondents in a survey expressed satisfaction with the overall performance of the government. By August 2000, that number had plunged to 30 percent. Three years later, in the wake of the botched handling of the severe acute respiratory syndrome (SARS) outbreak and the controversy over Article 23 of the Basic Law (which provides the basis for the security law in Hong Kong), approval stood at 20 percent. Economic decline, deterioration of the rule of law, and foot-dragging on democratization also contributed to the sharp decline in public approval of the government.

This growing public discontent (and the accompanying belief that democratization could perhaps help address the issues of concern) served as an invitation for Beijing to become more involved in the governance of HKSAR. As Lam has argued, while Beijing had been "highly self-controlled in ruling Hong Kong in the early post-handover years," by 2003 China had shown a "growing tendency . . . to get involved in Hong Kong's affairs." The massive protest on 1 July 2003 over the attempted passage of Article 23, described as "one of the most controversial provisions in Hong Kong's constitution," forced Beijing to become more actively involved lest the HKSAR become a source of trouble for the CCP. Critics of Article 23 regarded it as one of the greatest threats to civil liberties, and argued that offenses like "subversion" and "secession" were alien to the legal system in Hong Kong. The CCP's enlarged definition of "state secrets" was also seen as problematic for the people of the SAR (Petersen). In some ways, the crisis over Article 23 was regarded as the litmus test of the "one country, two systems" formula, which "many Hong Kong people looked upon as a buffer against an interventionist state under Beijing" (Ku). The crisis eventually forced the government to make concessions on Article 23, representing a victory of Hong Kong's civil society over the pro-Beijing Hong Kong authorities and the Central Government.

Interestingly, the new National Security Law discussed in Chapter 5 contains many of the elements, in expanded form, that were to be included in Article 23, and the new law clearly states that residents of HKSAR, Macau (and Taiwan) are subject to it.

According to Ku, success emboldened the protesters, who then turned their sights on democracy, namely the call for universal suffrage, with further rallies on 9 and 13 July. Sensing trouble, Beijing stepped in. Among other signs of its greater involvement in the SAR, the SCNPC intervened in the controversy over universal suffrage, which residents had hoped would be implemented by 2003 (as of this writing this has yet to become a reality).

The civil mobilization against the perceived erosion of freedoms and liberties under Beijing rule that occurred in 2003 and the Central Government's response to that defiance are a demarcation line between "one country, two systems" as a promising formula and its being discredited in the eyes of the residents of Hong Kong. Subsequent to those developments, Beijing deepened its direct involvement in the SAR's affairs, thus contributing to further erosions of freedoms and liberties, delayed universal suffrage, and renewed efforts to co-opt, sideline, and eliminate various segments of society so as to harmonize the SAR with the Mainland. Those developments reaffirm the notion, as discussed, that the CCP would never allow HKSAR to undermine or destabilize the socialist system favored by Beijing. As Lo observed, "the mainlandization of the HKSAR, rather than the Hongkongization of mainland China, has become the phenomenon since the retrocession of Hong Kong began on July 1, 1997."

While Beijing made some attempts to hide its hand in Hong Kong, such subtlety was thrown out the window under Xi Jinping, an ideologue who has demonstrated his intention to strengthen the Central Government's control over all of China, including the peripheries.

Despite Beijing's promises, it isn't difficult to imagine that similar interventions would occur following the unification of Taiwan with China. The same rule that from the very beginning applied to Hong Kong would be used in Taiwan. What is surprising isn't that Beijing did what it did in HKSAR but that people were surprised when it took measures that it had already telegraphed. Perhaps even more surprising is the belief, held by some, that Beijing would treat Taiwan – whose society poses an even greater challenge to the Chinese political system – differently.

Under a more interventionist Beijing in the affairs of Hong Kong, the freedoms, liberties, and way of life that were purportedly to be protected under the Joint Declaration were slowly eroded. Influence was a one-way street: Those who had hoped that a liberal Hong Kong would promote political reform in China were proven wrong by a regime that instead strengthened its repressive measures. Since 2003, almost all indicators have shown a downward trend in the SAR, including the economy, the one aspect that in theory should have been allowed to continue to prosper.

Goodstadt observes that of the 159 articles in the Basic Law, "34 were devoted to entrenching the pro-business, laisser-faire policies of the colonial era, together with its financial and commercial structures." Conversely, social rights were "far vaguer and less comprehensive." As he put it, "Hong Kong, it seemed, was to be a world with little regard for welfare." A focus on growth by the unelected, probusiness government rather than on redistribution compounded the problem of poverty and wealth inequality. Between 1997 and 2009, the top 10 percent households in terms of per capita income saw their income rise by 64.7 percent, while the lowest 10 percent saw a drop of 22 percent.

Above all, the SAR's growing dependence on the Chinese economy increased its vulnerability to changes in the Chinese business environment.

Although the 1997 Asian Financial Crisis had a negative impact on the Hong Kong economy, the SAR's vulnerability stems from more structural problems. The collapse of the Hang Seng Index in 2007–2008, for example, was the result of the discovery that a promised "free walk" scheme, which had presumably been approved by China's State Administration of Foreign Exchange and would have allowed residents of the PRC – especially investors from Tianjin – to use their own currency to trade on the Hong Kong Stock Exchange, would not be authorized. News that the train would not arrive sparked a collapse in Hong Kong share prices from which the market has yet to fully recover.

The largest threat, however, stemmed from what Goodstadt describes as "the complex readjustments that Hong Kong firms were being forced to make in response to Mainland policies." To make things worse, "political sensitivities" meant that those challenges were rarely discussed publically. The fact that the headquarters of many corporations moved from Hong Kong and resettled in cities like Beijing and Shanghai, where they could establish better relations with their political masters, certainly underscored that new reality.

Nothing has tied the Hong Kong economy with China more than the Closer Economic Partnership Arrangement (CEPA, 內地與香港關於建立更緊密經貿關係的安排), signed in June 2003, and its supplements. Economists tend to agree that CEPA helped resurrect Hong Kong's economy after 2003. In a series of liberalization moves that would be familiar to the Taiwanese less than a decade later, CEPA allowed Chinese from a number of regions in the PRC to travel to HKSAR individually rather than as part of tour groups, helping the local retail sector, while Hong Kong banks and retail enterprises were able to operate on the Mainland and to compete with local firms there.

However, the agreement has also distorted the economy and contributed to wealth inequality, which has become a serious problem for the SAR. Luxury home prices have almost quadrupled since CEPA came into force, while rent on prime spots has nearly tripled. The high rent prices have elbowed out small and medium enterprises, which have been replaced by large chains and luxury shops that, it is claimed, cater to wealthy Chinese tourists, thus pushing up economic inequality. As with the ECFA signed between Taiwan and China, the money that has been generated by the agreement has tended to remain in the hands of ruling elites who are politically connected. According to Bloomberg, home prices in 2015 had more than doubled since 2009, in part as the result of money flowing in from China.

Although Hong Kong was already facing a serious problem of social inequality prior to handover and the CEPA, close economic ties have exacerbated the problem and contributed to discontent with the nondemocratic regime. In 2001, Hong Kong's Gini coefficient, a standard indicator of wealth inequality, was 0.525 (up from 0.43 in 1971), higher than in Japan, Taiwan, and South Korea. By 2011, that number had risen to 0.537, the highest since 1971 and, according to analysts, well above the 0.4 level that is normally associated with social unrest. According to Ming, one of the largest contributors to widening wealth inequality since retrocession has been growing cronyism, a situation that has its parallels in Taiwan since 2008.

Another problem that has been attributed to CEPA is the rise in social tensions caused by the large influx of Chinese tourists who, according to the *South China Morning Post*, are now competing with local residents for "everything from baby milk to flats and maternity services in hospitals." Every year, the city's 7.2 million people have to contend with approximately 40 million Chinese visitors, which has also exacerbated tensions between "impolite" Mainlanders and the "more refined" residents of Hong Kong. Even if some of the tensions can be attributed to the narcissism of small difference, they nevertheless exist, and sometimes things do get ugly. Hurt feelings have prompted Chinese Internet users to call for economic warfare against Hong Kong by boycotting the SAR for a month. Although this has yet to translate into action by Beijing, such advocacy points to the possibly that, at some point, Beijing could use HKSAR's reliance on the Chinese economy to punish it by turning off the spigot. This is something that the PRC has already done repeatedly against Taiwan by cancelling large tour groups following developments in Taiwan that were not to its liking. Targeted economic warfare, such as denying investment, tourism, and purchasing delegations to specific regions of Taiwan that are seen as inimical to Beijing, while rewarding those that are more aligned with its policies, is also a weapon that the PRC has at its disposal to keep Hong Kong and Taiwan in line.

Perhaps even more troubling is the territory's heavy reliance on the PRC for its water, food, and electricity. According to Law, 70 percent of the water used in HKSAR comes from Dongjiang, a river in Guangdong Province, while 90 percent of its fresh meat and vegetables and half of its electricity come from China.

Despite this exposure, the residents of Hong Kong who have not benefited from the closer ties with China, as well as those who have lost out, have increasingly come to associate their problems with the lack of democracy in the SAR. In other words, structural problems related to the economy, wealth inequality, curtailed liberties and press freedoms, and other social ills became more and more tied in with the notion that some form of democracy for the SAR – and here again there probably wasn't a consensus on what they meant by democracy – was needed. Among other things, this intensified the ongoing conflict over universal suffrage, which came to a head in 2014 with the Umbrella Movement. If there is one definition of democracy that the pandemocratic residents of Hong Kong seem to agree on, it is that they should have the ability to freely choose who runs the place.

The standoff was sparked by the holding of an unofficial referendum in June 2014 to mobilize support for the direct election of the Hong Kong Chief Executive, who since 1997 has been selected by 1,200 mostly pro-Beijing businessmen and politicians. Although the campaign received more than 800,000 signatures, Beijing responded with a white paper that denounced the prodemocracy camp as "unpatriotic" and reaffirmed the CCP stance on the politics of Hong Kong. Despite the demands of the activists, the Central Government remained uncommitted to implementing the kind of free universal suffrage by 2017 that the prodemocrats in the SAR were calling for. Soon afterward, the Occupy Central movement organized rallies and public disobedience campaigns in the SAR's business district.

Writing in *Fortune* magazine, Pei observed that the political crisis that ensued was a sign that the "one country, two system" model was "unraveling." If Taiwan should ever have paid attention to what was going on in Hong Kong, this was it.

As was pointed out in the discussion on the media in the previous chapter, a number of pro-Beijing corporations have become increasingly complicit in government repression of free speech. Often they have done so by denying advertisement revenue to media outlets that criticize the authorities or provide coverage of civil unrest. This is exactly what HSBC Holdings PLC and Standard Chartered PLC appear to have done in late 2013 when they pulled millions of dollars in advertisement from the *Apple Daily*, allegedly after being pressured by Beijing. The

Apple Daily and its parent company, Next Media, have been strong supporters of the protest movements in Hong Kong against Beijing's creeping influence in its domestic affairs. The two banks, which have substantial operations in China, denied they had been asked by Beijing to do so and said that the decisions reflected changes in advertising strategy.

Similarly, state-controlled China International Trust and Investment Corp. (CITIC, 中國中信), which in June 2015 attempted to invest in Taiwan's CTBC Financial Holding Co Ltd (中信金控), reportedly pulled advertisements from independent media in Hong Kong in 2013, ostensibly as punishment for their editorial line that was critical of Beijing and China's growing influence in HKSAR. Civic groups in Taiwan warned that by becoming the third largest investor in CTBC, CITIC could exert political influence in Taiwan.

Later that month, the SAR's Big Four accounting firms – Ernst & Young, KPMG, Deloitte Kwan Wong Tan & Fong, and PricewaterhouseCoopers – used what can only be described as scare tactics by placing advertisements in local newspapers warning that Occupy Central could force foreign investors to abandon Hong Kong altogether. Benny Tai (戴耀廷), one of the organizers of the protests, said at the time that the warning by the Big Four was evidence that "China is exerting all possible influence over all groups they can influence." Whether Beijing even needed to pressure large corporations to take such actions is debatable. Nevertheless, the tactic echoed later comments by the pro-Beijing government that the unrest would seriously damage Hong Kong's economy and unduly affect the tourism industry.

As we will see in the next chapter, the Ma administration used very similar scare tactics during the Sunflower Movement's occupation.

By September, tens of thousands of young protesters had taken to the streets in a blatant defiance of Beijing that few people would have believed possible. Still, despite 79 days of protest, which brought the city's business district to a standstill, C.Y. Leung (梁振英), the current chief executive, had not stepped down, as requested by the Umbrella Movement, and, more importantly, Beijing has not changed its stance on the mechanism by which the next chief executive will be picked. Although 2017 will be the first time that the residents of Hong Kong can vote for their leader, the "electoral reform package" issued by Beijing in August 2014 stipulates that all the candidates must first be approved by Beijing in order to ensure that nobody who runs in the election advocates for policies that the CCP does not agree with, chief among them more democracy or autonomy for HKSAR.

So after a months-long government-sponsored media blitz and alleged moves to buy off opposition lawmakers in Hong Kong, the so-called reform bill was put to a vote in the Legislative Council in June 2015. Against all odds, it was shot down with 28 votes against and only eight for, in large part due to the fact that all but a few of the pro-Beijing lawmakers walked out. Apparently, Jeffrey Lam (林健鋒), a member of the proestablishment Business and Professionals Alliance (經民聯), initiated the walkout, apparently to give Lau Wong Fat (劉皇發), another pro-Beijing member, time to join the session. Another possibility is that Lam intended to derail the vote altogether to give Beijing more time to persuade the pandemocrats to switch sides.

The pro-Beijing camp at the Legislative Council had bumbled, and the reform package was dead. Beijing responded by showing who was boss. The following day, Xinhua news agency reported that despite the veto, the National People's Congress, China's parliament, had announced that the electoral "reforms" issued by Beijing were still in force.

By 2015, the frustrations had reached such levels that Chin Wan (陳雲), an assistant professor of Chinese at Lingnan University in Hong Kong and the founder of the Hong Kong Resurgence Order, suggested in an op-ed for the *New York Times* that while the "one country, two systems" framework seems to tacitly recognize Hong Kong's uniqueness, "these two systems are too different to belong to the same country, and their relationship must be redefined." According to him, Hong Kong should receive treatment as a "federal entity."

Throughout the Umbrella occupation, young activists were physically assaulted and threatened by pro-Beijing crime syndicates, as occurred in Taiwan during the Sunflower Movement's occupation of the Legislative Yuan earlier that year. The involvement of gangsters doing Beijing's "dirty work" was very much in line with the recent attacks against Hong Kong journalists and editors who had refused to self-censor and had dared to criticize Beijing and its allies in HKSAR – among them Chen Ping (陳平), the billionaire publisher of *iSun Affairs* magazine (陽光時務), and Kevin Lau (劉進圖), the former editor of *Ming Pao* (明報), who were attacked with axes and meat cleavers in 2013 and 2014, respectively.

The drama that brought the SAR to a near standstill in the summer and fall of 2014 also compelled Beijing to tighten restrictions on who was allowed to enter Hong Kong. Prior to those events, only well-known critics of the Beijing regime like Tiananmen activists Wu'er Kaixi and Wang Dan (王丹), both of whom now reside in Taiwan, were denied entry into the SAR, as occurred in January 2011 when the pair applied for travel visas so they could attend the funeral of Szeto Wah (司徒華), a founder of Hong Kong's democracy movement. By summer of 2014, however, the number of individuals who were denied entry had expanded to include participants in Taiwan's Sunflower Movement, such as Lin Fei-fan (林飛帆), Chen Wei-ting (陳為廷), and Huang Kuo-chang (黃國昌). Huang was again denied a visa in January 2016. Tseng Chien-yuan (曾建元), an associate professor of public administration at Chung Hua University in Hsinchu, was informed in late May 2014 that his Mainland Travel Permit for Taiwan Residents had been cancelled, and he was sent back to Taiwan. Tseng, a board member of the New School for Democracy (華人民主書院), was planning to attend an international seminar at City University in Hong Kong to mark the 25th anniversary of the Massacre.

More difficult to explain was the refusal by Hong Kong authorities to allow Su Yeong-chin (蘇永欽), vice president of the Judicial Yuan and a younger brother of former National Security Council Secretary-General Su Chi (蘇起), permission to enter. The younger Su, who comes from the conservative camp within the KMT, was expected to deliver a keynote address at Hong Kong University's Faculty of Law on the subject of transitions from authoritarian rule. The fact that even conservative KMT members were being barred access to Hong Kong testified to the tightening of controls by Beijing, which given the growing unrest in the HKSAR, wanted to minimize the possibility of contact between civil societies in Taiwan and Hong Kong.

Maybe Beijing had reason to worry. After all, during the Sunflower occupation in March and April that year, Hong Kong students sent hundreds of letters of encouragement to the activists who were inside the legislature. And when the Umbrella Movement took to the streets, some of the activists wore activist T-shirts that originated in Taiwan or used techniques that had been tested and refined in Taiwan. A number of activists who took part in the Sunflower Movement, as well as academics who supported them, also traveled to Hong Kong during Occupy Central to monitor the situation and presumably to establish contact with the leadership.

As this chapter has demonstrated, the experience of Hong Kong prior to and since retrocession in 1997 provides useful guidance for Taiwan as it develops closer ties with China. While the former British colony's penetration by CCP organs sheds light on the underground techniques that Beijing is currently deploying against it so as to facilitate eventual unification, the erosion of freedoms and liberties that occurred after reunification and that led to escalating discontent from 2003 serves as a warning and a reminder that, no matter what Beijing says, Taiwan would never be allowed to maintain its way of life, let alone its democracy, under any political agreement reached with the CCP. Whether the Taiwanese people would countenance the curtailment of their liberties in exchange for membership in the PRC and a formal end to hostilities in the Taiwan Strait is for the Taiwanese themselves to decide. Recent developments in Taiwan, from the reemergence of activism to the consolidation of an entity that is based on notions of civic nationalism (the subject of the next two chapters), seem to indicate that they would not.

Bibliography

Baldwin, C, Rose, A and Kwok, D (2014) "Big Four Accounting Firms Warn Investors Could Leave HK Over Occupy Central Protests," *Reuters*, 27 June, http://uk.reuters.com/article/uk-hongkong-occupy-idUKKBN0F20W720140627

Chin, W (2015) "A Federation for Hong Kong and China," *The New York Times*, 14 June, http://www.nytimes.com/2015/06/15/opinion/a-federation-for-hong-kong-and-china.html?_r=0

Chung, L-H (2015) "中資入股中信金 民團憂後患," *Ziyou Shibao*, 24 June, http://news.ltn.com.tw/news/business/paper/892098 (in Chinese)

Curran, E and Yung, C (2014) "Hong Kong Newspaper Says HSBC, Standard Chartered Pulled Ads," *Wall Street Journal*, 16 June, http://www.wsj.com/articles/apple-daily-says-hsbc-standard-chartered-pulled-ads-due-to-chinese-government-pressure-1402923219

Goodstadt, L (2013) *Poverty in the Midst of Affluence: How Hong Kong Mismanaged Its Prosperity*, Hong Kong: Hong Kong University Press: 2

Ku, S-M (2009) "Civil Society's Dual Impetus: Mobilizations, Representations and Contestations Over the July 1 March in 2003," in *Politics and Government in Hong Kong: Crisis Under Chinese Sovereignty*, Sing, M, ed, Oxon: Routledge: 44

Lam, W-M (2007) "Political Context," *Contemporary Hong Kong and Politics*, 2nd ed, Lam, W-M, Lui, L-T and Wong, W, eds, Hong Kong: Hong Kong University Press: 4

Law, V (2014) "Hong Kong's Inconvenient Truth," *Foreign Policy*, 21 August, http://foreignpolicy.com/2014/08/21/hong-kongs-inconvenient-truth/

Lo, S-H (2008) *The Dynamics of Beijing-Hong Kong Relations: A Model for Taiwan?* Hong Kong: Hong Kong University Press: 7

Loh, C (2010) *Underground Front: The Chinese Communist Party in Hong Kong*, Hong Kong: Hong Kong University Press

Ming, S (2009) "Hong Kong at the Crossroads: Public Pressure for Democratic Reform," in *Politics and Government in Hong Kong: Crisis Under Chinese Sovereignty*, Sing, M, ed, Oxon: Routledge: 118

Pei, M (2014) "Why China's Hong Kong Model Is Falling Apart," *Fortune*, 1 July, http://fortune.com/2014/07/01/hong-kong-china/

Pesek, W (2015) "Hong Kong's Peg to Instability," *Bloomberg*, 14 April, https://www.bloomberg.com/view/articles/2015-04-14/hong-kong-s-peg-to-instability

Petersen, C (2005) *National Security and Fundamental Freedoms: Hong Kong's Article 23 Under Scrutiny*, Fu, H, Petersen, C and Young, N-M, eds, Hong Kong: Hong Kong University Press: 2–3

Tsang, S (2007) *A Modern History of Hong Kong*, Hong Kong: Hong Kong University Press: 236–7, 240

Tsang, D, Sun, C, Sito, S and Li, K (2013) "The Tricky Business of Trading Places, Thanks to Hong Kong-Mainland CEPA Deal," *SCMP*, 4 July, http://www.scmp.com/business/economy/article/1274790/tricky-business-trading-places

7

CROSSING THE RED LINE

The Sunflower phenomenon

Something extraordinary happened in Taiwan between the reelection in 2012 of Ma Ying-jeou to a second and last term and the dramatic events of March and April 2014, when hundreds of young Taiwanese, supported by tens of thousands of people, launched a three-week occupation of the Legislative Yuan in Taipei in protest against a controversial trade agreement with China. Although the Sunflower Movement derailed President Ma's plans to sign the Cross-Strait Services Trade Agreement (CSSTA), the truly extraordinary thing wasn't so much the unprecedented occupation of government buildings but rather the two years that led to it, during which a traditionally heterogeneous civil society came together to fight for a common cause in a manner that transcended political affiliations, "ethnicity," and social class.

In many ways, the Sunflower Movement was the natural progression – an almost inevitable one – to events that most media and the majority of Taiwan experts overseas had largely ignored. Interestingly, it is during those two years, 2012 and 2014, that a new force politicized itself and, through trial and error, grew into an entity that could directly challenge the government. Just as important, it is during that period that local activism fused with activism that was directed at China's creeping influence inside Taiwan.

The blatant disregard by Ma administration officials (both at the local and at the central levels) for public opinion, due process, and transparency on such matters as urban renewal, wind power, abuse in the military, workers' rights, large petrochemical refineries, same-sex marriage, nuclear energy, nuclear waste disposal, school textbooks, aboriginal land, and the preservation of the nation's cultural heritage succeeded in fusing anger over local issues with the administration's cross-strait policies. If, activists and victims concluded, the government cannot be trusted to handle local affairs in a just and transparent manner, how can we trust it with negotiations on national issues with an authoritarian regime that does not even recognize the existence of Taiwan as a sovereign entity? Moreover, reflecting the Hong Kong experience, those in charge of negotiating agreements with China tended to represent the elite within Taiwanese society and thus advocated policies that, while beneficial to politicians and the owners of large businesses with operations in the PRC, often left ordinary Taiwanese with precious little in terms of benefits but much more in terms of the potential risks to the way of life that they wanted to preserve.

The Ma administration's greatest blunder during the period leading up to the Sunflower Movement was to mismanage local issues that had little, if any, relationship to cross-strait issues. Its unresponsiveness and increasing reliance on law enforcement and the courts to counter dissent and by using those tactics in various contexts, the administration created the conditions that were necessary for civil society to adopt escalatory strategies. So the streets of Taipei and other locales nationwide became a training ground for young activists who cross-pollinated and helped each other out. Furthermore, thanks to new media like Facebook and Internet chat rooms, the activists learned from one another and developed coordination skills that would increasingly keep law enforcement authorities on their toes.

Those two formative years were crucial for the Sunflower Movement. In fact, many of the small organizations that eventually coalesced into the movement cut their teeth fighting on other issues, where they developed skills and during which charismatic leaders emerged who could mobilize larger groups. For all intents and purposes, the Sunflower Movement probably could not have existed had it not been for the two years of local activism that preceded it. This coming together of a politicized, empowered, and confident youth was an extraordinary counter to the usual claim that young Taiwanese were apolitical, lazy, and too disinterested in public affairs to defy their government. So when, sometime in 2013, a large enough segment of society decided that the Ma administration had crossed certain red lines in its negotiations with China – and there is no doubt that the CSSTA was such a red line – civil society had all the elements it needed to take action.

The speed with which they took over, the high levels of organization, and the seemingly structured leadership that almost immediately took charge of the occupation led many observers and officials in the Ma government to conclude that the activists had been trained by and were working on behalf of the opposition DPP. Had they been paying attention in the years prior to the occupation, those critics would have known that the DPP had nothing to do with it. In fact, the high mobilization that was experienced during that period was in part due to the DPP's inaction on a variety of issues.

Why the Sunflower Movement seemed to be so structured and organized was because, for the most part, the structure already existed. In reality, as we shall see, the first 24 hours of the occupation of the legislature were mostly unplanned, with activists quickly reacting to a shifting situation. Yet their years of experience in defying the government meant that once they had ensconced themselves inside the chambers of parliament, they were able to call upon a large network and launch the stunning operation that captivated the nation and in some instances the entire world for three captivating weeks.

Nor, for that matter, was the occupation "spontaneous," as a number of observers said in the days following the launch of the occupation, attacking the activists for supposedly breaking the rules of democracy. The problem is that with the exception of a few local journalists, the activists themselves and the government officials who did everything in their power to discredit civil society, nobody was paying attention as the situation slowly deteriorated. In the end, the Sunflower Movement was both a symptom of and the response to a series of controversies in the previous two years that led to a loss of faith in government institutions and the ability to correct the course using standard and legal procedures. In the eyes of many activists who in the days before 18 March pondered their next move, things had reached a point where they had to make one of two choices: capitulate or escalate. They chose the latter.

Despite the sudden interest among the media and foreign academics in Taiwan's civil society following the occupation, there is nothing new about activism in the country. In fact, its civil society is vibrant and has a long, rich, and enviable tradition of involvement in politics at the local and national levels and has become what Fell has described as "one of the most vibrant civil societies of any state in Asia."

Of course, under martial law there was little of what could be called independent associational life or civil society capable of challenging the party-state. The KMT enjoyed hegemonistic rule in Taiwan, and whatever groups existed outside government were organizations that had the KMT's imprimatur. However, as Fell observes, "Immediately before and after the lifting of martial law a large number of new social movements emerged to challenge the KMT regime on a range of political and social issues." These groups, Fell continues, "contributed to Taiwan's democratic transition by not only calling for social and political reforms, but also by eroding the KMT's dominant position in the country's associational life." As the political system liberalized and then democratized, social movements grew and diversified, playing a "critical intermediary role between the state and society."

Formed on 28 September 1986, the DPP was itself a regrouping of individuals who had operated outside the system (*dangwai*) and who had taken part in the nonviolent opposition – from 1977 through the mid-1980s – that contributed to Taiwan's peaceful democratization.

With its institutionalization as a loyal opposition, the DPP relinquished the mantle of civil society, which was soon assumed by other groups. Starting in 1987, Taiwan saw the emergence of many self-help organizations (*zili jiuji*, 自力救濟) that according to Chuang "illuminated a history of otherness in the process of democratization" and "contributed as much as the *dangwai* to the democratization" of Taiwan. In fact, as Chuang argues, "while the *dangwai*-turned-DPP was entrapped and paralyzed in institutional politics, the *zili-jiuji*-inspired social activism was still vigorously in search of their goals of justice, equality, and dignified ways of life."

For the most part, the self-help organizations focused on issues such as environmental pollution, conflicts of interest in the workplace, and the rights of marginalized groups. Besides their contributions to the resolution of various social ills, the *zili jiuji* also left a legacy that carried into the 1990s and that encouraged other groups outside the now institutionalized DPP to involve themselves in matters of democracy.

One such group was the Wild Lily Movement (野百合), which held a series of protests in March 1990 calling for the abolition of the National Assembly (國民大會) and an end to the Temporary Provisions Effective During the Period of Communist Rebellion (動員戡亂時期臨時條款). As a result of the protests and hunger strike, President Lee Teng-hui, who agreed to meet with the students, agreed to one of their demands by convening a National Affairs Conference in June and July 1990. Interestingly, many of the students who took part in the Wild Lily protests in 1990s, such as Fan Yun (范雲) and Wu Rwei-ren (吳叡人), would later serve as mentors to the new wave of political activism that emerged during the first and second terms of the Ma Ying-jeou administration, thus highlighting a thread of continuity that, with democratization, many observers thought had been severed. (In Fan Yun's case, she would later enter politics at the head of one of the small "third force" parties that emerged in the wake of the Sunflower occupation.)

In the Chen Shui-bian years, some of the activists who would later gain prominence during the protests against the Ma administration made their first appearances, participating in protests over the planned demolition of the Losheng Sanatorium (樂生療養院) in Taipei County's Xinzhuang District (新莊區) to build a mass rapid transit (MRT) warehouse. Protests over the planned demolition of the sanatorium, which since the 1930s had been home to hundreds of patients suffering from Hansen's disease, or leprosy, from all over Taiwan, and efforts to relocate them to a nearby hospital, began in 2004. In their handling of the controversy, Vice President Annette Lu (呂秀蓮) and Premier Su Tseng-chang did little better than Ma administration officials would nearly a decade later, when efforts to secure the integrity of Losheng and to ensure the dignity of its aging residents were still ongoing.

Another and much more overtly political movement that emerged during the Chen years was the Red Shirts, also known as the Million Voices Against Corruption, President Chen Must Go (百萬人民反貪腐倒扁運動) campaign, attracted the participation of individuals like former DPP chairman Shih Ming-teh (施明德) and future Taipei mayor Hau Lung-bin (郝龍斌). Leading to mass protests and the occupation of a space outside Taipei Main Station, the protests are closely associated with pan–blue political parties.

Now professors at the nation's most prestigious universities and research institutions, professionals, and parents, the Wild Lily "graduates" provided guidance, support, and focus for many of the young activists who formed the Wild Strawberries Movement (野草莓運動) that held nationwide protests in response to the breakthrough visit to Taiwan by Association for Relations Across the Taiwan Strait (ARATS) Chairman Chen Yunlin in November 2008 and that, among other things, demanded amendments to the antiquated Assembly and Parade Act (集會遊行法). One of the about 400 participants in the movement was Lin Fei-fan, a young man from Tainan who would reemerge four years later as one of the leaders of the

Alliance Against Media Monsters, which sought to block the acquisition of Next Media's Taiwan operations by a consortium led by the pro-Beijing Tsai Eng-meng. Already in 2008, the Wild Strawberries used live video streams to broadcast their activities to a global audience, a precursor to the much more formidable media campaign launched by the Sunflower Movement (and the Umbrella Movement in Hong Kong) four years later.

The sudden mobilization reflected the highly symbolic value of Chen Yunlin's visit and the displeasure with the large-scale police mobilization that accompanied the visit. Some activists also complained of police harassment prior to the landmark visit, and limits on press freedoms immediately drew attention to the lengths to which the Ma administration would go to facilitate fledgling exchanges with Beijing. Soon afterward, the Wild Strawberries faded into oblivion, having failed to achieve its goals. Between November 2008 and 2012, civil society appeared to have receded into the background, leading many people in Taiwan and overseas to accuse Taiwan – especially its youth – of being apathetic and apolitical. However, nothing that occurred during that period seemed to warrant drastic measures such as those that were taken during the Chen Yunlin visit. For one thing, subsequent visits by the ARATS chairman desensitized the Taiwanese public, which resigned itself to such exchanges. Moreover, the process of liberalization that began during that period, including the signing of the ECFA and other cross-strait agreements, was for the most part regarded as logical and within the bounds of acceptability. In other words, the cultivation of the low-lying fruits in the Taiwan Strait was acceptable to the majority of the public, and the protests that did take place on such matters were usually organized by the DPP or its smaller ally the Taiwan Solidarity Union (TSU) and therefore were regarded as the zero-sum games that politicians played.

Civil society, however, reemerged in 2012 after Next Media Chairman Jimmy Lai (黎智英) did what he vowed he would never do and agreed to sell his Taiwan operations to his ideological archenemy, Tsai Eng-meng. As with the Wild Strawberries, the Alliance Against Media Monsters benefited from the behind-the-scenes assistance of a number of veterans from the Wild Lily movement, who provided the intellectual heft while allowing a new generation of activists to take the lead publicly. The campaign against the monopolization of Taiwan's media industry also saw the emergence of another young charismatic leader, Chen Wei-ting, who would later spearhead protests against forced evictions and laid-off factory workers in Miaoli, and of course the Sunflower Movement's occupation of the legislature in 2014.

The impact that the success of the Alliance Against Media Monsters had on future activism in Taiwan cannot be discounted. By 2013, following a series of protests, workshops, and an online campaign meant to undermine the Want Want brand image, Mr. Tsai called it quits and pulled out of the attempted bid for Next Media. A few thousands of activists, aided by legislators, had faced off against one of the richest men in Taiwan and prevailed. Moreover, there was no doubt that their activism had made it difficult for the agencies in charge of evaluating the merits of the acquisition – the NCC (國家通訊傳播委員會) and the Investment

Commission (經濟部投資審議委員會) among them – to skirt their responsibilities, which is conceivably what would have happened had they not been pressured by civil society and journalist associations.

Thus emboldened, civil society turned its sights on other issues. Many of the participants in the Alliance Against Media Monsters involved themselves in other causes. One important aspect of what followed is that, with no exception, the protests transcended the notions of "ethnicity," political affiliations, and ideology that often have kept Taiwan in a state of perpetual division.

Chief among the causes during that period was urban renewal, which threatened communities in Taipei, Taoyuan, and Miaoli, among others. Although many of the land controversies had existed for years, local KMT mayors and commissioners were seemingly under renewed pressure from investors, land developers and the central government, to complete the projects. This sudden rush to complete the projects led to abuse of due process and human rights violations. This time around, an energized, attentive, and connected civil society was ready to pounce into action – and it did.

Two cases in particular, the demolition of the Huaguang Community (華光社區) in Taipei and the forced evictions in Dapu Borough (大埔), Miaoli County, set passions ablaze and the government on a collision course with civil society. Located on prime real estate next to Chiang Kai-shek Memorial Hall, Huaguang was an old community that since the early 1950s had been home to many Nationalist soldiers who had fled China after the Civil War and their families. By the twenty-first century, many of its residents, *waishengren* (外省人) and *benshengren* (本省人) alike, were elderly and ailing, and their offspring were poorly educated and of meager financial means. Huaguang, which sits on land belonging to the Ministry of Justice, had been the target of urban renewal projects for several years, but when the DPP was in power the government simply decided to delay the decision and pass the problem on to future administrations.

By early 2013, the government had run out of patience and wanted the residents out so that the bug-infested eyesore of a community could be razed and be replaced by a glitzy, "Roppongi-style" shopping complex. Many of the residents, however, refused to leave, fearing that the communal bonds that they had known since their childhood would be forever destroyed. Most of the residents, furthermore, did not have the financial means to move elsewhere, especially in a city where housing costs had risen exponentially in recent years. Whatever assistance the city government offered them to relocate was insufficient, and to make matters worse, such assistance was set to expire after three years, whereupon the residents would be on their own.

However, the government was unfazed. Not only did it give the residents an ultimatum, it sued those who refused to leave, fined local merchants for "illegally profiting," and froze their bank accounts. To add insult to injury, it sent the demolition bills to the residents and, as protests escalated, charged them for police overtime. Under tremendous stress, some elderly residents died. A number of residences were also set ablaze under mysterious circumstances, suggesting involvement by organized crime (the son of one of the elderly residents, who sent a letter to U.S.

President Obama hoping for assistance, was adamant that gangsters were behind the arson attack. Soon after the incident his mother, a resident of Huaguang, passed away).

In the end, the series of protests to save the community failed, and by 2014 Huaguang was no more. Struggling to make ends meet, its residents had been dispersed, and many of them continued their battle with the Ministry of Justice over the fines that were imposed on them for "illegally" occupying government land. And yet Huaguang was a key development in the reemergence of an activist civil society in Taiwan, bringing together "veterans" of the Alliance Against Media Monster and the sons and daughters of the Huaguang residents, as well as a variety of other self-help groups. It did not matter to the participants, who often clashed with police, that many of the residents of Huaguang were Chinese who had fled to Taiwan and who had voted for the KMT their entire lives. For young Taiwanese like Lin Fei-fan, who played a role as a foot soldier rather than a leader in the protests, this was a matter of justice and dignity, to which every resident of Taiwan, no matter how they self-identified, was entitled. Youth fought for men like the so-called Uncle Chiang (蔣伯伯), whose ramshackle house was virtually a Chiang Kai-shek museum. Ironically, it was a KMT administration – the same party that prided itself in its Chinese origins and that had provided the land to the Nationalist soldiers in the first place – that brought Huaguang, perceived as a "Mainlander" community, to its knees. The message was very clear: In this new era, even if you were *waishengren* and had been a staunch supporter of the KMT over the years, it didn't matter. Nobody was safe – not the Wang family (王家) in Shilin (士林) and certainly not the residents of vulnerable communities like Huaguang. Everybody was fair game when it came to the enrichment of an increasingly corporatist state and its clients.

And as the brokenhearted residents and activists looked at the ruins of the community, it dawned on them that this thirst for money created immense possibilities for the government across the Taiwan Strait that had no compunction in throwing money around to achieve its political objectives in Taiwan.

Around the same time, events came to a head in Dapu, a small borough in Miaoli County. Since 2010, the local government, led by KMT County Commissioner Liu Cheng-hung (劉政鴻), had been waging war against the residents to seize their land, farmland, and homes to build roads leading to a science park project nearby. With Miaoli, a primarily Hakka community, being one of the poorest counties in the country, Commissioner Liu knew that he could solidify his support by promising development and more money for his constituents. Treating the county like his personal fiefdom, Liu had tremendous influence on the local police force and used his position to facilitate his personal enrichment and that of his family. Those who resisted his desire for land suffered the consequences. A handful of officials, almost all of them involved in land issues, committed "suicide" under mysterious circumstances, with law enforcement refusing to make the autopsy reports public or even available to the families of the victims.

On 3 August 2010, Chu Feng-min (朱馮敏), a 73-year-old farmer, committed suicide by ingesting pesticide to protest the local government's efforts to seize

her house and land. Commenting on the suicide, Wu Den-yih (吳敦義), who
was premier at the time, attributed Ms. Chu's suicide to "chronic disease, maybe
even depression." Soon thereafter, a large group of protesters, mostly students and
academics, gathered in front of the Presidential Office in Taipei and held an all-
night vigil and symbolically planted crops on Ketagalan Boulevard. The protests
and national indignation eventually convinced Premier Wu to issue a document
"promising" that that the farmers' homes and land would be left alone (原地保留).

Three years later, weeks after the bulldozers and excavators had rumbled into
Huaguang, Commissioner Liu issued a renewed order for the demolition of the
remaining houses and land in Dapu. The order set 5 July as the deadline for the
residents' homes to be demolished and for them to vacate the area. Indicatively, by
then a land development company had opened an office right across from one of
the residences. Apparently, the promise made by Wu, who was now Ma's vice president, no longer held. In fact, Wu denied he'd ever made such a promise.

The families, who had initiated administrative lawsuits against the government,
held a protest in front of the Executive Yuan on 2 July calling on Premier Jiang
Yi-huah (江宜樺) to honor the promise made by his predecessor and call off the
planned demolitions. In scorching heat, the protesters gathered. Among them were
Chu Ping-kun (朱炳坤), the son of Ms Chu, Peng Hsiu-chun (彭秀春), and her
husband, Chang Sen-wen (張森文), who ran a small pharmacy that stood to be
demolished, as well as other residents of Dapu, students, academics, and lawyers. At
4 a.m. on 4 July – just as soldier Hung Chung-chiu was drawing his last breath –
police moved in and removed the protesters. In the melee, Mr. Chang collapsed, a
broken man who had failed to defend his family. The protesters gathered again later
that day, and after brief and highly emotional speeches, during which Mr. Chang,
still unconscious, was wheeled in on a wheelchair, a number of activists climbed
over the wall and briefly clashed with police.

For a while, the protests seemed to have succeeded in halting the planned
demolitions. The fifth of July came and went, and the houses were still standing.
However, the residents' hopes were dashed on 18 July when Commissioner Liu
dispatched demolition teams while the activists were holding another round of
protests, this time in front of the Presidential Office. Arriving at the protest site, a
wailing Ms. Peng, who had just learned that her home was no more, was pushed
in the melee between protesters and police and collapsed. As paramedics lifted
her into an ambulance, the anger among the activists was palpable. Moments after
the ambulance left, the clashes resumed. Dozens of protesters were taken away on
police buses.

Five days later, following a gathering on Ketagalan Boulevard involving many
of the same protesters and a large group of indignant figures from the artistic community, the protesters rallied near the Ministry of Health and Welfare, which was
being opened that day and where President Ma and Premier Jiang were attend-
ing a ceremony. Expecting trouble, the police deployment was substantial, and in
the ensuing clashes several protesters were dragged and sustained minor injuries,
including Hsu Shih-jung (徐世榮), a professor of land economics at National

Chengchi University (NCCU) and chairman of the Taiwan Rural Front. Photos of Professor Hsu being dragged away by police spread like brushfire over the Internet and contributed to the anger over the Dapu fiasco. Soon thereafter, it was revealed that the National Security Bureau (NSB) was involved in the policing efforts. Hsu, who faced obstruction charges, in turn filed lawsuits against the NSB and the Datong District Police Department.

Exactly one month after the demolitions in Dapu, a crowd of several thousands gathered on Ketagalan Boulevard for a protest against forced evictions. Dozens of self-help organizations from across the country were invited on stage to rally support for their cause.

What happened next clearly demonstrated that a line had been crossed in the public mind. Something had shifted, and developments in a small, little known borough in one of the poorest counties in Taiwan was transformed into a pivotal event in the history of modern activism in Taiwan. Faced with government indifference, civil society would retaliate with escalation.

Less than an hour after the 18 August ("818") rally concluded, thousands of protesters were occupying the grounds of the Ministry of the Interior, whose windows and façade were covered with eggs, stickers proclaiming "[T]oday Dapu, tomorrow the government" (今天拆大埔，明天拆政府), and spray paint. As would happen exactly seven months later at the Legislative Yuan next door, police were completely unprepared, outwitted, and overwhelmed by the young activists.

Exactly one month later, Mr. Chang left home early in the morning. Hours later, his lifeless body was found in a drainage ditch, 200 meters from their former home. Police ruled it a suicide, though suspicions remain that there might have been foul play. After all, for several months local gangsters had visited the Changs' pharmacy, where they would flash knives and handguns. The surveillance cameras that could have shed light on what really happened to Mr. Chang were off, and once again, the autopsy report was not made public. That night, an angry crowd gathered at the site of the Changs' former home. When Commissioner Liu attempted to pay a visit, he was hit on the side of the head by a brand new running shoe. Chen Wei-ting had scored a direct hit.

If there is one incident in recent years that has turned civil society against the government, it was the Dapu case and the death of Mr. Chang. Not once did the government apologize for the harm caused to the victims, and nobody in the administration expressed remorse at Mr. Chang's death (President Ma, it seemed, would shed tears only in memory of Chiang Ching-kuo). This kind of government indifference caused great alarm among the residents of Taoyuan, thousands of whom were facing the prospect of forced evictions and similar nightmares as plans accelerated for the Taoyuan Aerotropolis megaproject, in which Chinese investors and construction firms were presumably allowed to bid.

Those fears were allayed after Taoyuan County Commissioner John Wu (吳志揚), the son of Wu Poh-hsiung (吳伯雄), a Beijing-friendly former KMT chairman, was defeated by the DPP candidate in the 29 November 2014 elections. Similarly, the defeat of Sean Lien, the KMT candidate in Taipei in the same election, likely halted planned development projects that would have resulted in serious land expropriation and large protests in neighborhoods such as Songshan. Although other factors, such as general discontent with the KMT, conceivably had an influence on voter choice, the electoral outcomes in Taoyuan and Taipei are a clear demonstration of the positive effect that activism and the corrective that results from electoral retribution can have on social stability.

Above all, the moral outrage that was sparked by the events in Dapu and the central government's subsequent moves to shield County Commissioner Liu from court action and criticism, convinced civil society that they needed to escalate. Years of peaceful protests, appeals to government officials, and legal action had led to failure at the hands of an all-powerful government that seemingly had no patience for due process. What's worse, the DPP, which ought to have been a natural ally in these cases, was inattentive and failed to play a role, something that civil society would not forget or forgive.

By then, Commissioner Liu was probably the most reviled person in Taiwan, and yet he continued to be protected by the KMT in Taipei. Besides his actions in Dapu, Liu's image had also been tarnished by other developments in Yuanli Township (苑裡), where a controversy over the erection of several wind turbines very close to the homes of local residents, who claim they were not consulted by the government, led to protests. Police inaction when thugs hired by Infravest, the German firm that was awarded the contract when the DPP was in office, physically assaulted elderly residents and illegally blocked access to sites that are public property, raised serious concerns about the ability of law enforcement to ensure public safety. That the private security firm hired by Infravest had possible ties to organized crime and that the said triad had seemingly a close relationship with the head of the National Police Agency (內政部警政署) at the time certainly did not contribute to making people feel safe or convincing them that they could trust local police to do the right thing.

The NPA's image would be further undermined by its failure to intervene when groups opposing the legalization of same-sex marriage harassed and prevented the free movement of individuals in a public space during a rally on Ketagalan Boulevard on 30 November 2013 or at many of the protests against visiting Chinese officials when groups with ostensible ties to pro-Beijing crime syndicates physically assaulted members of social movements and proindependence political parties.

Lawsuits against many of the protesters, who were charged with "kidnapping," also raised questions about the courts' impartiality. The Yuanli self-help association held a series of protests in Taipei, at one point delivering a severed pig's head to the Ministry of Economic Affairs. Once again, many of the protesters were involved in other protests and would play a role during the Sunflower occupation of the legislature.

One other event that served as a catalyst during that period was the 4 July 2013 death of 24-year-old Army conscript Hung Chung-chiu of complications from hyperthermia-induced disseminated intravascular coagulation. The punishment meted out on the young man by his superiors, which led to his death a mere three days before he was to complete his obligatory service, and the military's bungling of the matter, including stalling, broken surveillance cameras, and outright lies, sparked mass protests and the emergence of a new civic organization under the name Citizen 1985 (公民1985), named after the military hotline. The group, which was led by individuals who had "met on the Internet" and who were reluctant to make their identities known, held its first protest outside the Ministry of National Defense on 20 July, attracting tens of thousands of people. A second rally, held on 3 August, brought together a quarter of a million people, many of them brandishing "big brother is watching you" placards with the large eye that had become emblematic of the movement. During that rally, several families of young men who had died while doing their military service came forth and expressed their anger at never receiving proper answers as to the circumstances that had led to their untimely deaths. By then, Minister of National Defense Kao Hua-chu (高華柱) had resigned over the controversy. His replacement, Andrew Yang (楊念祖), seemed dedicated to properly addressing the controversy over Hung's death and making those responsible accountable, but facing resistance from within the embattled military establishment (in part because he was a civilian), he was quickly unseated when revelations that he had plagiarized an academic article were made public, in part with the help of DPP legislators. In all, Yang served as minister of national defense for a mere six days. President Ma, who had never hesitated to refuse a request by cabinet officials to step down, didn't think twice about granting Yang's request. Soon afterward, a member of the military establishment took over the helm of the ministry.

Despite its ability to attract large crowds and foreign media attention with well orchestrated rallies, Citizen 1985 was not uncontroversial. One of the main criticisms leveled against it was the tight control that its staff imposed at protest sites, which often prevented media personnel from moving around. The absence of large police deployments at the protests – in stark contrast with the substantial deployments that inevitably accompanied much smaller protests by self-help groups over forced evictions and other issues – also encouraged speculation that Citizen 1985 may have struck a deal with the authorities. Many observers argued at the time that the predictability and overly peaceful nature of the rallies organized by Citizen 1985 defeated the purpose of keeping the government on its toes. Responding to the accusations, Liulin Wei (柳林瑋), one of the organizers, argued that Citizen 1985 aimed to create a safe environment so that young people and families would not hesitate to come out and support the cause.

There certainly is some validity to this argument, and in fact such grooming may have familiarized some of the tens of thousands of young people who would eventually gather around the Legislative Yuan during the Sunflower occupation, in which a more radicalized Liulin Wei also played a leading role.

Still, the Citizen 1985 never achieved its objectives. Then punishments against those who were responsible for Hung's death were minor, and many of the reforms that the organization called for were never implemented. When the KMT blocked those, Citizen 1985 failed to follow through or to escalate. Such an outcome demonstrated that large crowds were not, on their own, sufficient to sway a government that did not intend to be influenced by public opinion, in stark contrast with the much smaller, "guerrilla-style" protests organized by other movements, such as the Black Island Nation Youth Alliance (黑色島國青年陣線), formed around that time to oppose the CSSTA, which the leaders of Citizen 1985 often reviled as "low class" and "violent."

Nevertheless, as with the tragic events in Dapu, the Hung case captivated a national audience and increased awareness in the public that the government could not be trusted with the fundamentals. Human rights were being violated, and, worse, people were dying as a result. Those developments largely contributed to the loss of trust in local and central government officials – much more, in fact, than the poor economic performance that many outside observers usually mention to explain President Ma's drop in approval rates.

The public anger at government officials led to various protests calling on President Ma and other members of his cabinet to step down. It also gave rise to flash protests in which protesters lobbed shoes at government representatives, culminating in a shoe collection event at Sun Yat-sen Memorial Hall in Taipei and the siege of a long-delayed KMT congress in Taichung in November 2013, where hundreds of protesters threw footwear at the pictures of government officials. Other direct actions that were originally planned on that day were cancelled after the prounification gangster-turned-politician Chang An-le vowed to dispatch thousands of his supporters to protect Ma administration officials and attempted to bribe the organizers of the protest, a self-help association for laid-off factory workers. Wherever they went, government officials faced spontaneous protests; young students, academics, mothers, and other activists hounded representatives of a government that was quickly losing the trust of the people. Here again, the resentment transcended the blue–green divide, though there is no doubt that as 2014 approached, the protests increasingly took on a more political hue over the question of China, in large part due to government efforts to pass the CSSTA.

Despite the mounting rage, little did people know just how transformative the year 2014 would be, a year pregnant with events that would shake the KMT at its core and derail plans for a series of cross-strait deals that would have further drawn Taiwan into Beijing's embrace.

The first signal that escalation and more dramatic events lay ahead occurred early in the morning of 25 January, when Chang Ter-cheng (張德正), a 41-year-old truck driver and former Air Force officer, crashed his 35-tonne truck into the Presidential Office. The government quickly played down the incident and claimed that Chang was mentally unstable and ostensibly angered by personal circumstances (he had a troubled marriage and had recently lost in an alleged child abuse case). What the authorities conveniently did not mention, however, is that in a letter that he distributed to the media prior to his act, Chang listed a series of grievances. Besides the "unfairness" of the court that had handled his case, he mentioned government corruption, widening inequality, and a judicial system that is skewed in favor of the rich and the powerful. More specifically, Chang singled out the demolitions in

Dapu, Corporal Hung Chung-chiu's death, and the "preferential treatment" given to government officials who engage in corruption.

Chang was probably onto something. The previous year, about a thousand lawyers across Taiwan had signed a declaration outside the Ministry of Justice condemning police action and the series of lawsuits that the authorities had filed against young activists over protests in the past couple of years. At the same event, the lawyers announced they were offering pro bono services to the activists – which they did repeatedly in the ensuing months, fishing them out of jail, informing them of their rights, and stepping in when riot police went into the Executive Yuan. The fact that the people who know the law best were offering their services *free of charge* to thousands of young individuals who, according to the authorities were constantly engaging in "illegal" activities, said a lot about the situation and may have helped sway public opinion in favor of the activists.

Despite his personal problems, there was no doubt that Chang was translating public anger and felt compelled to do something (he nevertheless planned his "attack" in a way that minimized the risk of casualties). Those who, a few months later, expressed disbelief at the suddenness and spontaneity of the Sunflower occupation had obviously not been paying attention to developments in Taiwan. All signs were there.

One group in particular that harnessed the momentum created by other movements was the Black Island Nation Youth Alliance, the most direct precursor to the Sunflower Movement. The members of Black Island, which was created in response to the CSSTA, accused the negotiators of having reached a "black box" agreement that endangered Taiwan's sovereignty and liberal-democratic way of life. Among the sectors that were to be opened to Chinese investment under the deal were banking, health care, tourism, film, telecommunications, and publishing. Though technically reciprocal, it was clear that the influence on those sectors would largely be one-way, with authoritarian China in a position to undermine freedom of speech in Taiwan while Taiwanese firms would face serious censorship obstacles in China. Many small sectors in Taiwan also feared that they would be unable to compete with China-invested firms in the service sector and would be forced out of business.

The agreement was signed in Shanghai on 21 June 2013 by representatives of ARATS and the SEF; the CSSTA was to be immediately sent to the legislature for ratification. Right away, critics pointed out that the CSSTA had been negotiated in secret. Indicatively, even KMT legislators – especially those from districts where firms in the service sector stood to be negatively affected by the pact – expressed surprise at its scope and complained that they were never consulted. In the weeks and months that followed, business representatives, trade groups, academics, and activists accused the government of failing to consult them or to promise the necessary safeguards to ensure that the targeted sectors would not be unduly affected. In response, the Ma administration adopted the same refrain that had gotten it into so much trouble over the past year: The policy was fundamentally sound, but it had done a poor job explaining it to the public. In other words, changes to the policy were unnecessary; the government only needed to convince the public which, presumably, wasn't intelligent enough to understand what the government was doing on their behalf.

The Black Island Nation Youth Alliance held its first protest in front of the Executive Yuan on 24 June. It wasn't a promising beginning. Only two dozen or so activists participated. They flashed a few placards, chanted slogans, and left. The small gathering was duly ignored by the media.

Yet Black Island, again drawing from the experiences of previous movements and the participation of some of its members in recent activism, refined the art of the small, guerrilla-style street activism. By dint of sustained efforts – flash mob protests outside the legislature and other government buildings, workshops, websites, and so on – Black Island began attracting the attention of media and academics. And, of course, of law enforcement, which deployed increasingly large contingents to meet the protesters, who nevertheless often succeeded in slipping by police officers at the Legislative Yuan. Had it not been for the ability of Black Island activists to keep the government on its toes and their flair for the dramatic, there is a strong likelihood that the CSSTA would have been ratified without a glitch.

Eventually, Black Island and the many NGOs, academics, and former Ma advisers who rallied to the cause, forced the government to compromise by holding a series of public hearings, to be chaired by the KMT and the DPP (eight by each party). It soon became clear, however, that the KMT intended to use the hearings as a one-way communication channel, in which the government explained the contents of a policy that it had no desire to change. After all, as everybody knew, the public hearings were nonbinding. Moreover, while the DPP-led hearings proceeded reasonably well, those chaired by the KMT – all eight were held within the space of a week – often excluded the very elements that feared most for their survival if the CSSTA were implemented. Many groups were not invited; others learned that a hearing was about to be held at the last minute and were therefore unable to attend. Black Island activists were denied entry, sparking protests, which were held back by a substantial police force.

Still, the hearings meant that the CSSTA could not be implemented by the end of 2013, as the Ma administration had planned.

The government then made what looks like a second compromise by agreeing to a clause-by-clause review of the agreement. Critics of the government saw the move as reasonable. Supporters of the government – investors and many of the firms that stood to benefit from the CSSTA – countered that trade agreements worldwide never underwent such reviews and that it wasn't unusual for trade pacts to be negotiated behind closed doors. Of course, what those individuals failed to mention was the fact that so-called black box agreements worldwide tended to be negotiated between countries that, while not necessarily "equals" in terms of comprehensive national power, did not deny the other's existence, as is the case in the relationship between Taiwan and China. Although much more powerful than its partners, the U.S., for example, never threatened to take over Mexico and Canada while negotiating the North American Free-Trade Agreement (NAFTA).

The exceptional nature of the cross-strait relationship and Beijing's full-spectrum strategy to undermine Taiwan and eventually absorb it are factors that outside observers who were critical of Black Island and the Sunflower Movement often neglected, surprisingly, treating the CSSTA as if it were a normal agreement between two sovereign states negotiating as equals. But for the Taiwanese who feared for the future of their country, the CSSTA was a red line that ought not to be crossed. Things were going too far, and this time the impact of the CSSTA was not abstract, as had been the case with previous agreements signed with China.

The threat was real: It could be quantified in jobs lost and the ability of the CCP to slowly infiltrate Taiwan's media, telecommunications, advertising, publishing, and translation industries, all of which are critical components of a healthy democracy and the ability of the public to access information that is often denied to the citizens of repressive states like China.

Those who favored the quick passage of the CSSTA need not have worried too much about the clause-by-clause review. After all the hearings and consultations were held, Chang Ching-chung (張慶忠), a motel-operator-turned-KMT-legislator who was now presiding chair of the legislature's Internal Administrative Committee, said the agreement could not be amended and had to be adopted "as a whole."

When the legislature reconvened in March 2014 to negotiate the matter, KMT legislators blocked the process, leading to clashes in the legislature over a period of three days. DPP legislators, who did not have enough seats to block the process with their votes, responded in kind, leading to recriminations on both sides. As was often the case on major issues like relations with China, the legislature served as a battlefield in which there could be no winner.

Meanwhile, outside the legislature, activists gathered and launched a sit-in.

Then, on 17 March, with the DPP occupying the podium inside the legislative chambers, Chang, citing Article 61 of the Legislative Yuan Functions Act, announced that the review process had gone beyond the 90 days allotted for review. The agreement should therefore be considered to have been reviewed and be submitted to a plenary session on 21 March for a final vote. The Executive Yuan immediately "congratulated" Chang for successfully reviewing the agreement, even though no review had ever been held. Experts later noted that Article 61 did not apply in this case, as the CSSTA was a component of the ECFA, which was regarded as a "prospective treaty" (准條約) and not an executive order, in which case Article 61 *would* have applied. With 65 members in the 113-seat legislature, the KMT was assured of victory. The pact could be implemented as early as June 2014.

The following night, on 18 March, about 200 protesters led by Black Island fought their way into the ill protected Legislative Yuan and occupied its chambers.[1] Using chairs and whatever furniture they could find, they barricaded themselves inside the building and with the help of a handful of DPP legislators, warded off efforts by police to expel them. They had no plan, and the young men and women who found themselves in this extraordinary situation did not expect to remain ensconced in parliament for more than a few days.

In the end, they were in there for three dramatic weeks, rallying tens of thousands of people to their cause and the outside support of millions, including communities overseas. The initial phase of the occupation was not the result of careful planning; in fact, it doesn't appear that an occupation was part of the plan. But once they had barricaded themselves inside the building, the years of training – the networking, organizing, logistics, propaganda – gave them the wherewithal to quickly turn things around and give the occupation an air of unity. Soon afterward, drawing from their contacts, the activists established a communications center, a medical clinic, and a recognizable leadership, with Lin Fei-fan and Chen Wei-ting, by then recognizable figures to the public, at the top.

Had it not been for the coming together of civil society that had occurred in the previous two years, it is very likely that the occupation would have failed within days. Instead, it served as a rallying point, with dozens of NGOs, associations, and tens of thousands of people, some of them acclimatized to protesting by the "safe" and "controlled" Citizen 1985 rallies, joined the cause, turning the entire area around the Legislative Yuan into a war zone, outdoor classroom, concert site, and rallying point where ordinary citizens could express their fears, their anger, over the services trade pact and what they saw as the government's dangerous flirtations with Beijing. Months of persevering by Black Island, during which they were arrested, ridiculed, and reprimanded, had also succeeded in turning the CSSTA controversy into a recognizable issue, one that could no longer be ignored by the public or the media. Through small and unpredictable protests, they proved that size didn't matter. They outwitted the government and won the first round of the battle for hearts and minds. Just as importantly, they kept the issue alive. And when the situation reached a crisis point, there were plenty of young men and women who, worrying about their future, were willing to step in, either by joining the occupation or by filling the ranks of supporters who launched a sit-in outside the legislature or by helping disseminate information on social media.

As days turned into weeks, the fact that a majority of the population supported the actions of the activists, who eventually came to be known as the Sunflower Movement, was proof that the apprehensions about the trade pact and the Ma administration's future plans for engagement with Beijing had reached a point where people would say, "Go no further." For about six years, the Taiwanese had countenanced the liberalization of the cross-strait relationship, but all along they knew that things could go only so far. When President Ma crossed over that line, they fought back. Had there not been large public support for the Sunflower Movement, it is conceivable that its leadership would have felt compelled to abandon their plans. Instead, public support, along with the tens of thousands of people who formed a protective ring around the Legislative Yuan, provided the confirmation they needed to forge ahead and to take the battle to the Ma administration – and all the way to Beijing.

Even when the Sunflowers made the tactical error of launching an occupation of the Executive Yuan, whatever negative impact this had on public perceptions was immediately counterbalanced by government overreaction in its efforts to evict the protesters. Having thus misjudged public opinion, the Ma administration unleashed riot police units and water cannons, falling into the age-old trap of using disproportionate force against a weaker group, which was sure to benefit the government's opponents. This, too, was an art that young activists had refined over the months preceding the occupation of the Legislative Yuan. Activism is a battle for hearts and minds, and no matter what the Ma administration said, calling the protesters "violent," "irrational," and "easily manipulated" or, as in Hong Kong later that year, the dire warnings by corporations of economic collapse, it didn't stick. Throughout the occupation, a public majority continued to rally behind the Sunflowers. Accusations that the Sunflowers were unemployed youth with nothing better to do were also completely false, as the majority of them were either full-time university students or had jobs, showing up at the protest site between shifts.

Only in such a context, therefore, could the Sunflower Movement have emerged unscathed (bruises notwithstanding) from a move at the Executive Yuan that could very well have been extremely costly in terms of public support. Five days later, between 350,000 and half a million people answered the Sunflowers' call and surrounded the legislature and neighboring streets in what may very well have been one of the largest rallies in Taiwan's democratic history.

Perhaps nothing highlighted the strength of the Sunflower Movement more than the fact that the decision to vacate the legislature was made by its members rather than by the government. Having succeeded in obtaining some of the concessions from the administration that it had sought – among them that an oversight mechanism be implemented before the CSSTA could be reviewed – the movement ended the occupation on a high note, as the mood outside the Legislative Yuan made perfectly clear on 10 April, where tens of thousands of supporters cheered the activists as, emaciated, tired, dirty, they trickled out of parliament. Society had prevailed over a government that had failed to listen to and to reassure the ordinary man and woman on the street.

The ramifications of the Sunflower Movement were far-reaching and long lasting, despite President Ma's claims to the contrary. At this writing, the CSSTA has yet to be implemented and was unlikely to come into force before President Ma stepped down in May 2016. A subsequent trade-in-goods agreement was also stalled, and plans to open reciprocal representative offices appeared to have been put on ice.

Beyond stopping President Ma's cross-strait policy in its tracks, the Sunflower Movement isolated Ma and nearly split his party. Only by co-opting his internal critics by making them deputy chairmen of the KMT did Ma prevent a mutiny. Finally, there is no doubt that the events of March and April 2014, with the addition of two years of incessant activism by civil society, influenced the outcome of the 29 November 2014 nine-in-one elections, in which the KMT received a much deserved drubbing. Once again, civil society had proven that it could act as a check on government when everything else – appeal mechanisms, a loyal opposition, and so on – had failed. Although this is an instrument that should be used sparingly lest society descend into populism, there are times in a nation's history when drastic measures are necessary. The CSSTA – what it stood for and the context in which it was being pushed on the Taiwanese – was such an occasion. The success of, and support for, the Sunflower Movement also lent credibility to its leaders' warning that they would once again take action in the future if the government attempted to cross certain lines. The fact that very little real effort has been made on the government's part to implement the CSSTA since the events in early 2014, then, tells us that this threat was taken seriously, even if the administration won't admit it. And the government had every reason to take note of that warning; the Sun-flowers' quick turnaround in the hours immediately following their rush inside the chambers of the legislature was a clear indication that the activists had a whole infrastructure, a constellation of groups and individuals who would unite when needed, that they could rely on to consolidate their effort. Normally disunited, civil society had come together over the CSSTA, when the threat to Taiwan was judged to be real enough.

Whoever in the Ma administration retained the belief that the Sunflower Move-ment was an ephemeral phenomenon whose ability to shape events ended when the last activist crossed the exit of the legislature on 10 April was quickly disabused of that view when, a few days later, the government found itself with another seri-ous problem on its hands – this time over nuclear energy. Protests over the nuclear issue and construction of the Fourth Nuclear Power Plant had been going on for years and became more salient following the incident at the Fukushima Dai-Ichi nuclear power plant in Japan caused by the 11 March 2011 earthquake and tsunami. Despite the high unpopularity of nuclear energy and fears over the safety, proper maintenance, and reliability of Taiwan's existing nuclear power plants, the govern-ment pressed ahead with construction of the Fourth plant, which by April 2014 had already cost Taiwanese taxpayers upward of NT$283 billion (US$9.3 billion).

Undoubtedly, the recent successes of the Sunflower Movement reinvigorated the antinuclear movement, which launched a new wave of protests calling on the government to mothball the Fourth power plant and commit to a phasing out of nuclear energy in Taiwan, a position that the DPP had already adopted. Though the rallies did not differ from the many large ones that had been held in recent years – and that had been duly ignored by the government – this time around new factors were at play. First, former DPP Chairman Lin I-hsiung (林義雄), whose family fell victim to the KMT's White Terror (the KMT government's crackdown on society), launched a hunger strike and threatened to commit the ultimate sacrifice if the Ma administration did not end construction of the Fourth power plant. Lin, who has become something of a maverick in recent years and who certainly does not shun publicity, had planned to launch his fast just as the Sunflower Movement took over the legislature and had therefore decided to delay his action until the drama there had ended.

Though his move was not welcomed by everybody within the DPP, Lin's hun-ger strike attracted substantial publicity at a time when the government probably wanted things to return to normal and therefore helped the cause. However, even that didn't sway the government, leading to an extraordinary meeting between

President Ma and Su Tseng-chang, the DPP chairman at the time, during which Su displayed the kind of leadership and real emotions that many of his critics said they had not seen since he had taken over as party leader. This gave place to an extraordinary scene when Su, losing patience with Ma, switched from speaking Mandarin to Taiwanese, whereupon a visibly disarmed Ma turned to his aide, the Nantou native and Vice President Wu, to take over.

For a while, it seemed that Su's eleventh-hour intervention, as well as a 50,000-person-plus rally on Ketagalan Boulevard, had compelled the government to compromise. Following a meeting of KMT officials on 27 April, the party announced that work on reactors 1 and 2 of the power plant would be halted and that the power plant would not be activated. However, critics pointed out that the government, not the KMT, had to make the decision. Moreover, the KMT's use of the term "mothball" rather than "terminate" when referring to construction at the Fourth power plant, also raised doubts as to the long-term commitment to that promise (in a Facebook post later on, President Ma wrote that the nuclear option should never be completely closed to future generations).

Unsatisfied with the government's response, thousands of activists – including many families with young children – left Ketagalan Boulevard and descended upon Zhongxiao West Road, in front of Taipei Main Station, one of the city's main arteries and a center of commercial activity. They were soon joined by thousands of other protesters, who were to be "contained" by rows of police officers. However, the authorities were wrong-footed, and once again the Sunflower activists were at the center of it all. Hiding in the underground maze of Taipei Main Station and adjacent shopping malls, the activists suddenly emerged and materialized behind the police lines, which were immediately surrounded and overwhelmed. Soon, the entire area had ground to a halt, paralyzing a key part of the city and taking on an air of permanence that certainly caught the attention of the authorities.

Unlike the large and peaceful protests on the nuclear issue that had taken place over the years, it was impossible to ignore this one. By threatening to shut off a part of the capital, civil society had once again chosen to escalate. And as with the controversy over the CSSTA, the various groups that took direct action had public opinion behind them. An invisible string was now connecting the antinuclear movement and a chain of events that had begun in 2012 or perhaps even 2008. Without these, it is unlikely that the antinuclear movement would have achieved what it did in April 2014. And without the momentum created by the Sunflower Movement, it is unlikely that the government would have taken it seriously enough to back down.

The Ma administration sent in the water cannons, but it was an act of despair, for surely it knew that doing so would further undermine its image with the public and draw more negative publicity internationally. The streets were cleared, Lin ended his hunger strike after nine days, and the nuclear controversy faded into the background.

With elections right around the corner presenting an opportunity for voters to punish the Ma administration – as they did, costing Ma chairmanship of his

party – civil society pulled back and began focusing on educating the population and recruiting new members for the future. Facing a Ma administration that,
for all intents and purposes, had been neutralized and thus was unable to impose
unpopular policies on the nation, civic groups once again became heterogeneous
and began fighting one another. Many of the foot soldiers who had made the Sunflower Occupation possible began complaining that they did not receive the recognition they deserved while the recognizable figures, people like Lin Fei-fan and
Chen Wei-ting, had turned into "superstars" who were now traveling the world.
All of this was natural; there was nothing to focus on, nothing that made cooperation seemingly more essential than competition for resources and recognition. And
with no action, no drama, to report on, the personalities of the now public figures
were scrutinized, shedding light on incidents in their past that, if only momentarily,
forced them to disappear.

Despite the recrimination and controversies that have emerged since the end of
the occupation, what the Sunflower Movement has demonstrated, however, is that
Taiwan's civil society had what it takes to come together under extraordinary circumstances, that it could accomplish exactly what Beijing is most afraid of: the joining of disparate causes. As research by Hsu Szuchien (徐斯儉), a professor at National
Tsing Hua University's Institute of Sociology, an now president of the Taiwan Foundation for Democracy, has demonstrated, what came to be known as the Sunflower
Movement was, in the beginning, a gathering of several dozen organizations that
more often than not did not usually work well together, though the seeds of cooperation had arguably been sown in the previous two years. The genie is out of the
bottle, and anyone in government who believes that he or she can still get away with
ignoring an energized and experienced civil society will be taking a tremendous risk.

Besides everything that has just been discussed, the Sunflower Movement and
its precursor groups have left two other legacies that are just as important as their
ability to keep the government in check. And both have been largely ignored.

The first is that the Sunflower Movement succeeded in breaching the wall
of international indifference that for far too long has kept Taiwan in a state of
isolation. All of a sudden, Taiwan was newsworthy and exciting. Days into the
occupation, foreign media that normally pay little attention to Taiwan were parachuting correspondents into Taipei to report on the events there. In the weeks
and months that followed the occupation, several conferences were organized
around the globe to discuss the movement or Taiwan's civil society. This author
alone spoke at six such conferences, on three different continents, in 2014 alone,
including in Singapore, where activists face severe repression and can only dream
of the liberties that we enjoy in Taiwan but that far too often we take for granted.
Several researchers have since come on visits to Taiwan to meet activists and write
dissertations on the subject. After years of isolation resulting from Chinese propaganda and efforts by Taipei to portray the cross-strait situation as a new era of
"peace," civil society had put Taiwan on the map again. As we saw earlier, there
also is good reason to believe that events in Taiwan eventually influenced events
in Hong Kong and Macau.

The second legacy of the recent wave of activism in Taiwan is that it has encouraged young people to play a role in politics. Since the end of the occupation of the Legislative Yuan, many young men and women who had protested on the streets since 2012 have joined political parties or began their own. Under Chairperson Tsai, the DPP has opened its doors to dozens of young activists as part of her efforts to rejuvenate the party and reconnect it with society. Although, as we saw, such efforts have encountered some resistance from the more conservative elements within the party, there is no doubt that this is a step in the right direction. The emergence of a third force has also allowed young individuals, academics, and artists who remain wary of joining the much hated "system" to enter politics and to run for office. Some of them have already been elected, becoming local players in their communities. Zoe Chen (陳薈茗), a young mother of two and an activist involved in the protest against wind farms in Yuanli, is one of them. She ran in the 29 November elections and won. She is now *lizhang* of Fangli Borough (房裡).

Many others ran for legislative seats in the January 2016 elections. Their decision to join the system and to try to change it from the inside has attracted criticism – sometimes vicious – from their former comrades. The skepticism was not unwarranted. After all, where was the DPP, they asked, when people's homes were being threatened with demolition or when local police were roughing up elderly residents and farmers at a wind turbine site, only for their local officials to show up after the fact, when the homes were no more and when people had died? It was difficult to trust the party when one of its elders, former Vice President Annette Lu, who briefly showed up at Mr. Chang's funeral, didn't lift a finger to help the victims while accepting a position as adviser to foreign companies that were seeking to secure a slice of the pie in the Taoyuan Aerotropolis project that would likely result in thousands of evictions. For many people in civil society, for the thousands who had taken to the streets over the years, the DPP and the KMT were equally bad, and everything party representatives did was nothing but selfish politics. The little man always lost out.

Nevertheless, a large enough number of activists concluded that it was essential that young men and women enter politics in order to breathe new life into a system that had calcified over the years. While there will always be a need for "outsiders" who eternally combat the system, there is also a need for activists to join politics so as to bridge the two worlds and help translate the demands of society into viable policies for the betterment of the nation. Politicians cannot do it on their own; neither can eternal critics. A healthy democracy needs both, and the young men and women who have made the decision (difficult, no doubt) to jump into the world of party politics should be encouraged rather than accused of treason or selfishness, as many have been of late.

In the end, the recent activism in Taiwan, which ultimately led to the emergence of the Sunflower Movement, was both a symptom of and a contributor to a new type of nationalism that had slowly been consolidating in Taiwan, especially among its youth. To this we now turn.

Note

1 For a comprehensive retelling of the different stages of the occupation, see 「這不是太陽花學運: 318 運動全記錄」允晨文化實業股份有限公司 (2015).

Bibliography

Chuang, Y-C (2013) *Democracy on Trial: Social Movements and Cultural Politics in Postauthoritarian Taiwan*, Hong Kong: The Chinese University Press: 12

Cole, M (2011) "Taipower's 'Dirty' Nuclear Plants Raise Concerns," *Taipei Times*, 5 April, http://www.taipeitimes.com/News/taiwan/archives/2011/04/05/2003499964

——— (2015) *Black Island: Two Years of Activism in Taiwan*, Charleston, SC: CreateSpace Independent Publishing

Fell, D (2012) *Government and Politics in Taiwan*, Oxon: Routledge: 171

8

A NEW AGE

Civic nationalism, resilience, and legitimacy

Defining nationalism is easier said than done. At its core, nationalism is an ideology, what Haas has called "assertions about the nation's claim to historical uniqueness, to the territory that the nation-state ought to occupy, and to the kinds of relations that should prevail between one's nation and others."

The problem of definition is also at the core of the conflict that has existed and that will continue to exist in the Taiwan Strait. As this chapter will attempt to demonstrate, not only are Taiwanese and Chinese nationalisms fundamentally different, they also derive from different interpretations of what nationalism is. While Taiwanese nationalism has tended to follow the Western concept of the state as a *modern institution*, China approaches the matter from a *civilizational* angle, one that is steeped in Confucian traditions, "bloodline," and a deep sense of victimhood that has in turn infused nationalism with paranoia and xenophobia.

By being civilizational, Chinese nationalism also knows no borders, which explains why, regardless of where they are geographically, those who identify as Chinese often feel an obligation to uphold the honor of the "mother country." This nationalism is defined by blood and DNA, thus making it impossible for other nations – like Taiwan – to exist in that context. The only exceptions to that rule are Tibet, Inner Mongolia, and Xinjiang, three classic cases of colonialism that will be the source of unrest for many years to come.

Fueled by a system that encourages a sense of victimization at the hands of foreign powers and an attendant xenophobic sentiment, Chinese nationalism has also fostered a sense of superiority, of Chinese tending to have "high IQs" and "the best brains," a legacy of the "rich, 5,000 years of history left them by their ancestors."

In his study of Chinese nationalism, Gries warns against taking what he calls a "social psychological" approach to nationalism. Instead, Gries chooses to use Elie Kedourie's definition, which makes nationalism "very much a matter of one's self-view, of one's estimation of oneself and one's place in the world." Although there is some merit in that proposition, it is difficult to reconcile this rather benign view of Chinese nationalism with the stridency with which it has tended to be expressed everywhere, from the international stage to classrooms in the West. While nationalism can be a personal process, it simply cannot be dissociated from the social and political context in which it exists. Chinese nationalism has turned into *exceptionalism*, a development that has been strongly cultivated by the CCP as a means to bolster its legitimacy (such exceptionalism isn't so exceptional as American nationalism, which its image as the indispensable nation has made perfectly clear). As Wang argues, "The link between historical memory and the rise of nationalism is essential to note because myths, memories, traditions, and symbols of ethnic heritage are what gives nationalism its power. Perhaps even more important is the way these idealizations of the past can be rediscovered and reinterpreted by modern nationalist intellectual elites."

The contrast between the essence of Chinese nationalism and the "national community" as it exists in contemporary Taiwan could not be starker. Whatever Taiwanese nationalism *is*, it has none of the emphasis on extraterritoriality and exceptionalism that is seen across China. In a sense, this contrast has also played a role in defining Taiwanese nationalism – through a negation: what it is *not*. It is *not* strident, expansionist, or marked by a belief in racial exceptionalism. It does *not* make it a patriotic responsibility for every Taiwanese or descendant of a Taiwanese to defend the "motherland" abroad (overseas Taiwanese tend to very quickly sever their ties with the homeland or their parents). And while it has traditionally been exclusivist along "racial" or ideological lines, it is less and less so and has become more embracing.

Why, despite the cultural, linguistic, religious, ideological, and "blood" similarities that exist between Taiwan and China, Taiwan's nationalism has remained so distinct from its counterpart across the Taiwan Strait is a matter of both geography and history. Also fewer than 200 kilometers separate Taiwan proper from China, we should not underestimate the impact that Taiwan's existence as an island has had on the identity formation of its people. Besides the fact that the Taiwan Strait created a physical barrier over the decades, insulating it from China, the relatively small size of Taiwan has facilitated the travel, communication, and exchanges necessary for the consolidation of a shared identity, even if defining it has remained a challenge (doing so in China, a country that is 267 times the size of Taiwan and with a population of 1.4 billion people, is understandably a much more onerous task, which may explain the long tradition of authoritarian rule there simply to try to keep the continent-sized jigsaw puzzle together).

That is not to say that the collective memory in Taiwan is not, as it is in China, influenced by past traumas (e.g., the 228 Massacre of 1947) and humiliations (e.g., severed diplomatic relations, loss of seat at the UN). Here too, Taiwanese have suffered at the hands of foreigners, most significantly the Japanese and the Chinese, two phases of colonization that resulted in repression and a series of massacres. Those experiences served only to exacerbate the islander desire to be left alone. And while those traumas are undeniably part of the national consciousness, they have not been played up extensively by the authorities, and they have not translated into the kind of vengeful nationalism that has arisen in China and other places.

We should note, too, that many of the early Chinese who came to Taiwan in the sixteenth and seventeenth centuries chose to make a fresh start on Taiwan to get away from the constant state of warring back in China, a phenomenon that is akin to the Europeans who, despairing of the future, left the Old World for the New. Very early on, therefore, a sense of "otherness" already existed. Later on, the half century of Japanese colonial rule (1895–1945) further severed Taiwan from China by imposing Japanese laws, culture, and language on the inhabitants of Taiwan, giving rise to the first nationalist movements that sought independence for Taiwan. Importantly, this period was also characterized by deep reforms of Japanese society and the adoption of Western technology, legal systems, and systems of governance. Though Taiwan remained a colony, there is no doubt that some of those influences were passed on to and in turn internalized by Taiwanese society.

After World War II and the end of the civil war in China, Taiwan was colonized anew, but very quickly the Cold War put it in the Western camp, facing off with world communism in which China – by then the PRC – was one of the principal actors. So even when Taiwan was ceded to China (Chiang Kai-shek's ROC), its experience continued to be separate from the "Mainland." Moreover, the political system that was implemented by Mao Zedong, followed by the disaster of the Great Leap Forward and insanity of the Cultural Revolution, further alienated the people in Taiwan while reinforcing their separate identity – even the KMT members who still hoped to "retake" the Mainland one day. Later on, the abandonment of this dream cut the umbilical cord that tied the Nationalists in Taiwan with China.

The Tiananmen Square Massacre in June 1989 and the tightening grip of the CCP on Chinese society under Xi Jinping, also disabused those who still believed the idea that China was on the "right track" and heading toward Western-style democracy. Those events made it clear that China remained a hard, violent, and often merciless society, whereas Taiwan was becoming a society with a very low threshold of "acceptable" violence, as the uproar over the crackdown at the Executive Yuan in March 2014 made clear.

The alliance between the U.S. and the KMT, which had begun while World War II was still raging, also slowly acclimatized the bureaucracy and military leadership in Taiwan to Western ideas. Many officials or their offspring earned advanced degrees at top U.S. universities – decades before their counterparts in the PRC, which under Mao Zedong had closed itself off to the Western world, could do so. During the Cold War and the White Terror in Taiwan, many Taiwanese also fled to the West, where they rebuilt their lives, earned an education, and internalized Western notions and values, which would also become part of the shared national experience. After martial law was lifted, some of those individuals returned to Taiwan and brought back their Western experience with them – an experience that included life and participation in multicultural and democratic societies. Those who did not return nevertheless stayed in touch with family members in Taiwan and in the process communicated some of the liberal–democratic values that existed in their adoptive countries.

Liberalization under Chiang Ching-kuo and democratization under Lee Teng-hui deepened the process of identity formation. However reluctantly it may had done so at first, even the KMT was forced to adjust itself to the new reality to ensure that it could compete in democratic elections. The fact that it did not fold and that after the first transition of power in 2000 it was able to make a comeback at the polls in 2008, is evidence that it understood the necessity of reinventing itself, however stacked the system may have been in its favor.

During all those years, Taiwanese nationalism often found expression in terms of ethnic identity, an us-versus-them that was reflected in the deep divide in Taiwanese politics. For years – and to some extent this is still true today – the green camp, led by the DPP, served as the defender of Taiwanese nationalism while the blue camp, headed by the KMT, was a bastion of "Mainlanders" with their supposed pro-China and prounification beliefs. According to an extreme version of this narrative, which certainly had its share of adherents, "real" ethnic Taiwanese could be trusted to protect Taiwan, while "fake" ones in the KMT were all potential traitors.

What was rarely mentioned, however, is the fact that, while the more vocal and exclusivist Taiwanese nationalism personified by the green camp and its supporters caught people's attention, a much more subtle and silent phenomenon was occurring in the other camp in Taiwan. As shown earlier, with the exception of a relatively small (and dwindling) group of individuals, the majority of people in the blue camp were coming to terms with the fact that Taiwan (or the ROC) was home. Home certainly was not the repression, one-party authoritarianism, censorship, and expansionism that continued to exist in the PRC. Home was democratic, free, safe, imperfect, and at times messy, but it was home, and those values were part of the many variables that defined who they were, what citizenship in Taiwan (legally the ROC) meant. While the emotional attachment to China was stronger among the many who were forced to flee to Taiwan after the Nationalists were defeated in 1949, their offspring were born in Taiwan, which had a substantial effect on how they defined themselves and their community. They may have been of Chinese cultural heritage and steeped in their parents' history and traditions, but their only experience of home was Taiwan. To many of them, China was to Taiwan what England is to Americans, Canadians, or Australians – a source of culture and traditions but a fundamentally alien political entity nonetheless, however much one might be fascinated by them. Later on, the offspring of those offspring were born after Taiwan had been liberalized and democratized. As such, freedom was the only thing they knew; it was a fact of life, something that one took for granted – even among those who, due to family pressure, automatically voted for the KMT candidates in local and national elections. As long as those freedoms and liberties continued to exist, there was no real need to worry too much about politics.

Still, the political parties continued to play the identity, or "ethnic," card. But it was clear that politicians did so far more for political expediency or to secure votes than out of a deep belief in a Manichean "Taiwanese"-versus-"Mainlander" battle for survival being waged across Taiwan. The KMT emphasized its proximity to the Chinese because, in their calculations, doing so would win them votes among those who feared tensions in the Taiwan Strait or who believed that the KMT was in a better position to help them make a profit in China. For its part, the DPP appealed to those who apprehended China or hated the KMT for personal reasons.

Those political games may have had their utility during elections, but over time it became clear that the artificial divide was detrimental to Taiwan by ensuring that it remained a house divided in perpetuity. Furthermore, while superficially the two main parties reflected two opposite "ethnic" groups, the views of the population were gradually moving toward the political center. This process was unacknowledged, but it was nonetheless real, built on foundations that almost every person in Taiwan could agree with: a liberal democracy with free access to information, human rights, and prosperity – and above all, the notion that Taiwan incarnated those ideals, as very few people still believed the ridiculous claim that the ROC contains all of the Chinese territory. Politicians could continue to make such claims for political agendas, but by the twenty-first century, those who believed that the ROC stood for a territory that goes beyond that which is associated with Taiwan were in a very small minority.

The deep divide was therefore increasingly seen for what it was: artificial and detrimental to Taiwan's ability to progress. It was easy to blame China for everything, but many of the things that kept Taiwan in a state of immobility were the result of a mental status quo that resisted change and progress. Not only did old politicians on both sides refuse to ever fully retire, they continued to exert influence on policy, more often than not leading the country in a direction that was opposite to the wishes of the majority – especially young people. Elders in both parties continued to be venerated, and, using various factions behind the scenes, they made sure that party leaders were unable to truly reform the parties. As a result, the two main political parties in Taiwan became increasingly disconnected from the wishes of the population they represented.

It is not surprising, then, that by 2013 most of civil society had concluded that the KMT and the DPP were both part of the problem. The public had had it with the "ethnic" card, which tended to be resurrected whenever a party faced defeat in the polls, and they'd had enough of the zero-sum games that politicians played and that doomed the nation to a perpetual state of stasis.

Essentially, what the two parties had failed to understand was that a new Taiwanese nationalism had been consolidating over the years, one that exploded onto the scene in 2014. The fact that the principal actors in that drama were all young people – people representing all of Taiwan's "ethnic" groups, moreover – was not accidental. Two major trends had led to this: first, a rising, albeit silent, inclusive nationalism that abstracted old notions of ethnicity; and, second, the policies of the Ma Ying-jeou administration, now seen to be threatening the very way of life that defined what it was to be a Taiwanese. Ethnic identity was no longer the sole concern for group boundary; in fact, ethnic identity had lost much of its currency and appeal. To be Taiwanese meant to be a participant in the democratic experiment that is Taiwan, regardless of one's ethnic background, language, social status, or voting tendencies. In other words, reflecting decades of engagement with Western culture, Taiwan was slowly becoming a multiethnic society that embraced a shared nationalism defined both by what it is and what it isn't.

Not so long ago, adult (ethnic) Taiwanese would warn their children or grandchildren to avoid communities like Huaguang, as those were filled with "Mainlanders." By 2013, youth representing all the ethnic groups in Taiwan were engaging in civil disobedience to preserve the community and ensure dignity for its predominantly Mainlander residents. Taiwanese, *waishengren*, Hakka, aborigine – they all cooperated and helped one another when one of the communities was threatened by government encroachment. Many young members of the Sunflower Movement came from very blue families and had huge fights with their parents because of what they did. Some of them were kicked out of their homes. Some had their computers confiscated or smashed to pieces, so that they could not continue to communicate with their friends in the movement.

That which they were fighting for, what brought them together, was the very definition of what it means to be a Taiwanese. Evidently, such values were markedly different from the variables that are used to define *Chinese* nationalism.

Taiwanese overseas, many of them who had fled Taiwan at the height of the White Terror, never to return, often had difficulty understanding that phenomenon, which is why they tended to be the most vocal critics of government plans to modify school textbooks to put greater emphasis on Chinese history. It was those groups that tended to warn that the Ma administration was trying to "brainwash" young Taiwanese, a feat that, for those of us who live every day with Taiwanese from all walks of life, is evidently impossible. For all their efforts to convince Taiwanese otherwise, China-centric administrations (and Beijing) will never "brainwash" young Taiwanese, who more than ever know who they are and who, furthermore, have access to all kinds of information. Case in point: Despite seven years of emphasizing the Chinese roots of Taiwan's society, various surveys have shown that self-identification trends have been moving in the opposite direction. More and more people identify as Taiwanese (or Taiwanese first and Chinese second) and fewer as Chinese (or Chinese first and Taiwanese second). The challenge of brainwashing people in an open society like Taiwan is an immense one; even closed societies like, say, Cuba under Fidel Castro, where information was much more restricted, had great difficulty selling falsehoods to their citizens, as my discussions with many a cab driver in Havana a few years ago made all too evident.

Overseas Taiwanese will often tell young Taiwanese or Westerners like me that we cannot understand how duplicitous and "evil" the KMT is because we are in the system and exposed to its powerful propaganda on a daily basis. Granted, many of those individuals were deeply traumatized by their experiences living in Taiwan during the White Terror, when many friends, family members, and coworkers were arrested, disappeared, or killed for criticizing the authorities. Such traumas can have long lasting effects on one's perceptions of the enemy. However, only someone who has not witnessed firsthand the extraordinary transformation that has occurred in

Taiwan in the last decades and even more so in recent years can argue that those of us who are here are oblivious to the KMT's tenebrous machinations. That simply is not true. The KMT is but a shadow of its former authoritarian self, and like the DPP it is riven by factionalism – including its "Taiwanese" faction, which has a lot of influence in the south.

Although pro-Beijing party elders like Lien Chan, Hau Pei-tsun, and Wu Poh-hsiung remain influential, their ability to direct the party is diluted by the many members who, like the rest of the population, have developed a truly "Taiwanese" identity as defined by a desire to uphold democratic ideals and the freedoms that the people here enjoy. The reaction of deep alarm among many KMT legislators to seemingly pro-Beijing remarks by Hung Hsiu-chu, the initial KMT presidential candidate in 2016, is a case in point (see Chapter 13). Before her removal, many members had expressed fears that by drifting so far away from the middle ground that appeals to the majority of Taiwanese, Hung risked "destroying" the party. Hung's ability to forge ahead with such views for several months was much more the result of cowardice within the KMT than acquiescence to or agreement with her beliefs.

The KMT's refusal to participate in rallies outside the Interchange Association, Japan's representative office in Taiwan, over the Senkaku/Diaoyutai dispute, at a time when Japanese citizens and companies were being attacked across China, is another example of the lines that most KMT members will not cross ("[W]e could not be caught dead with those pro-unification crazies," a former KMT legislator told me at the time).

Even deeper blue and ostensibly prounification parties have demonstrated their internalization of the values that define contemporary Taiwanese nationalism in their public exchanges by correcting – and sometimes berating – individuals who had failed to do so, such as Chang An-le experienced soon after his return to Taiwan in 2013. Most of the deep blue Hung supporters who protested outside KMT headquarters in October 2015, hours before she was replaced by Eric Chu in the 2016 presidential election, did so out of the belief that the party's eleventh-hour move was undemocratic and the conviction that Hung was the best person to uphold the ROC's democratic institutions, which they openly contrasted with the PRC (Cole).

Taiwan has therefore developed a kind of nationalism that is defined by civic values and the democratic system that, though imperfect, has been embraced by the majority of people in Taiwan. Although, as we've seen, Taiwanese nationalism existed before Taiwan became a democracy, there is no doubt that the democratic experience and expectations of its continuation are now important elements of what defines Taiwanese identity and patriotism. Notions of "ethic" or "racial" nationalism, meanwhile, have lost currency and are now generally regarded for the divisiveness that they tend to encourage. By now the KMT and the DPP should have realized that resurrecting the "ethnic" card is the surest way to a political dead end, as evidenced by the reaction to the Sean Lien camp's accusations that independent candidate for Taipei mayor Ko Wen-je was a "Japanese bastard." The lines have been blurred, so much so that ethnicity is no longer a determinant of one's political preference. Long ago, the KMT recruited (often through co-optation) Taiwanese at the grassroots, and in recent years a number of *waishengren* have played prominent roles in the DPP camp, serving as ministers in the Chen administration or as spokespeople during Ko's campaign for Taipei.

This is the new Taiwan, an increasingly inclusive society that, shaped by its idiosyncratic experience as an island-nation and facing an existential threat to its way of life, has been compelled to move toward the center. The more exclusivist and racial forms of nationalism that exist at both ends of the spectrum, both in the prounification and proindependence camps, will continue their spiral descent into oblivion as their proponents die of old age. Taiwan's future lies with its youth, a youth that is sure-footed and confident about its identity and the country they inhabit but that is increasingly apprehensive about their ability to counter the seemingly "inevitable" forces of unification with China.

This gradual rapprochement of the two camps in Taiwan, the obvious desire by most people in those two camps to maintain their way of life, and their identification as full participants in the Taiwan national experiment are phenomena that also haven't been fully understood by observers and experts abroad, who continue to attribute those desires to the DPP and the green camp. Rather than being divided, Taiwan is much more united on those questions, and this trend will likely continue as national identity continues to consolidate. Two things are worth mention: (1) Nationalism need not have a negative connotation (though Beijing, which describes this as "splittism," certainly wants us to believe that this is the case), and (2) increasingly one will find Taiwan nationalists in the blue camp, even if officially that nationalism is expressed in the context of the Republic of China.

As many of those young people said in the weeks prior to and during the Sunflower Occupation of the legislature in March and April 2014, they have only one passport and cannot go anywhere if China takes over. The coming together of the various segments of Taiwan's society means that the more pressure Beijing applies on Taiwan with regard to unification, the stronger the nationalist sentiment is likely to become. The example of Hong Kong, which as we discussed in an earlier chapter saw its cherished way of life suffer following retrocession, can only exacerbate the desire among Taiwanese to avoid a similar outcome, as is the intensification of a neo-Maoist campaign across China under President Xi, which goes counter to everything that defines modern Taiwan. In many ways, the latter reinforces the notion of nationalism as defined by what one is *not* or does not want to be.

Rather than lead to better understanding, the greater contact between people from the two sides since 2008 has also reinforced some elements of Taiwanese nationalism, a phenomenon that has also occurred, in a very vocal fashion, in HKSAR.

Despite the rapprochement that has occurred in the Taiwan Strait in the past seven years or so, and notwithstanding decades of substantial economic relations, *Taiwanese* and *Chinese* nationalism are erected on the pillars of two different ideologies – in Taiwan's case in Western traditions of the modern state and in China's on a civilizational perspective that transcends boundaries. Moreover, the two countries' very different histories and geographies have propelled nationalism in diametrically opposed directions. As the end products of those historical processes, Taiwan's youth are now the current and future actors in politics, and their coming of age will make unification more rather than less difficult to achieve for Beijing, which continues to insist that the two nationalisms, rather than contradicting themselves, can be reconciled.

Yan is correct when he writes, "Control over territory is just a part of gaining submission and it may lead to one's opponent developing nationalism and hopes for national restoration such that they become your most dangerous enemy."

Beijing's attempt to bring about "peaceful" unification with Taiwan, which very much requires it to square the circle, is the subject of the next chapter.

Bibliography

Cole, M (2015) "Taiwan's Pan-Blue Camp Is at War with Itself," *China Policy Institute Blog*, 7 October, http://blogs.nottingham.ac.uk/chinapolicyinstitute/2015/10/07/taiwans-pan-blue-camp-is-at-war-with-itself/

Gries, P (2004) *China's New Nationalism: Pride, Politics and Diplomacy*, Berkeley and Los Angeles: University of California Press: 8–9

Hass, B (1986) "What Is Nationalism and Why Should We Study It?" *International Organization* 40:3: 707

Wang, Z (2014) *Never Forget National Humiliation: Historical Memory in Chinese Politics and Foreign Relations*, New York: Columbia University Press: 26

Yan, X-T (2011) *Ancient Chinese Thought, Modern Chinese Power*, Princeton, NJ: Princeton University Press: 193–4

PART 3
Convergence or conflict?

9

NO TURNING BACK

What Taiwanese want versus Beijing's expectations

> When my generation comes of age, Taiwan's cross-strait attitude is going to be very different ... We want China to treat us like a country.
> — Huang Yen-ru, student leader

As we saw in the previous chapter, Taiwan and China have different ways of and use different metrics to define their nationalism, which reflect the separate histories and geographies that have shaped them over centuries. Inevitably, the separateness of those two societies has had an impact on the politics of the Taiwan Strait and on the reactions in Taiwan to Beijing's efforts to reconstitute an imagined China that serves as the wellspring of Chinese nationalism. The values, customs, languages, and histories that shape a place's identity can also serve as sources of friction when one's nationalism seeks to impose itself on another society, as the developments in Hong Kong since 2003 have demonstrated.

Our study so far has shown that despite Beijing's efforts, Taiwanese nationalism and Chinese nationalism are headed in opposite directions. If we look past the convenient rhetoric used by the Ma Ying-jeou administration since 2008, it is clear that reconciliation, let alone peaceful unification, are within reach. The seven years under President Ma may have served the needs of a rich elite on both sides of the Taiwan Strait, and undoubtedly they have made it easier for politicians from both sides to meet in person, but fundamentally the rapprochement has failed to create the conditions that would eventually lead to an agreement by the people of Taiwan to become part of the People's Republic of China.

In fact, the increasing contact between the two sides seems to have contributed to a deepening of Taiwanese nationalism and fears that further steps, such as the CSSTA, could endanger the liberal-democratic political system that all Taiwanese, regardless of their voting preferences, have grown accustomed to and cherish.

The recent wave of unrest in Hong Kong, sparked by the residents' thwarted efforts to obtain universal suffrage, press censorship, a widening wealth gap, Beijing's meddling in local affairs, and the frictions caused by the millions of Chinese citizens who visit the SAR every year, among other things, have further reinforced the view among Taiwanese that a similar fate could await them if they were to unite with China. Moreover, the unmistakable indications that the Chinese Communist Party under President Xi Jinping has adopted a much harder line on civil liberties, press freedoms, controls of the workplace and in the education system, and measures taken against ethnic minorities within China's borders have undermined whatever appeal closer political ties with China may have had among the Taiwanese. The neo-Maoist line that President Xi seems to have espoused, either by design or, as some China watchers now believe, because the situation in China is spinning out of control, is hardly the best way to win the trust of the people in Taiwan, as was the news in July 2015 that several dozens of rights lawyers and advocates had been arrested or "disappeared" in a nationwide sweep targeting a supposed "major criminal gang." What Youwei, a scholar based in China who writes under a pseudonym, has described as "an extremely efficient apparatus of 'stability maintenance'" is anathema to what ordinary Taiwanese believe in and want for themselves.

Now, it is important to point out that the refusal to unify with China under the current or future conditions is not *a priori* the result of an "anti-China" sentiment or solely the territory of a "small group" of "splittists" in the DPP who oppose the "reunification of the motherland." All of this is CCP propaganda that, sadly, has had some traction overseas. As we saw in our discussion in the previous chapter, Taiwanese nationalism is far more widespread in Taiwanese society than is usually believed. Rather than be limited to a "small group" of people who invariably "hate" China, the desire to retain an independent status and, just as importantly, the way of life that Taiwan has enjoyed over the past three decades, finds expression in the two main camps of Taiwanese politics. The great majority of the people who vote for the DPP *and* the KMT are thus in favor of a distinct political existence for Taiwan and one that, if the HKSAR precedent is any example, likely could not continue should Taiwan be annexed by the PRC.

The latest Taiwan Mood Barometer Survey by the Taiwan Indicators Survey Research (TISR, 台灣指標民調) highlights that sentiment and reflects a continuation of trend lines that have developed over the years. Of the people surveyed, 14.6 percent said they wanted "Urgent Independence for Taiwan," while 7.8 percent supported "Status Quo for Now, Independence Later," and 13.0 percent wanted "Status Quo for Now, Consider Independence Later." In the middle, 30.2 percent said they wanted an "Eternal Status Quo."

Meanwhile, 5.8 percent of respondents in the TISR survey said that they supported the "Status Quo for Now, Consider Unification Later," while 5.5 percent said "Status Quo for Now, Unify Later," and 4.2 percent wanted "Urgent Unification." Nineteen percent did not know or did not have a response.

What these figures tell us is this: 35.4 percent of respondents are in the independence camp, 62.3 percent in the status quo camp, and 15.5 percent in the unification camp. Moreover, as TISR observed, the younger the respondents and the higher their education level, the more they supported independence.

The 4.2 percent of respondents who want "Urgent Unification" are clearly a marginal force in Taiwan and likely are elderly individuals who have a strong emotional attachment to China. The steady drop in that category over the years seems to dovetail with the rate at which those individuals are passing on. In that category, we can also include those who for ideological and perhaps financial reasons support immediate unification, which again is not representative of the majority view.

Furthermore, among those who support eventual unification, most predicate that position on the expectation of the future democratization of China, which given current trends there is certainly not going to happen anytime soon.

Meanwhile, two things are worth mentioning about the status quo camp. First, the current status quo is, for all intents and purposes, the existence of Taiwan (or the ROC) as a sovereign and independent state in everything but name. In other words, this is support for independence minus the "dangerous" word "independence," a vague concept that has allowed Taiwan to continue to exist as a sovereign entity despite lack of international recognition and the China threat. The second element that needs mentioning about the status quo camp is that it is likely the intellectual refuge for those who, were it not for the military threat facing Taiwan, would openly support immediate independence. As such, an important addition to surveys like the TISR's would be to ask the same question under two different scenarios: the current one, where a declaration of *de jure* independence would risk military invasion by the PLA, and another one in which the military variable is taken off the table – in other words, choice without coercion. It is very likely that, under the second scenario, support for immediate independence would rise dramatically. What this indicates is that most Taiwanese support independence but that they are hedging against Chinese coercion.

One more thing is worth mentioning about the relatively low support among the Taiwanese for *de jure* independence. As they already enjoy all the benefits of statehood, there is little incentive for them to push for anything beyond the status quo. They have passports that are recognized all over the world (and that now feature visa waiver in several countries); they elect their officials and have access to world markets. In other words, much like the citizens of other countries, their lives are regulated by state institutions. The only additional benefit that *de jure* independence would have for Taiwan would be its ability to join international institutions like the UN as a full member. However, since nonmembership does not have a serious impact on their lives, official status and membership are not main national priorities. It would be nice, no doubt, but the value is more symbolic than real. *De facto* independence is therefore sufficient for them.

We can assume that the 14.6 percent of Taiwanese who support immediate independence take matters such as UN membership seriously, but their numbers pale in comparison to the 30.2 percent of the people who favor a perpetual status quo, under which UN membership for Taiwan will likely remain an elusive dream. This does not mean that those who favor the status quo are against the idea of a sovereign Taiwan; it simply means that for them, the added benefits of official state-hood, such as UN membership, are not worth the trouble.

Once we juxtapose the numbers from the TISR survey with the percentage of the vote that President Ma received when he was reelected in 2012 (51.60 per-cent) and elected in 2008 (58.45 percent), it is clear that many of the people who voted for him and the KMT are in the status quo camp (as were, presumably, the 15.5 percent who are in the unification camp). In fact, what this tells us is that *most* of the people who voted for the Beijing-friendly Ma are in the status quo camp; otherwise he would have been trounced in both elections. Such numbers show that a vote for the KMT does not necessarily correlate with support for unification with China. In fact, it does not. Other considerations, such as perceptions that the KMT was in a better position to ensure stability in the Taiwan Strait and to man-age the economy, that it would be less corrupt than its predecessor, or that it could help "repair" ties with the U.S. played a much larger role in voter decisions in both 2008 and 2012.

It must also be said that the refusal by the majority of Taiwanese to be part of China does not on the whole stem from a hatred of China or a refusal to recognize its legitimacy. Despite the Ma administration's insistence that the only legitimate government of China is the ROC, the great, great majority of the people in Taiwan (again regardless of their voting preferences) have reconciled themselves to the fact that the PRC exists and that it is here to stay. Beijing has used its vast propaganda architecture to make us believe that "hatred" is the main motivator behind the refusal to merge with China: Those who oppose reunification are "unpatriotic," "China bashers," or they are being manipulated by Western "neoimperialist" forces that seek to keep China forever bottled in. All these claims stem from the xenopho-bic and paranoid streaks in Chinese nationalism and furthermore serve to *delegiti-mize* self-determination as an option for Taiwan. Instead, opposition to unification is, according to the CCP, the outcome of irrationality, emotion, or duplicity – all negatives.

Beijing's propaganda campaign has scored some successes on that point. For one thing, it is not unusual for international media to prefix references to the DPP as "anti-China" in their headlines, even though the party (especially under Chairper-son Tsai) has put substantial effort and goodwill in recent years into opening chan-nels of communication with Beijing and realizes, like everybody else, that the giant elephant next door cannot be ignored.

The same intellectual bias affected reporting on the Sunflower Movement in 2014, which was also often characterized and headlined as being "anti-China." Some of the small groups that fell under the Sunflower umbrella were indeed ideologically opposed to Taiwan having anything to do with China. However, we should note that just as many of those small organizations were against globalization and trade liberalization and thus not specifically against China. Overall, the Sun-flower Movement therefore was not, as the headlines claimed, "anti-China." Most of its leaders, and those who rallied to the cause, are intelligent enough to know that there is no avoiding trade with China, the world's second-largest economy that already accounts for more than 40 percent of Taiwan's external trade. Instead, what the movement was against was poorly negotiated deals that threatened to undermine Taiwan's democratic institutions and ultimately its sovereignty. In other words, the activists were not opposed to deals with China *per se*, and in fact, if they had been, we would have seen Sunflower Movements throughout President Ma's first term and the first two years of his second. What they opposed was the political ramifications of a bad deal negotiated by individuals who were unaccountable to the public with an authoritarian regime that does not recognize the legitimacy of Taiwan as a sovereign state. As long as trade deals with Beijing were not seen to be crossing certain lines, Taiwanese society – and the more activist among them – were willing to give President Ma the benefit of the doubt. As they were not "anti-China" and did not deny its existence, they were for the most part comfortable with a process that they regarded as a natural normalization process between two states.

Many had also believed the government's claim that the trade deals would resuscitate Taiwan's economy, which had been moribund for the past decade or so. By 2014, however, few were those who believed that the salvation of Taiwan's economy resided in closer economic and perhaps political ties with China. Six years of rapprochement and more than 20 cross-strait agreements later, the economy was still "moribund." Salaries were lower than they had been a decade earlier, young graduates had difficulty finding good jobs, youth could not afford to buy a home in the capital, and the wealth gap was widening in favor of an elite that had captured most of the benefits of growing trade with China. Rather than directly blame China, critics of the Ma administration concluded that the problem was instead structural and stacked in favor of a politically connected few who seemingly had no compunction in damaging Taiwan's democracy if doing so meant further personal enrichment.

These two elements – the political ramifications of a far-reaching services trade agreement and the realization that trade deals with China had only a marginal impact on the health of Taiwan's economy – gave the Sunflower Movement the legitimacy it needed in the eyes of the public. Those who joined the occupation of the legislature out of sheer hatred for China represented a tiny minority.

So what do the Taiwanese want, and how does this stack up against Beijing's expectations?

Most Taiwanese, especially the country's youth, have no problem whatsoever with Taiwan conducting business with China, with academic exchanges, or even with young Taiwanese going to China to find better paying jobs. In other words, they are perfectly fine with treating China as a normal country, as a source of ideas, innovation, and wealth, in a manner that is very similar to the relationship between Canada and its much more powerful neighbor to the south.

Just as with the thousands of Canadians who cross the border into the U.S. to make a better living and to put their skills to greater use, the Taiwanese are willing to do so with China, and furthermore they do so with the full confidence that this will not in any way affect their self-identification or their commitment to Taiwan as loyal citizens.

Indicatively, recent research on the *taishang* demonstrates that this group of China-based Taiwanese businesspeople, which has been much demonized by the green camp as a Chinese Trojan horse, is far more heterogeneous in its political views than is often believed. The fact that these entrepreneurs seek to protect their investments and will vote for the party back in Taiwan that, in their view, offers the best policies to ensure the continuation of their operations in China, does not mean that they have abandoned their commitment to Taiwan's democracy or that they no longer identify as Taiwanese. In fact, rather than being traitors, many of them are probably highly patriotic and convinced that their operations are contributing to Taiwan's prosperity (that is not to say, however, that some of them have not been coerced or used by Chinese authorities to send signals that suggest support for unification).

Of course, none of this would be possible if Taiwanese were not clear about their identity and the legitimacy of the country they call home. But that issue is largely settled, and that is why China and cross-strait relations are never at the top of the list when the public is asked which issues they would like politicians to prioritize. If Taiwanese were uncertain as to their identity and relationship vis-à-vis China, we would expect those issues to be at the very top of their priority list. Instead, what matters most to them are the economy, food safety, and so on – in other words, the stuff of nation-building. Why China is often regarded as the number one priority of the Taiwanese is because Beijing and the international community have made it so. China constantly imposes itself on Taiwan, while governments abroad are unable to discuss Taiwanese politics without immediately asking, "But how will Beijing react?"

China can also play up the nationalism card regarding Taiwan during periods of high instability in the PRC, an age-old tactic that serves to redirect popular anger against an underperforming government toward an external object and that would make it difficult for the Taiwanese to ignore Beijing (besides Taiwan, the historical hatred of Japan, as well as territorial claims in the East and South China Sea, can also provide such a "distraction").

However, in general, most people in Taiwan could not care less about how Beijing will react. They just want to live their lives as free men and women. What Taiwanese want, especially its youth, is normal relations between the two sides. In other words, what they want is the actualization of what is already very clear *in their minds* but certainly less so in China and within the international community. Two forces, one *positive* and one *negative*, have led to this.

First is the consolidation of a Taiwanese identity and its attendant nationalism, which has dispensed with the incertitude that characterized much of the previous decades. As we saw earlier, the generation of people in Taiwan that was still emotionally attached to China has been dying off and has been replaced by people whose only experience of citizenship has been with Taiwan; for the younger ones, we can add democracy to that notion of citizenship. It is all they know.

Consequently, Taiwan's ambiguous status, which has erected endless barriers against Taiwan's ability to participate in the international community or to being treated as an equal by other (and often much smaller) nations, is no longer acceptable as people realize that the so-called status quo in the Taiwan Strait has become dynamic – incrementally in Beijing's favor. As Bush argues, while President Ma's pledge to "safeguard the sovereignty of the ROC" may have been a "clever way to create a two-China solution ... one danger, of course, is that this 'keep hope alive' tactic in the medium term might require Taipei to make concessions that have negative strategic consequences for the long term."

Thus the higher support, as the TISR survey shows us, for *clarity* (independence) among the young and highly educated and for the legitimization of otherwise escalatory movements, such as the Sunflowers, that have taken direct action when the government was seen to be threatening Taiwan's institutions.

It goes without saying that such normalization and the recognition of Taiwan as a legitimate sovereign entity in the international system imply a desire for self-determination. In turn, this will necessitate countering the widely accepted notion that Taiwanese self-determination is both *illegal* and that it constitutes secession "without consent or constitutional authorization" (Buchanan). Beijing's rhetoric notwithstanding, Taiwan is not a case of secession, as its legal status does not fall under China, and especially not under the PRC, which as a successor state no longer recognizes the existence of the ROC. And yet in their exercise of finding solutions to resolve the Taiwan issue, both Beijing and many surely well-intentioned academics abroad have done so under the premise that Taiwan somehow falls under the territorial boundaries of China and that therefore the Taiwanese independence movement is a *secessionist* movement. Until this is properly countered, whatever self-determination is to be offered to the Taiwanese will fall within the confines of the Chinese state as defined by Chinese nationalism.

Of course, as the HKSAR example has made amply clear, such a perspective quickly runs into difficulties when it applies to the self-governance of subgroups within China. According to Buchanan, international law should "grant" the unilateral right to secede only as a "remedial" and "last-resort response to serious injustices." In other words, "international law should unambiguously repudiate the nationalist principle that all nations (or 'peoples') are entitled to their own states." This emphasis on preserving "territorial integrity" and encouraging "alternatives to secession" is hugely problematic in the context of China. For one thing, it is not even possible to agree on territorial integrity: Beijing claims that Taiwan is an indivisible part of China, while the Taiwanese and their supporters abroad disagree. Unless Taiwan manages to convince the international community otherwise, it will continue to be regarded as a province or territory of China – and so far Beijing has been winning that battle. The second problem with Buchanan's argument is one of definition. How does one define "serious injustices," who gets to decide, and at what point does this legitimize, under international law, a move toward unilateral secession? If, as I suspect, for Buchanan the phrase "serious injustices" means rampant human rights violations and the use of indiscriminate force by the state, then it goes without saying that societies like Hong Kong today or Taiwan after unification undergo a gradual erosion in their freedoms and liberties, where human rights violations do not result in a bloodbath, are pretty much doomed.

The first ("positive") force, therefore, seeks clarity on Taiwan's status and to counter the view that Taiwanese independence forces are secessionist. Taiwan is a state, it is normal, and it should be recognized as such in its exchanges with China and the international community. Such recognition would evidently have tremendous repercussions on the conditions under which the Taiwan issue can be resolved, as Taiwan would not have to make some of the concessions that would be necessary should a resolution occur under conditions that define it as a subunit of China. This desire for clarity stems both from a greater understanding of what has been happening in HKSAR and from the realization that whatever agreement is reached between Taipei and Beijing that places Taiwan in a position of subjugation will necessarily comport losses in terms of Taiwan's freedoms, liberties, and ability to control its future.

This is conceivably what the 14.6 percent who want "Urgent Independence for Taiwan," the 7.8 percent who support the "Status Quo for Now, Independence Later," the 13.0 percent who want the "Status Quo for Now, Consider Independence Later," and the 30.2 percent who want an "Eternal Status Quo" believe in. In other words, based on the TISR survey, 65.6 percent of the population of Taiwan is probably in favor of a clear status and self-determination for Taiwan, hardly an illegitimate sentiment shared by only a minority of so-called splittists.

The second ("negative") force, therefore, is in reaction to Chinese encroachment on Taiwan's democracy. Irrespective of whether one agrees with the first element just discussed – that Taiwan is a normal state whose desire for self-determination does not constitute secessionism – the second force seeks to counter the negative influences that closer ties with China may have had or will have on Taiwan's way of life and democratic institutions (the "mainlandization" of Taiwan). This is Taiwan's firewall, which would manifest itself even in the context of Buchanan's "alternatives to secession." Although this places less emphasis on the clarity on Taiwan's status that seems to be sought by younger Taiwanese, this nevertheless poses a challenge to Beijing in that the conditions under which a political arrangement could be reached would necessitate the kind of concessions on the CCP's part that it simply is not willing to make (more on this in the next chapter).

Those views are probably shared by the 9.7 percent of respondents who in the TISR survey favored either "Status Quo for Now, Consider Unification Later" or "Status Quo for Now, Unify Later" (the 4.2 percent who seek urgent unification either do not care for Taiwan's democratic institutions or assume that they could somehow obtain a much better deal than the one that was given to Hong Kong).

Despite all these conditions in Taiwan, Beijing maintains that the only offer to Taiwan is the "one country, two systems" framework that has been used to incorporate and to regulate Hong Kong since 1997. Needless to say, this system is already coming apart at the seams in HKSAR and has no viable future in Taiwan, a society with a very different history from Hong Kong's and that furthermore already enjoys the fruits of democracy and freedoms that had been denied the residents of Hong Kong even under British colonial rule. Beijing's shooting down of the Dalai Lama's so-called Middle Way, which sought "genuine autonomy within the framework of the constitution of the People's Republic of China," is also indicative of a mindset that cannot countenance the notion of real autonomy for certain regions within the PRC (Beijing's response was, "The only sensible alternative is for the Dalai Lama and his supporters to accept that Tibet has been part of China since antiquity, to abandon their goals of dividing China and seeking independence for Tibet").

Even if we were to treat "one country, two systems" as a "broad concept" that can be used "creatively" to "tackle Taiwan's political destiny" (Lo), such an agreement would still entail some loss to the Taiwanese in the form of concessions on and presumably the abandonment of things that they already enjoy – such as, for example, the ability to conduct foreign relations. Meanwhile, none of the benefits that would presumably accrue, such as closer economic integration, access to Chinese markets, and so on, can be obtained via other means, such as an actual FTA between two sovereign states under World Trade Organization rules. The only real "benefit" that would stem from unification would be the removal of the threat of force against Taiwan, though this would have to be weighed against the high likelihood of a pacification campaign across Taiwan, as well as all the other ills that have already been observed in Hong Kong since retrocession. This makes for a very tough sale to the Taiwanese who seek the continuation of their way of life.

What reinforces these views in the second ("negative") variable is that marginal prounification agents like Chang An-le and the New Party's Yok Mu-ming aside, even deep-blue academics who have been selected by the KMT to engage in talks with their Chinese counterparts at various academic conferences cannot find common ground on which combination of Chinese characters to use to describe the complex relationship between Taiwan in China. In other words, academics whose ideology is presumably closest to that of the Chinese are unable to agree with the Chinese on how to describe the relationship, much less on the path to resolution of the conflict in the Taiwan Strait. And those are just academics engaging in wordplay and intellectual pursuit, who do not need to "sell" their views to a political party that is responsible for the electability of its candidates – let alone to the general population.

The agreed-upon, even if tacitly so, national identity of the Taiwanese in both camps is also one of the reasons why there has been such low public support for a proposed "peace agreement" with China, as became clear to President Ma when he floated the idea during his reelection campaign in 2011. For most Taiwanese, there is no need for such an agreement, as Taiwan is not at war with China: It recognizes its existence, does not threaten military invasion, and is perfectly willing to engage in normal business and diplomatic relations with it. Why sign a peace accord when one is already at peace with the other side, knowing full well, furthermore, that such an accord would in no way reconcile Beijing to Taiwan's aspirations for self-determination or diminish the Chinese threat of military invasion to combat the "evil" of "secessionism"?

Most Taiwanese, in both the green and the blue camps, are aware that a peace agreement would serve other, mostly symbolic, purposes that the CCP would exploit to further draw Taiwan into its embrace or to isolate it within the international community. Among other things, it would add to the chorus of voices in the West that have been calling on Washington to end arms sales to Taiwan under the TRA. There would be much wider support for a peace agreement with China if such an agreement indeed lowered tensions in the Taiwan Strait and provided benefits to Taiwan.

Although Hao is partly right when he argues that Taiwanese consciousness has "brought forth prejudices and discriminatory attitudes against the Mainland Chinese and a strong belief in Taiwanese independence," it is clear that the elements of Taiwanese nationalism run far deeper than mere discrimination against the "other," with the implication that better understanding of the people on both sides is all it would take to resolve the issue of Taiwan once and for all.

The fault in Hao's argument is that he seems to believe that the inability of the two sides of the Taiwan Strait to attain reconciliation is primarily due to a misunderstanding, which leads to prejudice, narrow views, and assumptions of the worst in the other. Writing in the early days of the Ma administration, Hao observed that the ability of people in Taiwan and China to cross the Taiwan Strait and to learn more about each other remained limited. The situation has changed markedly since then, and yet the divide remains. In fact, it appears to have widened significantly. And if Hao's counterpart at the University of Macau, Chen Dingding, is right, the exposure of the millions of Chinese who have visited Taiwan since 2008 to a democratic system will have hardened their belief that democracy is not suitable for China. This would be perfectly fine if the Chinese were happy to leave Taiwan alone, but given the nature of Chinese nationalism today, that is not the case. Consequently, since Taiwan is regarded as a part of China, its democracy is a problem and one that, like HKSAR, would have to be aligned with the rest of China – not so much, as we saw earlier, because democracy in Taiwan poses an existential threat to China (it does not) but rather, as we will see in the next chapter, because the Chinese body politics cannot currently absorb the contradiction that a democratic province within would create.

Meanwhile, the millions of Taiwanese who visit China every year, added to the 2 million or so who already work there on a semipermanent basis, have had plenty of occasions to learn more about the Chinese and to dispel the prejudices and racism that supposedly fuels Taiwanese nationalism and support for independence. Yet here too, there is no sign that such contact has had any impact on those individuals' identity or support for the continuation of Taiwan as an independent, democratic, and sovereign state.

If greater exposure to the "other" helps end prejudice, that is certainly a welcome effect; however, to assume that a lack of understanding of the other is the only thing that stands in the way of "reconciliation" – which furthermore connotes a mere family split – is naïve at best.

Still, Beijing and pro-Beijing media in Taiwan constantly play that tune, as they did following the protests that surrounded TAO Minister Zhang Zhijun's visit in June 2014. Paraphrasing reports in Taiwanese media that, as we saw in an earlier section, have been taken over by pro-Beijing businesspeople, the TAO wrote on its website, "Affected by some protesters, Zhang's route was changed on the last day of his visit. Mainstream newspapers on the island *all expressed* regret and appealed to 'introspect what hospitality is,' and 'learn to listen' to different opinions." It then added, "The *United Daily News* said that violent clashes are not equivalent to freedom, and 'to listen and understand discrepancy' is what Taiwanese people should reflect on."

According to this highly distorted view (for one thing, not *all* newspapers expressed regret, only the pro-Beijing ones, and the violence was perpetrated by pro-Beijing gangsters who physically assaulted peaceful protesters at the sites), the problem lies with the Taiwanese who "refuse to listen to different opinions" – a rather risible contention given Beijing's fixation on inevitability and the indivisibility of one China, which refusal to adhere to can now, under new regulations, land people in jail and ruin their careers. The CCP has been waging war on freedom of speech across China and threatens war if the Taiwanese refuse unification, but the root of the conflict in the Taiwan Strait, the propagandists tell us, is the unwillingness of some Taiwanese to listen to "different opinions." Right.

Rather than a misunderstanding, the real problem in the Taiwan Strait is that the Taiwanese are on a path to self-determination, which a succession of Chinese governments has refused to recognize. No amount of understanding will change the fact that the majority of people in Taiwan do not want to be part of a Chinese state, period, regardless of the political system that exists there. Most Taiwanese recognize that they may be culturally Chinese and have Chinese ancestry – both elements that are in fact celebrated and that contribute to Taiwan's great cultural, literary, architectural, and culinary richness – but such recognition does not necessarily entail a contradiction, at least not under the Western model of nationalism that has been adopted in Taiwan. Under its understanding of nationalism, Taiwan is to China just as the U.S., Canada, or Australia are to the U.K., as descendants of the English with several cultural, linguistic, and value similarities and yet confidently citizens of a separate nation-state.

Those examples also help in understanding why the compatibility of political systems also does not necessarily create a desire for unification. None of the three former British colonies has expressed any desire for reunification with England, nor, for that matter, has American democracy engendered any desire among their neighbors to the north to unify with the U.S., despite the geographical proximity and the even greater dependence of Canada on the U.S. economy than that of Taiwan vis-à-vis China.

Of course, it would be less of a problem if Beijing operated under the same definition of nationalism as Taiwan. But it doesn't. Its civilizational approach to what it believes to be the nation (or rather the "world-society," which transcends the idea of the nation) is what really stands in the way of "reconciliation" in the Taiwan Strait. Unable and unwilling to consider *de jure* independence for Taiwan as one of the possible solutions to the conflict, Beijing therefore continues to insist that a solution to the Taiwan issue must fall within the parameters of some form of union under one China – in other words, whatever the outcome, Taiwan will inevitably be part of China *in some way* (see Chapter 11). Whether ordinary Chinese believe this or are merely regurgitating CCP propaganda (after all, it *is* against the law to encourage "separatism") and whether regime change that brought to power a government that does not emphasize China's sovereignty over Taiwan would make acceptable the notion that Taiwan can exist as a sovereign neighbor are questions for which the answers have yet to be discovered. Still, we should not assume that the CCP "knows," let alone that it can speak on behalf of, all 1.4 billion Chinese. In other words, a truly peaceful solution to the Taiwan "question" could lie with the people rather than with a party-state that has made reunification one of the instruments legitimizing its existence.

Beijing's current rigidity on the Taiwan issue and its unwillingness to recognize the dynamics within Taiwanese society that militate against unification were made very clear in its latest defense white paper, which states that it is the "responsibility" of every Taiwanese compatriot to make sure that reunification happens and to combat "secessionism." As we saw earlier, the new National Security Law of the PRC makes similar claims and demands not only of Chinese citizens but of the Taiwanese as well.

As the trends discussed in this section indicate, the CCP has been unable to win the hearts and minds of the Taiwanese, while threats and coercion have more often than not been counterproductive. Meanwhile, as Wang and Tsering argue, economic determinism – throw enough money at a problem and hope that it will go away – has proven itself to be a failure, even in places like Tibet, and will certainly fail in convincing the people of Taiwan that they would be better off as citizens of the PRC.

However much it may hope that Taiwanese negotiators could play the role that the British government played during the negotiations on the terms of retrocession in the 1980s – in which the residents of the enclave were treated very much as inert matter – Taiwan's democracy, its opposition parties, civil society, and voters won't allow it. Beijing's best bet, therefore, is to adopt a rigid line and to create conditions such that Taiwan will feel it has no choice but to capitulate, to concede defeat by cutting as best a deal as it can . . . on China's terms, evidently.

One other, more long-term option for Beijing would be to reverse the seemingly unstoppable trends through dilution: by encouraging Taipei to modify its laws so that more Chinese spouses and perhaps Chinese workers can establish themselves in Taiwan permanently and obtain voting rights. There is no doubt that over time a large influx of Chinese in Taiwan could change the face of Taiwanese politics and turn things around in Beijing's favor. But that is a remote prospect for the time being, and one that furthermore would be contingent on the government in Taipei.

Although this seems outlandish at present, we cannot entirely rule out the possibility that at some point in the future, some form of political accommodation, based on what Hao has described as "cosmopolitan citizenship," *could* become acceptable to people on both sides of the Taiwan Strait, and the socialization of the two sides would certainly help create the conditions for such an agreement (Hao proposes "hybrid federalism" and "confederation"). However, such a scenario is not even remotely feasible under the current conditions and could very well never be. Besides China's idiosyncratic nationalism and the nature of its political system, another obstacle exists and will continue to do so as long as the CCP insists on maintaining a tight grip on Chinese society. To this we now turn.

Bibliography

Blanchard, B (2015) "China Calls on Dalai Lama to 'Put Aside Illusions' About Talks," *Reuters*, 15 April, http://www.reuters.com/article/2015/04/15/us-china-tibet-idUSKB N0N608720150415

Buchanan, A (2004) *Justice, Legitimacy, and Self-Determination: Moral Foundations for International Law*, Oxford: Oxford University Press: 331

Bush, R (2013) *Uncharted Strait: The Future of China-Taiwan Relations*, Washington: Brookings Institution Press: 40

Gold, M (2015) "Taiwan Youth to China: Treat Us Like a Country," *Reuters*, 30 June, http://www.reuters.com/article/2015/06/30/us-taiwan-china-youth-idUSKCN0PA2W320 150630

Hao, Z (2010) *Whither Taiwan and Mainland China: National Identity, the State, and Intellectuals*, Hong Kong: Hong Kong University Press: 139–169

Lo, S-H (2008) *The Dynamics of Beijing-Hong Kong Relations: A Model for Taiwan?* Hong Kong: Hong Kong University Press: 227

Schubert, G (2010) "The Political Thinking of the Mainland Taishang: Some Preliminary Observations from the Field," *Journal of Current Chinese Affairs*, 1: 73–110

Taiwan Affairs Office (2014) "Taiwanese Newspaper Appealed to 'Learn to Listen,'" *Taiwan Affairs Office*, 29 June, http://www.gwytb.gov.cn/en/CrossstraitInteractionsand Exchanges/201406/t20140630_6427970.htm

Taiwan Indicators Survey Research (2015) June, http://www.tisr.com.tw/?p=5523#more-5523

Wang, L and Tsering, S (2009) *The Struggle for Tibet*, London: Verso

Youwei (2015) "The End of Reform in China: Authoritarian Adaptation Hits a Wall," *Foreign Affairs*, May/June: 3

Yu, V (2015) "Chinese Police Detain More Than 100 Lawyers and Activists in Weekend Sweep," *South China Morning Post*, 13 July, http://www.scmp.com/news/china/policies-politics/article/1838240/chinese-police-detain-scores-lawyers-and-activists?page=all

Zhao, T (2011) "Rethinking Empire from the Chinese Concept 'All Under Heaven' (Tianxia, 天下)," in *China Orders the World: Normative Soft Power and Foreign Policy*, Callahan, W and Barabantseva, E, eds, Washington and Baltimore: Woodrow Wilson Center Press and Johns Hopkins University Press: 23

10

THE TRAP THAT CHINA SET FOR ITSELF

Beijing is stuck. One of the principal components of the CCP's legitimacy, which both stems from and fuels Chinese nationalism, is the leadership's emphasis on the need to end the so-called century of humiliation at foreign hands, of which the continued existence of Taiwan as a separate entity serves as a painful reminder. As Sandby-Thomas observes, "[T]he issue of Taiwan's sovereignty is central to the CCP's nationalist credentials." "Reunification" is therefore one of Beijing's core interests, the formulation of which, of course, has always rested in the hands of the CCP. Whoever argues otherwise would immediately be accused of "splittism," one of the three evils as defined by the Chinese leadership, and face severe punishment, especially under the new national security laws adopted in July 2015.

Consequently, the discourse on the Taiwan issue has been and will continue to be limited to a list of possibilities for resolution in which Taiwan would ultimately be part of one China. There simply is no room for the simplest solution — recognizing Taiwan as a sovereign nation.

Arguably, one China could mean several things. It could leave ample room for creativity and yield formulas that might stand a better chance of persuading the people of Taiwan to consider some sort of a joint future with China. As Hao argues, anything from "hybrid federalism" to "confederation," to which we could add a variation on the EU model, should in theory be possible.

Instead, Beijing remains insistent that only one formula — "one country, two systems" — will ever be on the table.

As we saw, "one country, two systems" has left no doubt as to who is the ultimate boss in either system, and as we have seen, it will inevitably lead to the mainlandization of the territory in question. Recent developments in HKSAR have also highlighted a marked tightening of Beijing's grip on the territory, so much so that the "one country, two systems" formula that exists in Hong Kong today is not the formula that the residents of the former British colony – and the authorities in London – believed they were implementing in 1997.

The strengthening of Beijing's authority in Hong Kong has coincided with the installing of Xi Jinping as CCP secretary general and president of the PRC. Whether for reasons of ideology or because Xi has, despite himself, been forced to take a hard line amid possibly mounting instability in China, the result has been the same: "one country, two systems" increasingly looks like "one country, one system." As we saw, from the beginning the CCP had made it clear that it would never allow Hong Kong (or Macau) to threaten the socialist system that was installed by the CCP across China. Not only that, but over time it was inevitable that Beijing would seek to align the system in HKSAR with that in the Mainland – especially after signs of trouble emerged in the territory that risked spilling into neighboring parts of China proper and may have received some support across China.

Given what we have learned about Taiwanese nationalism and identity in the preceding chapters, there is no doubt that the "one country, two systems" formula is a nonstarter in Taiwan. In fact, if we exclude pro-Beijing hardliners, not even those who support eventual unification with China agree that the formula is appropriate for Taiwan. Something much more "generous" and far more permissive than what has been extended to HKSAR would be necessary to convince more people in Taiwan that unification *may* be worthwhile (though as we have seen, Taiwanese identity may have consolidated to a point where any offer, however generous, is insufficient).

Oddly enough, given the multiple opportunities to "better understand each other" that have arisen since 2008 and that Hao maintains could facilitate "reconciliation," Beijing has stuck to a position on unification that has no future in Taiwan and that has run into serious difficulties in HKSAR. Two realities explain why this is so, and stupidity certainly is not one of them.

First, Beijing will never agree to anything that suggests the existence of "two Chinas" or two states on each side of the Taiwan Strait. Hence its refusal to recognize the existence of the ROC. This is an ideological bottom line that directly results from China's *civilizational* nationalism and that clashes with the Western type of nationalism existing in Taiwan. The CCP under Secretary-General Hu Jintao may have allowed President Ma's KMT to get away with its insistence that for Taipei, one China means "one China, with different interpretations," but this was hardly a sign of flexibility on Beijing's part. As long as rapprochement was occurring, the Chinese leadership did not pressure Taipei to drop the *different interpretations* part, even if it gave rise to the possibility that there are two Chinas. But there was never any doubt about what Beijing thinks one China means – and that is *one* China, the PRC, with the CCP firmly in control. Consequently, while the "different interpretations" word game may have had its utility while Taiwan and China continue to exist as separate political entities, such language was never used on the Chinese side, and furthermore it would inevitably be struck out from any final agreement on reunification.

The second point is far more complex, as it undermines Beijing's ability to explore other possible solutions to the Taiwan issue. Essentially, Beijing's problem is not one of imagination but simply that the current political system in China makes it impossible to make a better offer to Taiwan without risking that the entire house of cards will come down. In fact, this problem is directly related to the reasons why, despite high hopes at the international level and the emergence of a middle class, China's *political* system has not liberalized and even less democratized. Keeping China together is an extraordinarily difficult balancing act that may in fact require some form of authoritarianism. This would certainly explain why, over its 5,000 years of history, this continent-sized imperial system has always been condemned to either dictatorial rule or warlordism and disorder. Even today, when China has become a "normal" state in the Westphalian sense of the word, any leader who wants to keep the country together must do so with high levels of institutional controls. It is no surprise, then, that the annual budget for the People's Armed Police is higher than that of the People's Liberation Army.

The additional restrictions on press freedom and Internet censorship, the growing instances of foreigners who are denied entry into China or who are expelled, rising paranoia and accusations of foreign meddling in China's internal affairs, and the new national security laws that were adopted in June 2015 are hardly developments that inspire confidence in the stability of the PRC. In fact, all are the tools that are normally used by regimes that fear they are about to lose control. What is needed under such circumstances is what Zheng has called an "organizational emperor" – the CCP as a new emperor ruling over all of China and as a continuer of those traditions.

Faced with the centrifugal forces of modernity and globalization, the CCP has had little option but to seek to homogenize the political system across China, regardless of the local ethnic composition, which not only explains its campaign of "ethnic cleansing" in Xinjiang and Tibet, but also, as we discussed earlier, the mainlandization of Hong Kong.

It is therefore easy to imagine just how much of a problem Taiwan would be if it were to be incorporated into China in its current form. Beijing is already struggling to cope with the contradiction that HKSAR has created in the system of Chinese politics, and its response to date has inclined more toward repression than accommodation. Consequently, if Taiwan is to be integrated into the PRC, it must do so under a formula that doesn't threaten the stability of China – but here's the catch: The only formula that meets that requirement is "one country, two systems," which no Taiwanese will accept.

Notwithstanding the likelihood that even better offers would likely be turned down by Taiwan, there are several formulas that, at the intellectual level, should have more appeal. As mentioned, federalism is one of them, along with other formulas in which the Taiwanese have much greater freedoms than those that are enjoyed in HKSAR. The problem with this is that such an offer would probably turn Taiwan into a poison pill. Ironically, as long as Taiwan is not part of the PRC, its liberal democracy does not pose an existential threat to China. However, if Taiwan were to become a province of China, its political system, just like Hong Kong's, would have to be harmonized (i.e., mainlandized) with that of the PRC to an extent that the contradictions arising from unification no longer threaten national stability.

There are two principal reasons for this. First, as with the case of Hong Kong, the CCP will never allow political influences to go in any direction other than from Beijing toward the periphery. Put differently, influence is one-way and inevitably will lead to the mainlandization of politics in the territory, as has clearly occurred in HKSAR. Such dynamics are preemptive and prophylactic, meant to ensure that territories that enjoy special status and "autonomy" (HKSAR, Macau, Tibet, Xinjiang, Inner Mongolia) do not influence change in other parts of China.

This is why, for example, Beijing has refused to offer the residents of Hong Kong the kind of universal suffrage that they want, one under which the candidates would not be preselected by Beijing and that could in theory allow candidates running for office to do so on an independence platform.

The second reason is related to the first, in that unification of Taiwan with China under *preferential* terms for Taiwan – for example, the ability to directly and freely elect their leaders, to maintain their democratic way of life, and so on – would inevitably create resentment in other parts of China and calls for similar freedoms. In other words, the incorporation of Taiwan under such terms would be a cause for similar (and perfectly legitimate) demands across China (starting with Hong Kong and other more "modernized" areas like Shanghai), which would threaten to topple the CCP, challenge its legitimacy under multiparty politics, and likely contribute to great instability, if not the creation or threat of breakaway territories ("Grant us the same rights and liberties as Taiwan, or else we secede"). If anyone has doubts about the kind of nightmares that awaken Chinese leaders at night, such a scenario is it.

Another possible concession that Beijing would make to sweeten the deal of unification would be large money transfers to Taiwan, which not only would also fuel resentment among people across China but also take away large sums of capital that could be put to much better use in the poorer areas of China, where, despite the Chinese economic boom, conditions remain very much in the third-world category.

Undoubtedly, the prospect of "losing" Taiwan is an accomplishment that no Chinese leader would want to add to his or her résumé. But a far greater nightmare still would be to become a "Chinese Gorbachev" by launching a process that ultimately leads to the dismantlement of the entire system. Thus, preserving the integrity of the PRC and the primacy of the CCP under a socialist system will always trump the desire to reunify with Taiwan, however much of a core interest that might be.

Following the collapse of the Soviet Union and communist states in Eastern Europe in the 1990s, the CCP Politburo held several meetings on the subject, and research institutes, including the Chinese Academy of Social Sciences (中國社會科學院), were asked to prepare studies to find out what "went wrong" in the U.S.S.R. and how to avoid a similar outcome in China, where, as the Chinese saying goes, "A single spark can start a prairie fire." Many studies concluded that Mikhail Gorbachev, General Secretary of the Central Committee of the Communist Party of the Soviet Union, had carelessly implemented reform, which had opened the door for Western-backed "peaceful evolutionists" to destroy the U.S.S.R. from within. As Wang Renzhi (王忍之), a former chief of propaganda, once observed, following the path of European democratic socialism would be a step further on "the slippery slope to political extinction of the CCP" (Shambaugh). Despite the changes in China, the leading role of the CCP and of democratic centralism remains non-negotiable. Interestingly, two U.S. institutions that were singled out as having played a role in toppling communist regimes in Poland, Czechoslovakia, Bulgaria, Hungary, and Romania – the National Endowment for Democracy (NED) and the National Democratic Institute (NDI) – were also accused by Beijing of fostering instability in Hong Kong in 2014.

Following the logic of the "lessons learned" from the collapse of the Soviet Union, it is very clear that the CCP would regard allowing the unification of a democratic Taiwan with China as opening the door to the same "peaceful evolutionists" who collapsed the U.S.S.R. And, of course, if the Taiwanese were granted the right to freely choose their leader (or to continue to do so, that is), why couldn't the rest of the Chinese? The scenario is antithetical to the CCP's one-party-state ideology.

Evidently, the U.S.S.R./Eastern Europe analogy fits imperfectly with the situation in the Taiwan Strait. Above all, rather than deal with "peaceful evolutionists" in their midst, through unification, China would be inviting one into its home, which many CCP supporters would rightly regard as suicidal.

All of this explains Beijing's insistence on the "one country, two systems" formula for Taiwan. Everything else, any better offer, would simply be too threatening to the stability *of the rest of China* after unification.

Another major problem for Beijing in the highly unlikely scenario that it would "grant" the unification of Taiwan and China under preferential terms is that the PRC would suddenly be absorbing 23 million people who have experienced freedom and democracy – many of them having experienced nothing else in their entire lives. Consequently, Taiwan would inevitably be a constant irritant, and Beijing's many opponents (those who would continue to oppose unification on any terms) would, if their freedoms are indeed respected under the exceptional terms of unification, be highly empowered, mobile, relatively wealthy, and connected. By absorbing Taiwan, China would potentially make it easier for Taiwanese dissidents to link up with like-minded individuals across China, which is something that Beijing certainly does not want to facilitate, as the denial of entry to several Taiwanese students and academics following the unrest in Taipei and Hong Kong has demonstrated. The kind of pacification that would be necessary to silence such opposition would be highly problematic and would inevitably attract international attention.

Rather than face such problems, Beijing would therefore prefer to absorb Taiwan under much more restrictive conditions, such as those that now exist in HKSAR, which takes us back to a situation where Beijing's offer is unpalatable to the majority of the people of Taiwan (again assuming that a "good" offer would convince them to join China). This is why Beijing's offer has been "one country, two systems" . . . or else, and why we are unlikely to see any other proposal unless the CCP decides to liberalize and democratize China and to devolve power to the regions in federalism style, which are all unlikely prospects for now.

So Beijing will stick to its "one country, two systems" offer while continuing to do everything it can to undermine Taiwan's democracy, isolate it internationally, and whittle away at public morale, with the hope that Taipei will capitulate and agree, however resignedly, to terms of unification dictated by Beijing. Additionally, the more Taiwan resists such pressures (e.g., civic activism, the election of officials and governments that are more careful in their dealings with Beijing), the likelier it is that Beijing will turn to the instruments of political warfare and subnational elements such as gangsters, discussed in Chapters 5 and 6, to continue the process of integration.

This prospect makes the utility of Taiwan's "democratic firewall," as well as the need to further strengthen and consolidate Taiwan's democratic institutions and civil society, all the more compelling. The best way to react to Beijing's attempts to secure unification through underhanded means is to respond by strengthening and enlarging that which China is trying to undermine.

The option of a military invasion to resolve the matter remains on the table, but as we will discuss in Chapter 12, that will always be considered as a last-resort option that Beijing, PLA bluster notwithstanding, would much rather never have to call upon.

Of course, besides the systemic limits imposed on the situation, we must also factor in Chinese pride as a component of an increasingly racialist form of nationalism. Why would "bad" Chinese, whom the CCP defeated in the civil war, along with the others who were "deformed" by half a century of Japanese colonial experience, be rewarded for their long refusal to "reunite" with the motherland with concessions granting them privileges that the Chinese authorities will not even extend to patriotic Han Chinese?

Lastly, despite the deep ideological commitment that seems to exist across China for the reunification with Taiwan, we cannot disregard the utility that continued conflict has had for certain sectors of the Chinese system – primarily the intelligence and defense sectors in China. As a highly emotional core issue, Taiwan provides the perfect pretext for the PLA, defense contractors, intelligence agencies, and propaganda departments to request larger budgets, better equipment, and more influence, a phenomenon that is certainly not limited to China. Governments the world over used the Cold War, and after that the threat of international and home-grown terrorism, to justify wildly expanded defense and intelligence expenditures.

In other words, some people in China probably don't want the Taiwan issue to be resolved, ever. Continued conflict in the Taiwan Strait is beneficial to the PLA, which otherwise would have to find other enemies to justify its continually growing budgets, a growing military-industrial complex, and the acquisition of advanced weaponry, such as S-400 air defense systems and Sukhoi Su-35 combat aircraft, from Russia. Moreover, since, contrary to what Pillsbury argues, it is doubtful that China intends to become a *global* superpower, where it would have to compete with and try to displace the U.S. and its alliance system, Beijing is therefore limited to a list of regional enemies, of which Taiwan and Japan are the most convenient, and the ones able to arouse an emotional response from Chinese citizens.

One of the principal instruments that Beijing has relied upon to break the will of the Taiwanese who resist the forces of unification, as well as to encourage the view within the international system that Taiwan is not worth defending, is propaganda. At the heart of this multifaceted propaganda campaign is the concept of *historical inevitability*, the subject of the next chapter.

Bibliography

Cole, M (2014) "National Consolidation or Poison Pill? Taiwan and China's Quest for 'Re-Unification'," in *China and International Security: History, Strategy, and 21st-Century Policy*, Chau, D and Kane, T, eds, Santa Barbara: Praeger: 3–20

Pillsbury, M (2015) *The Hundred-Year Marathon: China's Secret Strategy to Replace America as the Global Superpower*, New York: Henry Holt

Sandby-Thomas, P (2011) *Legitimating the Chinese Nationalist Party Since Tiananmen: A Critical Analysis of the Stability Discourse*, Oxon: Routledge: 122

Shambaugh, D (2008) *China's Communist Party: Atrophy and Adaptation*, Berkeley and Los Angeles: University of California Press: 50, 81

Zheng, Y (2010) *The Chinese Communist Party as Organizational Emperor: Culture, Reproduction and Transformation*, Oxon: Routledge

11

THE MYTH OF INEVITABILITY

In the language of social science, China's propaganda strategy against Taiwan is known as "framing." Using mass media, political leaders, organizations, education, and other devices, Beijing has sought to frame the argument on Taiwan by shaping the concepts and theoretical perspectives that define the discourse on the issue. In other words, framing sets out to define a version of "reality" and to reinforce that definition with others so that it becomes *the* reality. The core axes of Chinese propaganda on the subject are that (1) Taiwan is an inalienable part of China and (2) that reunification is inevitable.

Although, as we saw in our discussion of Chinese nationalism in an earlier chapter, this version of "reality" seems to have become accepted by the Chinese side, not everybody outside China agrees. It is clear, based on the consolidation of a multicultural and multiethnic Taiwanese identity, that many people in Taiwan do not agree with either of the tenets of Chinese propaganda regarding Taiwan.

However, while it might be difficult to shift perceptions on the first axis, the second one is much more vulnerable to the influence of propaganda, which applies not only to the Taiwanese but also to the many analysts and China "experts" abroad. Simply put, while the CCP might find it hard to convince the people of Taiwan that Taiwan has always been part of China – and now that it is part of the PRC – it believes that a sustained propaganda effort can convince most Taiwanese and outside observers that, to quote a famous sci-fi TV series, "resistance is futile."

The object of this chapter is to demonstrate that this deterministic view of "historical inevitability," which in a very different context the American art historian Bernard Berenson once compared to a Moloch that is devouring us, is false, that it is a "doubtful" and "dangerous" dogma that tends "to make us accept whatever happens as irresistible and foolhardy to oppose" (Berenson).

A perfect example of the Chinese government's use of the concept of inevitability appears in its 2015 defense white paper, where it says, "The Taiwan issue bears on China's reunification and long-term development, and reunification is an *inevitable trend* in the course of *national rejuvenation*" (italics added).

China may no longer be communist, and in fact it appears that the CCP even considered changing its name early in the twenty-first century by removing the word "communist" to reassure the international community, but we must never forget that the party has nevertheless retained many elements of its foundational Marxist-Leninist worldview, a position that has been reaffirmed by the ideological "reawakening" encouraged by the so-called New Helmsman, President Xi Jinping, since 2012. Thus, although the party has selectively retained the aspects of Marxism-Leninism and Mao Zedong thinking that fit its current needs, the important ideological elements remain and continue to inform how the CCP views and seeks to shape the world around it.

Those who believe that China is now merely honoring Marxism "in the breach" (Service) are advised to go back to a speech by President and CCP Secretary-General Xi in August 2013, in which he called for the revival of "ideological purification" and a reinforcement of the "four cardinal principles": upholding the socialist path, the people's "democratic dictatorship," the party leadership and Marxism-Leninism, and "Mao Zedong thought." Xi has also laid to rest any hope that the party might undergo "peaceful evolution" by saying that "the nature of the party will never change . . . our red *jiangshan* [heaven and earth] will never change color" (Lam).

The notion of *inevitability*, which is at the core of Marxism-Leninism, therefore continues to figure prominently in the CCP's view of the world and propaganda efforts.

As Berlin wrote in his influential 1954 essay "Historical Inevitability," Marxism posits that:

> [m]en do as they do, and think as they think, largely as a 'function of' the inevitable evolution of the 'class' as a whole – from which it follows that the history and development of classes can be studied independently of the biographies of their component individuals. It is the 'structure' and the 'evolution' of the class alone that (causally) matters in the end.

Three elements – historicism, positivism, and monism – are of particular importance as we evaluate party propaganda efforts against Taiwan. *Historicism* means that the CCP (and the country) is moving toward "a determined historical objective along a predefined path of historical development" (Creemers) for the realization of the "Chinese dream" (i.e., a "reunified China" and a utopian society). *Positivism* is the means to accomplish those goals. It is the idea that "social reality, like nature, is undergirded by a single set of objective, intelligible laws and rules that cannot merely be used to understand reality, but also to control and change it, in order to achieve progress." "Scientific research" is necessary to define "objective laws" and implement "core scientific legislation." Tellingly, more than his predecessors Jiang Zemin (江澤民) and Hu Jintao, President Xi is, as Lam describes him, "committed to defending what he regards as *self-evident truths*" (italics added). *Monism*, meanwhile, stipulates that there is "only one set of legitimate values, preferences, and interests in a society," all of which are, of course, determined by the CCP (Creemers).

It is easy to see why, despite its foreign origins, this ideological triumvirate would appeal to authoritarian governments and "organizational emperors" such as the CCP. This ideology gives CCP policies a veneer of "natural laws" and inevitability; it guides policy and provides the tools to control and change reality toward the accomplishment of "legitimate" and "universal" goals that are arrived at via the discovery of indisputable scientific laws. As one of China's core values, the fact that Taiwan is part of China that must be reunified is also an "objective" and "legitimate" rule.

The vehemence with which the Chinese hold and express such beliefs (after all, they are "laws of nature") can therefore be very convincing to foreign interlocutors. It also makes trying to reason with them and, even worse, *disagreeing* with them a most onerous affair.

As Stokes and Hsiao have observed, propaganda "seek[s] to persuade an audience to embark on a course of action that 'everyone else is taking' in order to reinforce a natural desire to be on the winning side. Inevitable victory calls upon those not already on the bandwagon to join those already on the road to certain victory."

To the extent that it has shaped the discourse on Taiwan, we can argue that Beijing has succeeded on the second axis. With the exception of the minority of government officials and academics who argue that Taiwan should strive for *de jure* independence or who postulate a two-Chinas solution to the impasse in the Taiwan Strait, all other future scenarios and proposed mechanisms for conflict resolution situate Taiwan as part of and inevitably subsumed into China with the center residing in Beijing. Consequently, even the most generous proposals, such as a federalist arrangement, still result in Taiwan's losing some of the independence it currently enjoys by tying its fate to a central government in the PRC capital.

As we saw in the first section of this book, whoever argues otherwise has tended to be ostracized from the academic community, has seen his or her access to China or institutional funding melt away, and has encountered insurmountable pitfalls in trying to get published in "respectable" journals. Journal articles – *Foreign Affairs* and *International Security* among them – and books have made the case for "ceding" Taiwan to China, but the same highbrow publications would never agree to publish an article in which the author argues that Taiwan's destiny should be separate from China or, blasphemy, that it is already independent.

Only "irrational" and "small groups" of people continue to argue that Taiwan is or should be independent, and furthermore they are suspected of espousing such views out of sheer "hatred" for China or because of their associations with forces that conspire to keep China in perpetual weakness. Those, however, are "outsiders" who will never be in the in-group that recognizes Beijing's position regarding Taiwan and that, as a result, is showered with a variety of rewards, from access to the CCP leadership to the funding of research centers.

So the discourse has been framed, and its strictures are constantly reinforced via a system of self-censorship and punishments orchestrated by China and the international network of dependencies it has woven over the years. Thus, whatever choice Taiwan is given, it is a false choice, one between a maximalist position and a set of less than optimal outcomes that nevertheless dovetail with the desired outcome – a tactic long used by presidential advisers who want to shape the decisions of a president. Absent from all those choices is the option that the other party does not want to be considered. In the context of the Taiwan Strait, that option is independence, both in its current form and that of *de jure* independence.

A second component of Beijing's propaganda strategy seeks to reinforce the notion of inevitability by playing up China's strengths while emphasizing the weaknesses of its opponents. Thus the sustained signaling, which focuses on the following themes:

- The Taiwanese military has lost its quantitative and qualitative advantage in the Taiwan Strait, and the military gap will only continue to widen in China's favor;
- Taiwanese soldiers would drop their weapons the moment PLA forces landed on the beaches;
- The military it corrupt and completely penetrated by a seemingly ubiquitous Chinese intelligence apparatus;
- Taiwan can simply be "bought" because greedy Taiwanese would never say no to money;
- Great power politics and the rise of a new hegemon dictate that concessions must be made to accommodate the emerging power;
- Democracy is not the only game in town and perhaps we should show greater understanding toward the Chinese system;
- Taiwan would "fall" before the U.S. could intervene;
- Taiwan's security partner, the U.S., is overstretched, unwilling/unable to counter the growing threat of China's Anti-Access/Area Denial (A2/AD) capabilities and unwilling to risk nuclear war with China over the defense of Taiwan, which is of marginal interest to Washington but a core interest of Beijing; and
- Why should U.S. soldiers risk their lives defending faraway Taiwan when the Taiwanese themselves would not fight to defend their country?

If, as the propaganda goes, Taiwan's prospects are so dire, why resist? Why argue for its defense when doing so will poison the Sino-U.S. relations and undermine cooperation on other pressing issues, such as the North Korea nuclear program, global warming, or the territorial disputes in the East and South China Seas? Moreover, why risk U.S. cities, a carrier battle group, or airbases in Okinawa over a country that has no willingness to fight and whose majority of people agree they are Chinese? The military aspects of this equation will be discussed in greater detail in the next chapter. For the purpose of this chapter, is it important to note that most of the preceding claims, which are repeated in books, interviews, academic conferences, and official exchanges, rest on unproven assumptions that often have been internalized uncritically by foreign audiences whose inability to comprehend the dynamics in Taiwan is furthermore exacerbated by Chinese propaganda and fears of "angering" Beijing.

Such notions are furthermore reinforced by the patron–client system that Beijing has been trying to establish with Taiwan, in which those who understand early on that unification is "inevitable" and therefore that it is not to be resisted reap the benefits of greater access to China, while the laggards who refuse to face reality suffer the consequences. Better, then, to bandwagon and take the course of action that "everybody else is taking."

All of this, of course, rests on myths. However inconvenient this might be to the business elite in the Taiwan Strait whose ability to secure further enrichment is contingent on smooth cross-strait relations and to the political leaders worldwide who hope that the Taiwan issue could be neutralized once and for all so that this moral irritant will no longer nag at their consciences, there is absolutely nothing inevitable about unification. In fact, if current trends are maintained – and there is every reason to believe that they will – the only thing that appears to be inevitable is the resumption of tensions in the Taiwan Strait after eight years of relative (but in the end superficial) calm.

Chinese propaganda and Beijing's ability to "frame" the discourse on Taiwan's future will succeed only if we allow it to succeed. Far too often, countries that, after establishing diplomatic relations with China, adopted some form of a one-China policy have let Beijing define their policy, when in reality it is theirs to define. However much Beijing may insist that countries "agree" that there is only one China and that Taiwan is part of China, the texts of the agreements say otherwise. Most countries either "take note of" or "acknowledge" Beijing's position on one China and Taiwan's relationship thereto. Yet taking note of or acknowledging Beijing's position is very different from saying that Beijing is right or that it is one's policy. To believe so is to yield one's prerogative to set foreign policy. Countries can attempt to *influence* China's foreign policy through persuasion, coercion, and enticements, but we all agree that nobody but the leadership in Beijing has the right to set China' policies. So why, then, should we allow Beijing to decide other countries' policies on Taiwan?

Consequently, there is nothing to prevent other countries from adopting a two-state or two-Chinas formula to encourage the resolution of conflict in the Taiwan Strait or to disagree with Beijing that unification is the *only* solution. It clearly is not, and furthermore this is not the solution that the majority of the 23 million people who live in Taiwan would be comfortable with.

For far too long, the international community has allowed Beijing to frame the discourse on Taiwan, with the result that most governments, analysts, and journalists are unable to comprehend the dynamics within Taiwan that militate against unification and are unprepared to deal with outcomes in the Taiwan Strait that are far likelier to materialize than "inevitable" unification.

Ironically, when combined with the consolidation of Taiwanese nationalism that has been occurring in Taiwan, the traction that the myth of unification has had within the international community risks contributing to future conflict rather than helping to resolve it peacefully, as is ostensibly the universal wish. By narrowing the list of options available to Taiwan, Beijing and its international backers are encouraging a hardening of positions within Taiwan and fostering the conditions for a more militant form of resistance, as has occurred in other religious/territorial conflicts such as that between Palestinians and Israelis (the form of nationalism that the CCP has cultivated does have, ironically, religious and mystical undertones). Given that Taiwanese nationalism is not different from nationalism elsewhere, if they feel cornered, the Taiwanese will, like an animal fearing for its survival, escalate and lash out at its opponent.

So far, the international community has been lucky. The ambiguity that has surrounded Taiwan's status under the status quo over the years has been sufficient to keep these forces bottled up. After all, despite its unofficial status, Taiwan (or the ROC) was, for all intents and purposes, a sovereign state. However, efforts in recent years to change that status quo, especially since President Xi assumed near dictatorial powers at the helm of the CCP, as well as recent developments in HKSAR, have created a new sense of urgency among the Taiwanese who fear that Beijing might soon be willing to actualize the "inevitability" of unification.

The unrest that shook Taiwan in 2013 was a clear signal that Taiwanese nationalists were reacting to the perceived changes in the status quo and that they were willing to challenge Beijing directly if necessary – and that was only over a services trade agreement. The sense of powerlessness that for a long time seem to weigh down Taiwan's youth and that in turn reinforced Beijing's propaganda had seemingly been broken, probably for good. One can only imagine what would happen if China took steps that directly threatened Taiwan's sovereignty or its political institutions!

Of course, we can understand the significance and likelihood of future such disturbances only if we fully appreciate the legitimacy and scope of Taiwanese nationalism and the desire for self-determination, two variables that have been largely ignored – and in some ways reviled – by the international community.

Simultaneously, by encouraging Beijing to stick to its position on the inevitability of unification, the international community has made it almost impossible for voices within China that may see things otherwise to receive a hearing or not to be persecuted for airing such views. In other words, the global community has inadvertently propped up the hardliners within the CCP and have given Beijing *carte blanche* to silence whoever disagrees with the official line on Taiwan. The worst thing that the global community could do when it comes to China's future would be to reward Beijing for its intransigence by allowing it to reap the benefits of its hardline position on Taiwan. Such an outcome would just encourage similar behavior on other core interests, whose list will only grow as China's national power increases.

The best way to discourage such behavior is to treat Chinese myths for what they really are – propaganda – and not allow Beijing to determine the policies of other sovereign states.

The Sunflower Movement's occupation of the legislature in March and April 2014 seems to have had a beneficial effect on foreign perceptions and to have blown holes in the belief that the resolution of the Taiwan "question" should occur within the parameters of one China. In fact, soon after the end of the occupation, academics overseas were probably for the first time beginning to question the very foundations upon which they had studied relations between Taiwan and China over the years. Slowly, a few observers were reassessing the paradigms that illuminated their understanding of Taiwan. This was an achievement not of proindependence politicians, who tended to be regarded with apprehension and skepticism and whose efforts were often assumed to be little more than cynical politicking, but of society itself. By standing up to China, Taiwanese society had spoken and made it more difficult for the rest of the world to ignore the complex identity and nationalism that had developed in Taiwan over the years, a process that may very well have accelerated during the Ma years as contact with China became more frequent and the apparent threat of its encroachment more immediate.

As Berlin wrote, "it becomes the business of historians" – and that of political scientists, I would add – "to investigate who wanted what, and when, and where, in what way; how many men avoided or pursued this or that goal, and with what intensity; and further, to ask under what circumstances such wants or fears have proved effective, and to what extent, and with what consequences."

Of course, this is exactly what Chinese propaganda departments don't want us to do with regard to Taiwan.

These two fronts – a consolidating nationalism in Taiwan that refuses subjugation to China on one side and a "scientific" belief in an "objective" and ultimately "inevitable" process of unification on the other – is a recipe for future conflict. As both sides are unlikely to yield on those fundamentals, a "peaceful" resolution to the problem appears more distant than ever. And yet the CCP has a response for this as well, one that also relies on propaganda and that, thanks to the rapid modernization of the PLA in recent years, has managed to convince many observers abroad that resisting the "inevitable" is futile and in fact irresponsible: the threat of war.

Bibliography

Berenson, B (1952) *Rumour and Reflection: 1941:1944*, London: 116

Berlin, I (2013) "Historical Inevitability," in *Liberty*, Henry, H, ed, Oxford: Oxford University Press: 98–100

Brown, A (2010) *The Rise and Fall of Communism*, New York: Random House: 606

Creemers, R (2014) "Why Marx Still Matters: The Ideological Drivers of Chinese Politics," *China File*, 16 December, http://www.chinafile.com/reporting-opinion/viewpoint/why-marx-still-matters-ideological-drivers-chinese-politics

Huang, C (2013) "Xi Jinping Goes Back to the Future to Strengthen Party Control," *South China Morning Post*, 6 September, http://www.scmp.com/news/china/article/1310566/xi-jinping-goes-back-future-strengthen-party-control

Lam, W-L (2015) *Chinese Politics in the Era of Xi Jinping: Renaissance, Reform, or Retrogression?* New York: Routledge: 75–6

164 Convergence or conflict?

Service, R (2007) *Comrades! A History of World Communism*, Cambridge: Harvard University Press: 445
State Council Information Office of the People's Republic of China (2015) China's Military Strategy, Beijing, 26 May, http://www.china.org.cn/china/2015–05/26/content_35661433.htm
Stokes, M and Hsiao, R (2013) *The People's Liberation Army General Political Department*, Arlington: Project 2049 Institute: 6
Xinhua News Agency (2015) "中共中央關於加強和改進黨的群團工作的意見," http://news.xinhuanet.com/politics/2015–07/09/c_1115875561.htm

12

IS WAR THE ONLY OPTION?

China watchers worldwide have made a great deal of the PLA's modernization efforts over the past decade and a half, a development that coincided with the rise of China as one of the major global economic powers and, consequently, greater assertiveness on Beijing's part. As the beneficiary of years of double-digit growth in annual defense expenditure, the PLA embarked on a program to transform itself into a modern military capable of meeting various contingencies, including multiple scenarios involving Taiwan. All services modernized their equipment through the acquisition of advanced weapons from abroad (the main sources being Russia and Ukraine) and a rapidly expanding military-industrial complex at home.

As a result of all this transformation, the military balance of power in the Taiwan Strait gradually shifted in China's favor, a gap that was exacerbated by Taipei's inability to increase defense spending beyond 2.2 percent of its GDP and a seemingly growing reluctance on Washington's part, which at the time was endeavoring to develop a constructive relationship with the PRC, to sell them advanced weapons.

With modernization came greater responsibilities, and increasingly the PLA – especially its Navy (PLAN, 中國人民解放軍海軍) – began assuming additional roles, such as conducting patrols outside China's coastal areas and holding exercises in the West Pacific. Little by little, the PLAN was transforming from a green-water navy into a blue-water one, capable of operating well beyond China's shores. Although the PLAN was to play a greater role in the defense of the PRC's territorial claims in the East and South China Seas, modernization and transformation remained largely geared toward a role in a Taiwan scenario and preventing outside forces from intervening in the Taiwan Strait. The same dictate applies to the other PLA services – its Air Force (PLAAF, 中國人民解放軍空軍) and Army (中國人民解放軍) – as well as the Second Artillery Corps (第二炮兵部隊), which is in charge of China's missile arsenal and nuclear deterrent. The Second Artillery in particular, which by 2015 was aiming an estimated 1,500 short- and medium-range ballistic missiles at Taiwan, continued to figure in Beijing's military plans against the island, though in recent years its medium-range ballistic missile (MRBM) deployment has also begun to target other countries within the region.

China's growing territorial disputes with its neighbors, primarily over the Senkaku/Diaoyutai Islands in the East China Sea and nearly the entirety of the South China Sea, provided a rationale for forced modernization, as did the growing requirement for Beijing to develop the capabilities necessary to ensure its maritime domain and sea cargo routes, which were essential to secure its access to energy. Still, much of that transformation occurred with Taiwan in mind, and many of the new assets acquired by the various branches of the PLA would play a role in a Taiwan contingency.

What is also interesting is the fact that, despite the election of Ma Ying-jeou in 2008 and his policy of rapprochement with China, the PLA continued to prepare for war against Taiwan and to build up the arsenal it would need to take action if called upon to do so. As relations improved between the two sides, even the Second Artillery refused calls to dismantle its missile bases directly facing Taiwan as a precondition for peace talks or even as a gesture of "goodwill" toward Taipei. Thus, despite the détente, Beijing once again proved that its approach to Taiwan remained multifaceted, with all the fronts at its disposal engaged in efforts to bring about reunification. Consequently, as negotiators from the Straits Exchange Foundation (SEF) and the Association for Relations Across the Taiwan Straits (ARATS) met and as cross-strait agreement after agreement was signed, cyber attacks increased, espionage operations intensified, political warfare and propaganda campaigns were fully mobilized, and the PLA continued to hold drills simulating an invasion of Taiwan. The olive branch was extended, but immediately behind it the sword was drawn.

Despite the indisputable qualitative improvements that came with modernization, the PLA remains a fledging force that has not seen actual combat since 1979, when China launched an ill-fated invasion of Vietnam. Questions remain about how effective communication and decision making would be when split-second decisions need to be made during combat situations, as well as about the ability of Chinese generals to orchestrate highly complex joint operations. Additionally, the untested PLA remains very much a Frankenstein monster, comprised of systems of systems acquired abroad, reverse-engineered, or produced domestically. As Cheung concludes in his study of the Chinese defense industry, "The uneven state of development of the defense industry is likely to continue for the foreseeable future, with pockets of excellence existing in a broader landscape of technological mediocrity."

Therefore, as Bush and O'Hanlon observed a few years ago, "The Chinese military's aspirations to conduct 'local wars under high-technology conditions' remain aspirations more than realities."

Meanwhile, "formidable" new A2/AD weapons, such as the DF-21D (東風-21D), presumably pose a threat to U.S. carrier battle groups that would play a critical role in defending Taiwan, but the missile remains unproven, and as far as we know it has never been tested against a moving target at sea.

The PLA seems formidable, but, without transparency, we simply cannot know. And given the strict media controls over reporting on the Chinese military and the denial of access to foreign journalists, we rarely, if ever, hear about the accidents, failures, and blunders that often are the focus of media in open societies, a phenomenon that also contributes to defeatism on the Taiwanese side, whose media feast on the mishaps of the Taiwanese military.[1]

Therefore, leaps of modernization notwithstanding, the PLA does not know – could not know – how well it would perform in actual combat against its opponents, some of whom, like Japan and Taiwan, have enjoyed decades of assistance from and have jointly trained with the battle-hardened U.S. military. Aware of its shortcomings, Beijing has had to bluster to give its opponents the impression that it is larger and more powerful than it actually is. In other words, it has engaged in propaganda. All the attention that was paid to PLA modernization (and to the commissioning of the *Liaoning*, its first aircraft carrier) in journal articles by doomsayers in Washington and Tokyo, as well as at the many conferences that were organized on the Chinese military, helped with this campaign.

The trick was to inflate the strength of the PLA so that China's smaller opponents would not dare challenge it as it flexed its muscles within the region. In other words, to win without a fight, a military strategy that, though often associated with Sun Tzu (孫子), has in fact been espoused by warriors (and the animal kingdom) since the beginning of time. And nowhere was the propaganda campaign in fuller swing than against Taiwan, one of China's core interests.

As with propaganda aimed at political and intellectual targets in Taiwan and elsewhere, Beijing's military propaganda campaign operated under the "law" of "inevitability." Once again, resistance was futile, as the PLA had become too powerful to defend against. The campaign sought to discredit the Taiwanese military as a fighting force, portraying it as decadent, corrupt, unwilling to fight, and forced to defend the nation with equipment that was comparatively older than the PLA's. According to this view, Taiwan would fall within days, before the U.S. could even intervene – *if* it intervened, as the U.S.'s willingness to do so has also been a principal target of Chinese political warfare.

As icing on the cake, political warfare officers invited retired generals from the Taiwanese military to play rounds of golf in China or participate in cross-strait forums. Some of the participants, such as Air Force General Hsia Ying-chou (夏瀛洲), had their remarks quoted out of context by state-run PRC media, which served to further undermine morale in the active force and confidence within the Taiwanese population. Chinese propagandists also managed to convince quite a few defense experts that the Taiwanese can easily be "bought" or that the PLA knows the personal phone numbers of every fighter pilot in Taiwan – views that were then uncritically reproduced in articles in influential trade magazines and academic articles.

Meanwhile, Beijing emphasized its own capabilities and encouraged the view that the acquisition of new platforms by the Taiwanese military, such as F-16C/D combat aircraft, was pointless, as the Second Artillery Corps could quickly destroy them before they take off. A similar approach was taken to discredit Taiwan's early warning and air defense systems and put the survivability of its command centers and port facilities in grave doubt. Aggressive intelligence collection operations also played the twin roles of gathering classified information about Taiwan's air defense systems and communication channels with the U.S. while undermining confidence in Taiwan's ability to keep secrets when spy rings were exposed.

The latter puts Taiwan in a lose-lose situation because, when they are made public, successful counterespionage operations *still* reinforce the consensus that the Taiwanese defense establishment is completely penetrated by Chinese intelligence and therefore untrustworthy. Operations do not even have to be successful (i.e., to go undetected) for Beijing to reap the benefits in terms of making Taiwan's allies more reticent to sell it advanced weapons systems or to share sensitive information with it.

Although there is no doubt that the Taiwanese military faces extraordinary challenges [we could ask Hung Chung-chiu (洪仲丘) if he were still alive], the situation is not as dire as it seems. In fact, recent PLA war planning manuals indicate that there is substantial skepticism within the Chinese military about the PLA's ability to conduct successful operations against Taiwan – especially the kind of amphibious assault that would be necessary to seize control of the island.

For all its vaunted capabilities, the Second Artillery Corps has never conducted simultaneous test firings on the scale that would be necessary to wipe out all of Taiwan's air defense systems, airstrips, ports, C4ISR (command, control, communications, computers, intelligence, surveillance, and reconnaissance) architecture, counterforce capabilities, as well as government offices, in a single strike. Nor, for that matter, does it have enough launchers to do so, a common mistake among alarmists who tend to confuse the number of *warheads* with the number of *launchers*.

While outgunned, the Taiwanese military nevertheless packs a substantial deterrent against an invading army. It is unlikely that there is still a single member of the Taiwanese military who believes that Taiwan can confront China *symmetrically* on a boat-against-boat, plane-against-plane basis. The time when Taiwan could do so has long passed, and Taipei's defense doctrine and war preparations have adapted accordingly. The key to Taiwan's defense against the PLA lies on two pillars: (1) taking the "limited option" (coercion) off the table and (2) deterrence.

With strong encouragement by the U.S. military, Taiwan has been hardening its military facilities and has invested in redundancy and repair kits to increase survivability and the ability of those facilities to continue operating after an initial attack. Such efforts have been complemented by the acquisition of PAC-2 and PAC-3 ground-based and SM1 and SM2 ship-borne air defense systems from the U.S., as well as the indigenous development of the Tien Kung (天弓) I, II, and III surface-to-air missiles by the National Chung-Shan Institute of Science and Technology (NCSIST, 國家中山科學研究院). Consequently, we can state with a certain level of certainty that the "limited strike" option is probably no longer a viable one for the PLA or that its chances of success should not be taken for granted.

By denying China the ability to resort to limited military options to influence policy decisions, Taipei is forcing Beijing to consider other, more escalatory options that are of much greater complexity and are likelier to result in a backlash by the international community. This includes a military embargo against Taiwan, which would inevitably affect global trade and the ability of cargo vessels headed for other countries to transit strategic sea passages, as well as an invasion of Taiwan, which would very probably turn the international community against China and prompt an intervention by both the U.S. and, as is increasingly likely, Japan.

Moreover, despite all the doom and gloom in recent years about Taiwan's ability to ward off an attack by China, we should note that amphibious assaults are among the most difficult of all military operations, irrespective of how modern and capable is the force making the attempt. Taiwan's beaches are particularly inhospitable for attempted landings, and the meteorological conditions in the Taiwan Strait, characterized by high winds and seas and a preponderance of typhoons, are often bad and would affect the operations of the flat-bottomed craft normally used to facilitate the offloading of troops and cargo. Regardless of how well the PLA planned it, such an assault would likely result in very severe losses for the PLAN in the transit. As B. Cole has stated, "the lack of suitable landing areas for beaching craft limits the conduct of a traditional amphibious assault." Although troops "may be ferried ashore via helicopter or air-dropped from fixed-wing transports," B. Cole writes, "their heavy equipment must be carried in surface craft."

U.S. doctrine for amphibious assaults, B. Cole continues, is that "the assailant possess a 5:1 advantage in troops over the defender, a ratio difficult for the PLA to establish should Taiwan be forewarned."

All of this is not to say that China could not prevail in an amphibious assault (and indeed geography also undermines Taiwan's ability to defend itself against such an attack) but rather that projections of a "quick" and "clean" win by the PLA overstate Chinese capabilities and tend to ignore the many variables that would make such an operation both highly complex and potentially very costly, factors that the Chinese leadership (assuming that it calculates risks and benefits "rationally") is well aware of. We should also add that while the capabilities gap has widened in China's favor, Taiwanese force development and war preparedness have not been static.

The context in which such offensive operations would be launched, furthermore, would be one of already high apprehensions about China's rise, which, unlike what Beijing had promised, has been anything but "peaceful" in recent years. As such, a PLA invasion of Taiwan in 2015 would conceivably spark a different response by the international community than it would have a mere five years ago, when global leaders were still giving Beijing the benefit of the doubt.

Without doubt, Beijing's recent adventurism in the East and South China Seas has benefited Taiwan and encouraged countries like Japan and the U.S. to reassess their military relationship with Taipei, which until very recently had been in decline. As an example of this, in May 2015 the U.S. House and Senate Armed Services Committees both passed initiatives in calling for increased bilateral military exchanges, such as inviting Taiwan to participate in the Rim of the Pacific Exercise (RIMPAC) and Red Flag exercises.

Taiwan's deterrence is contingent on both its ability to inflict "unacceptable" pain on an invading force and that country's economic interests, international reputation, and stability *and* on the likelihood that allies would assist it in its hour of need. Thus, although deterrence undeniably has a strong military component – from the ability to destroy forces crossing the Taiwan Strait to attacking naval bases, airstrips, and radar sites in China – it also involves many other types of operations, from cyber attacks in order to disrupt the telecommunication and banking sectors across the PRC to a propaganda campaign to turn world opinion against Beijing. Developing closer relations with regional allies, who as we just saw may now be more amenable to exploring cooperation with Taiwan, is also another way for Taipei to increase its deterrence.

Ultimately, the key to successful deterrence is to convince the enemy that invasion would be too costly – in human, material and financial terms, as well as in the ramifications for China's international reputation. In other words, victory for Taiwan lies in war avoidance, in making sure that Beijing does not calculate that a major war could be won quickly and cheaply.

While a strong deterrent diminishes the likelihood that Beijing will decide to launch an attack against Taiwan, it also undermines China's propaganda efforts by exposing its bluff. More than anything, this is what the CCP does not want to see, as its principal strategy for Taiwan revolves on the idea that, faced with the forces of historical inevitability, Taipei will capitulate and agree to unification on terms dictated by Beijing. If, however, Taiwan does not believe that the PLA has the capabilities to launch a successful invasion, and if it concludes that Beijing, aware of the PLA's limitations, is unwilling to take its chances with a project that risks leading to catastrophe, then all that propaganda will fall on deaf ears, and the threat of war will lose some of its effect on the political calculations of the Taiwanese, support for independence, and so on. That is not to say that the people of Taiwan would suddenly stop taking the Chinese military threat seriously but rather that the myth of invincibility would be bust, which in turn would have a major impact on morale and the willingness of the Taiwanese to fight.

If Chinese reactions to these claims are any reaction, Beijing takes very seriously the possibility that Taiwan and its allies could see through the lies and not be deterred by the PLA's alleged invincibility. Days after one of my articles was published in *The National Interest* on the need to strengthen Taiwan's deterrent, Wang Hongguang (王洪光), a retired PLA lieutenant general and former commander of the Nanjing Military Region (since January 2016 part of the East Military Region), responded with a long-winded and vitriolic article in the Chinese-language edition of the CCP-run *Global Times* (環球), in which he accused me of being "mentally retarded" and of "low I.Q." Having thus established my credentials, Wang proceeded to explain how the PLA could annihilate Taiwan if it wanted – in other words, resistance was futile, and anyone who disagreed with the objective "law" needs to have his head checked.

Or, as some military analysts told me after the incident, I had touched a raw nerve within the PLA by calling its bluff.

Responding to the occasional recommendations by experts that Taiwan should be ceded to China because the latter has become "too powerful" and "too important," Taiwan's allies have often responded by comparing Beijing to Nazi Germany before World War II. Using that historical example, the critics warn that appeasement is not the proper way to respond to China's claims regarding Taiwan and that giving in to its demands would only encourage future expansionism. While the merits of that argument will be discussed in a later chapter, the Nazi analogy is definitely wrong on one aspect: As the historian David Faber observes in *Munich, 1938: Appeasement and World War II*, Adolf Hitler felt that the agreement that was reached with British Prime Minister Neville Chamberlain, which ceded parts of Czechoslovakia to Germany, had cheated him out of the delights of armed conquest. "That fellow Chamberlain has spoiled my entry into Prague," Hitler complained after the pact was signed. In other words, Hitler wanted his formidable military to crush his opponents, and knew he had the means to do so.

The difference with China is that Beijing has no such confidence and that it would rejoice in appeasement working in its favor and for Taiwan to be abandoned and ceded to China without a fight (the economic situation of the two countries is also markedly different and serves as a disincentive for recourse to force on Beijing's part). That, after all, is at the very core of its entire propaganda effort.

So is war in the Taiwan Strait, as the title of this chapter asks, the only option, especially if, as the rest of this book has argued, the relationship is moving in the direction of greater tensions? The answer is clearly no. China is unwilling to take the risk and will not have the capabilities it needs to ensure victory for several years to come. The changing geopolitical context that has resulted from the slow realization that China might not be the "responsible stakeholder" that the world had hoped for also creates opportunities for Taiwan that, if seized upon, could bolster its war avoidance strategy and make war even less likely.

One scenario that is rather perplexing is the "Crimea" precedent, in which major instability in Taiwan (say, following fraudulent elections) would compel Beijing to send in the PLA on a "humanitarian" mission to protect "Chinese compatriots," much as the Russian military did when it dispatched forces to the Crimean enclave and later to Ukraine's Donbas region in order to ensure the safety of ethnic Russians against the predations of Ukrainian ultranationalists (substitute those with proindependence ultranationalists in Taiwan). In such a context, Beijing's ability to convince the international community that it is acting out of altruistic and humanitarian considerations would be contingent on the effectiveness of its propaganda apparatus and the level of global ignorance about the state of politics *in* Taiwan. While perhaps far-fetched, such a tactic has a precedent, one that, moreover, was created by an ally of Beijing and over "near-abroad" territory that is of strategic "buffer" value against perceived external threats: NATO enlargement in Russia's case, the increased presence of the U.S. and Japan in China's case.

And the "buffer," of course, has all the airs of a traditional landgrab, which, to be legitimized, compels Beijing to weave its long historical narrative about the "Chinese dream" and the inevitability of reunification. As Wachman argues, "The geostrategic perspective about Taiwan makes it seem that the PRC's ambitions for security and prosperity – goals that dovetail with a hunger for national rejuvenation and prestige – hinge on unifying the state. Taiwan is presented as the key." Or as Friedberg writes, "If it is to establish itself in a position of unquestioned predominance in East Asia, China must find a way to bring Taiwan back, and push America out, while keeping Japan down."

Other scenarios, in which the CCP, facing instability at home, would embark on military adventures to "distract" the population and redirect public anger at an external enemy, are also possible and have been used throughout history. However, given that victory is the surest way to recapture public support and boost nationalistic pride, it is unlikely that Beijing would choose Taiwan as the object of such adventurism. For the reasons that we have seen, an invasion of Taiwan presents no certainty of success and would impose high costs. Instead, weaker opponents, such as the Philippines and Vietnam, would be better candidates for distractions, and China's territorial disputes with them provide the necessary context.

As China continues to modernize its forces and hopes for Taiwan's eventual ("inevitable") capitulation, what remains to be seen is whether the emergence of a new type of nationalism in Taiwan, one that is defined by an increasingly shared identity that transcends ethnicity and politics, will have an impact on the ability of the military here to attract young men and women to serve in the force. Although much work needs to be done to make service in the military an appealing career choice – increasing wages and addressing morale, image, and career advancement issues – we can nevertheless expect that rising nationalism would result in more young Taiwanese displaying a willingness to serve their country by joining the military.

As the China threat becomes more concrete to many potential recruits who are too young to remember the last time that China flexed its military muscles against Taiwan (during the 1995–1996 Missile Crisis), enlistment could increase. In other words, unlike, say, Israel, young Taiwanese have no first-hand experience of what it feels like to be attacked by the enemy; for most of them, the China threat has been an abstract and theoretical one, a view that probably has undermined the military's effort to attract volunteers.

If the results of a 2015 survey by Academia Sinica are any indication, such an attitudinal change may already be occurring. According to the survey, which was conducted by the Institute of Sociology in January and February of that year, between 50 and 60 percent of respondents said that they supported maintaining conscription to enhance Taiwan's military strength. Among those aged 30–39, support was at 70 percent. Fear of China's growing military strength and apprehensions over perceived weaknesses in Taiwan's military preparedness were ostensibly behind the unexpectedly high support for retaining some form of conscription, after years of being told by the Ma administration that compulsory service should be phased out in line with public expectations.

Thanks to a rising nationalism, after years of failing to meet its recruitment goals for transition to an all-volunteer force (it would eventually meet its goals after those were halved), the Taiwanese military could find itself in a more favorable environment, with young men and women displaying renewed commitment to defending their country, perhaps in the spirit of those who took risks by defying the authorities over the CSSTA and other controversies. However, for this to be successful, the military establishment will, like political parties, have to transform itself so as to better reflect the values and identity of those who will fill its ranks. As with politics and general trends in society, the military's traditional ties to "Mainlanders" and consequent attachment to China will diminish as older soldiers retire and are replaced by men and women whose attachment is to Taiwan. As new soldiers who were born in the late 1980s and 1990s join the military, their sense of duty and their understanding of what needs to be defended will inevitably be influenced by their experiences as citizens who have known nothing but life in a liberal democracy.

The military will have to reflect those values and should give serious consideration to dispensing with old traditions and the celebration of a ROC military that has little, if any, appeal among young people born in Taiwan. Celebrations over the Nationalists' victory against the Japanese in World War II are hardly the best way to recruit young soldiers, especially when the celebrations run in parallel with those that are being held across China in 2015 to mark the PLA's victory (revisionism alert!) against the Japanese aggressor. That is not to say that such events should not be marked or that the sacrifices of the Nationalist soldiers should not be recognized. But as a recruitment tool, this is very bad policy. Most young Taiwanese could not care less, as those distant events occurred in what, to them, is a foreign country. For their parents, that same military is a reminder of its role as a tool of repression after Chiang fled China and relocated on Taiwan.

Similarly, future administrations should reconsider the emphasis that President Ma has placed on Taiwan's claims to nearly the entirety of the South China Sea. Those territorial claims are a legacy of the ROC constitution of 1947 and therefore of little relevance to the contemporary needs and expectations of the Taiwanese. Although we can assume that Taiwanese would generally be willing to risk their lives defending the nation and its way of life, it is difficult to imagine that anyone would be willing to do so over Taiping Island (太平島), an islet that, due to its distance, is probably indefensible anyway, let alone smaller features in the Spratlys (南沙群島). No amount of hardship and combat duty bonuses warrants taking soldiers away from their principal mandate, which is to defend Taiwan against external aggression.

The military must therefore repair and modernize its image and views as a fighting force for *Taiwan*. Traditional media and the public at large can also play a role in this by ceasing to constantly ridicule the armed forces and showing more respect for the men and women who, every day, put their lives on the line for the nation.

Note

1 Revealingly, the only aspect of the PLA that does get negative coverage in state-controlled Chinese media is corruption in the military, as this is part of President Xi's "campaign against corruption" cum war against his opponents within the system.

Bibliography

Bush, R and O'Hanlon, M (2007) *A War Like No Other: The Truth About China's Challenge to America*, Hoboken: John Wiley & Sons: 104

Cheung, T-M (2014) *Forging China's Military Might: A New Framework for Assessing Innovation*, Baltimore: Johns Hopkins University Press: 274

Cole, B (2007) "The Military Instrument of Statecraft at Sea: Naval Operations in an Escalatory Scenario Involving Taiwan: 2007–2016," in *Assessing the Threat: The Chinese Military and Taiwan's Security*, Swaine, M, Yang, N-D, Medeiros, E and Skylar Mastro, O, eds, Washington: Carnegie Endowment for International Peace: 187–8

Cole, M (2015) "Taiwan's Master Plan to Defeat China in a War," *The National Interest*, 31 March, http://nationalinterest.org/feature/taiwans-master-plan-defeat-china-war-12510

Faber, D (2008) *Munich, 1938: Appeasement and World War II*, New York: Simon & Schuster: 428

Friedberg, A (2011) *A Contest for Supremacy: China, America, and the Struggle for Mastery in Asia*, New York: W.W. Norton: 174

Hong, Z-C (2015) "蕭美琴提驚人調查 恢復徵兵民支持度高," *Lienhe bao*, 20 April, http://udn.com/news/story/1/848260-蕭美琴提驚人調查-恢復徵兵民支持度高

Wachman, A (2007) *Why Taiwan? Geostrategic Rationales for China's Territorial Integrity*, Stanford: Stanford University Press: 152

Wang, H-G (2015) "南京战区原副司令员：台独若挑起战争，大陆该如何用武力统一」王洪光，環球," *Huanqiu*, 10 April, http://mil.huanqiu.com/observation/2015-04/6141845.html

13

THE 2016 ELECTIONS

A return to uncertainty?

So far, everything that we have seen indicates that a more Taiwan-centric identity, with liberal-democratic values at its core, has been consolidating across Taiwan and taking society as a whole toward a multiethnic and cultural middle ground. The inclusive nature of this emerging Taiwanese nationalism, as demonstrated by the composition of the Sunflower Movement, also stems from a deepening fatigue with the traditional and highly divisive politics in Taiwan, which has forced the main political parties to modernize their stance. The new dynamics have whittled away the more politically extreme outliers (deep green and deep blue) and have given rise to a general consensus about what Taiwan *is* that has often transcended political hues.

As the results of the 29 November 2014 nine-in-one elections made perfectly clear, those who, in the wake of the wave of activism that had hit the nation by storm in the previous year, failed to meet public expectations were assured of disaster at the polls. Society had already sent a warning by taking direct action. If that warning was not heeded, voters were more than willing to use the instrument of retributive democracy to punish laggards or politicians who refused to modernize their views. And in those elections, the KMT clearly was lagging behind public expectations.

The disastrous showing by the KMT on that day led to hopes that the party, in which fissures over the Sunflower occupation and the CSSTA had already begun to turn into cracks, would mend its ways so as to better reflect public wishes and the new reality in Taiwan. President Ma's ouster as KMT chairman, his replacement by Eric Chu, and Chu's ostensible early efforts to rid the party of the conservative voices that had weighed down the party in the November elections all seemed to indicate that the KMT was on the road to reform – reform by electoral necessity, perhaps, with the January 2016 presidential and legislative elections approaching.

For all intents and purposes, Ma had been neutralized, and since he could not run for a third consecutive term in 2016, it was assumed that the party would select a candidate that tended more toward the political center – in other words, a candidate who would perhaps be a little more "careful" than President Ma had been on engaging China and who was less associated with the "Mainlander" faction within the party.

If the KMT, after eight years of lackluster performance and dragged down by low public support, did not field a candidate who reflected this new civic nationalism, then there were very good chances that the DPP would make a comeback – in fact, as the elections approached, it now seemed possible that the DPP would, for the first time in its history, obtain a majority of seats in the legislature. After a somewhat disappointing run for the presidency in 2012, DPP candidate Tsai Ing-wen was back and had done relatively well in gauging public sentiment. As we have seen, she brought several young men and women (a good number of them from social movements) into the party and showed her willingness to work strategically with the "third force," as well as independent candidates in the 2016 legislative elections. Although more conservative members of her party took offense at such flexibility, Tsai's decision not to field a DPP candidate in Taipei in the November 2014 election and to tacitly support Ko Wen-je, who was running as an independent, paid dividends: The KMT lost the capital, and in Ko the DPP had found an ally.

On cross-strait relations, Tsai has also adopted a more centrist position by vowing to maintain the status quo under the existing ROC constitutional order and to seek continuity in the relationship with Beijing. By neutralizing the issue of the "independence clause" in the party charter and instead using the 8 May 1999 Resolution on Taiwan's Future, which states that the ROC/Taiwan is already an independent state, Tsai was signaling that she did not intend to make the Taiwan issue (and by rebound China) a major issue in her campaign. In fact, reflecting the public sentiment, she wanted to focus on the economy, food safety, the social safety net, and so on – in other words, on nation-building. On China, therefore, Tsai's position looked strangely like that of her predecessor, who throughout his presidency made the status quo a principal pillar of his China policy. Where Tsai and Ma differed, however, was in their positions on the so-called 1992 consensus, whose one China clause remains unpalatable to her DPP constituents. Still, on that issue, Tsai chose to focus on substance by promising the continuation of constructive relations with China and stating that a meeting between negotiators from the two sides did occur in 1992, adding that this was a "historical fact."

For her critics within her own camp, Tsai was not green enough and sounded too much like President Ma, which, though unfair, nevertheless indicated that the DPP candidate had moved toward the center politically – not necessarily a bad move if the DPP is to attract swing and light blue voters. Tsai's detractors, alarmed by her ostensible deemphasizing of the quest for *de jure* Taiwanese independence, warned of the "KMT-ization" of the DPP, which in the first half of 2015 compelled old-guard members like Peng Min-ming (彭明敏) and "deep greens" within society.

Tsai's critics overseas, in such organizations as the World United Formosans for Independence (WUFI, 臺灣獨立建國聯盟), also deplored her reluctance to take the lead on some controversies such as the protests in 2015 over the "minor" revisions to high school textbook guidelines initiated by the Ma administration and to act more like the DPP "used to do." What those critics ostensibly failed to understand, however, was that as the largest opposition party in the country at the time, the DPP had become *institutionalized* and could not take to the streets as its founding members did in the 1970s and 1980s. Others, the new generation of social activists, now have that responsibility and did so, culminating in the occupation of the Ministry of Education in Taipei. To expect the DPP to play that role was both unfair and revealed a misunderstanding of how democracy works.

Despite the grumbling in the more conservative wing of her party, by late 2015 Tsai was at the apex of her power. The expectation abroad was that in 2016 Taiwan would have its first female president and that after eight years of absence, the DPP would be back in charge. If the KMT was to have any chance of turning things around and beating Tsai, it would have to field a formidable candidate, someone who had the ability to harness the forces that had been unleashed by a more inclusive society that was increasingly assured of and vocal about its Taiwanese identity.

Instead, and perhaps by accident since no party heavyweight seemed interested in running, the KMT default candidate was Hung Hsiu-chu, whose policies on China, as they are understood, seemed to go against all the trend lines within society. With her candidacy, which was made official on 19 July, it seemed that the KMT not only had failed to learn its lessons from the November 2014 disaster but that it had regressed by 30 years – so much so that critics began referring to the "New Party-ization" of the KMT, the New Party being prounification and entirely out of sync with the wishes of the majority of Taiwanese. As it became clear that Hung, ostensibly Beijing's favorite, would be the KMT candidate in the 2016 presidential election, a number of KMT legislators from both the "Mainlander" and "Taiwanese" factions threatened to quit the party and join James Soong's People First Party (PFP, 親民黨), announcing they would run against the KMT candidates in the legislative elections and thus threaten to split the blue vote. Several other KMT members, especially those in the southern parts of the country, were waiting to see what would happen to the party and made it clear that they would resign if Hung, who according to them was "destroying" the party, was not reined in or removed altogether.

By that point, it was very telling that even party elders at the KMT were trying to convince Hung to tone down her rhetoric, an intervention that became necessary after she stated her espousal of a "one China, same interpretation" (一中同表) policy that not only contradicted the official KMT position of "one country, different interpretations" (一國兩憲) but seemed to echo the official *CCP* position on the matter. Her announcement that if elected she would sign a "peace agreement" with China and possibly end arms procurement from the U.S. alarmed many people within the KMT, while her flip-flopping on whether the ROC existed – Hung initially said that recognizing the ROC would create two

Chinas, which was "unacceptable" – raised eyebrows in many circles. After being pressured by party members, Hung eventually drifted back to the KMT's favored one China, two interpretations and 1992-consensus formulas, while continuing to adhere to her "one consensus, three connotations" (一個共識，三個內涵). Still, the candidate had revealed her ideology, and it was difficult to imagine that the apparent softening of her stance wasn't anything more than a tactical move ahead of major elections.

Although Taiwan's pluralistic political system ensures that people can legally express their preferences on all subjects, including on the kind of relationship that Taiwan should have with China, there were some fundamental problems with Hung's candidacy. The most blatant one, of course, was that hers were the views of a potential future president of Taiwan, whose policies should therefore aim to resonate with the majority rather than with a very small minority. The fact that her beliefs seemed to be diametrically opposed to the consensus that has been built across Taiwan and that they dovetailed so perfectly with the position of the authoritarian regime on the other side of the Taiwan Strait was problematic.

Strangest of all was the fact that the KMT, which over the decades has itself indigenized and understands the need to win elections by seizing the common ground, allowed Hung to become its candidate. This self-defeating outcome highlights the institutional problems that continue to prevent the KMT from truly reforming and that could very well lead to a second split of the party after the one that occurred during the Lee Teng-hui presidency in the 1990s.

While some observers were excitedly forecasting that Hung's emergence was a sign of the KMT's imminent collapse, such an outcome would ultimately not be beneficial to Taiwan, which instead should hope for a further deepening of Taiwanese consciousness within the party. One danger is that if all the "moderate" members abandoned ship, the KMT would once again be under the control of an old guard that is willing to cooperate with the CCP. Unless the bleeding out of its members leads to its actual collapse, Taiwan could end up with an ultra conservative and revisionist party that still controls vast assets that can be utilized to ensure its survival by undermining Taiwan's democratic institutions.

It is still difficult to understand what actually happened within the KMT and why influential Taiwanese figures like Wang Jyn-ping failed to stand up against Hung. Some political observers dismissed the whole matter as fecklessness on the part of the "Taiwanese" wing of the KMT. In mid-July 2015, five KMT members who had been openly critical of Hung's policies were expelled from the party,[1] a development that seemed to signal that the hard-liners had succeeded in seizing the reins even though Hung's chances of prevailing in the 2016 elections were slim. Whatever the cause of the crisis within the KMT, such dysfunctionality was nothing to celebrate over, especially if this opened another door for the CCP to exert its influence in Taiwan.

One such possibility was that Hung was intended to serve as an instrument of *incrementalism*: By adopting "extreme" positions that made the standard KMT line seem like the "new normal," the DPP would conceivably be compelled to move closer to, if not take ownership of, that new baseline, which while still unsatisfactory to Beijing, would nevertheless be closer to its goal than at a time when the DPP ardently advocated for *de jure* independence. Such a move would therefore take the mainstream DPP further away from its original ideology: in other words, it would be "KMT-ized."

It is difficult to know whether Hung's role was to force such a change within the DPP (after all, she did state that the aim of her running was to "reset" the KMT, which in her view had stalled in its efforts to deepen the relationship with China). Given the oddity of her candidacy, those are possibilities that are worth keeping in mind.

As we now know, a Hung presidential candidacy became so poisonous that KMT central felt compelled to intervene. With dismal poll numbers and the high likelihood that her unpopularity would damage the KMT's performance in the legislative elections, party heavyweights orchestrated an eleventh-hour replacement of Hung in October and replaced her with Chairman Eric Chu. Unsurprisingly, the unusual move attracted criticism from Hung's supporters, including Chang An-le and his prounification supporters, who protested outside KMT headquarters. In a sign of how deeply ingrained the values that make Taiwan have become, many of the protesters I interviewed during the 7 October rally deplored the "undemocratic" attempt to remove Hung, whom they regarded as the best candidate to protect their country – the Republic of China – against undemocratic China. Most Hung supporters present at the protest were also dismissive of Chang An-le and his followers and stayed away from them (Chang eventually rallied behind Chu and was present at the official opening of Chu's campaign office).

Despite the unorthodox manner in which the party dealt with the matter, the decision to remove Hung was probably the right thing to do, as the party wanted to avoid self-destruction. By then it was already clear that the presidency would be out of reach, but by replacing Hung there was still a possibility to stop the exodus of supporters that threatened disaster in the legislative elections. Despite his more moderate image, presidential candidate Chu's intervention was too little, too late. His numbers in the polls were initially only marginally better than Hung's and eventually dropped to even lower levels after a controversy over the "flipping" of military housing involving his vice presidential candidate Jennifer Wang (王如玄) turned to catastrophe. This time, rather than alienate southern supporters, it was old "Mainlander" veterans, traditionally safe ground for the pan-blue camp, who were disgruntled and threatened to walk away.

As expected, the road to 16 January was a tortuous one, in which character assassination and the necessary defenses often were substitutes for debate on actual policies and how those policies could contribute to the betterment of society. As discussed earlier, Taiwan's traditional media were partly responsible for this, if only for giving air time to talking heads such as then-KMT legislator Alex Tsai (蔡正元) and former legislator Chiu Yi (邱毅), who in November started making a series of allegations against the DPP candidate. The slander tactics used by the KMT opinion makers and spokespersons had little traction with the public, and in fact may have further eroded the party's appeal, as had occurred in Taipei in the lead-up to the November 2014 elections. Still, the cycle of attacks and counterattacks meant that very little time was spent discussing actual policies and subjects that mattered to Taiwan's future.

Although voters were more interested in hearing about domestic policies that will have a direct impact on their livelihood (the result, as we saw, of implicit nationhood), the China factor continued to loom large, with Beijing occasionally imposing itself on the debate, as did foreign governments and media who often regard Taiwan solely from the angle of its relations with China. The 7 November 2015 Ma-Xi meeting in Singapore, added to Chu's insisting that Tsai's China policy was "vague" and her status quo questionable, also ensured that China remained a hot topic for the elections.

Taiwanese turned a new page in their nation's history on 16 January by bringing the DPP back in power and, for the first time ever, awarding a majority of seats in the legislature. Under the prevailing conditions, by having adopted a more "centrist" position with the greatest appeal to the majority of Taiwanese, the DPP is best positioned to ensure social stability in Taiwan, though it too will likely face an activist civil society when it negotiates agreements, such as the TPP, that will inevitably threaten more vulnerable segments of society. But what about cross-strait relations? Based on the traditional understanding of cross-strait relations and on what the KMT and DPP critics want us to believe, Tsai's election should lead to the resumption of tensions between Taiwan and China. However, whether such tensions arise will be largely contingent on Beijing's reaction. Assuming that Tsai will commit to continuity and not take any actions that suggest a move toward *de jure* independence (and there is every reason to believe that she will respect that promise, despite the wishes of some deep greens), the only factor that could contribute to greater instability in the Taiwan Strait is Beijing. For example, in its latest defense white paper, China states that "the root cause of instability has not yet been removed, and the 'Taiwan independence' separatist forces and their activities are still the biggest threat to the peaceful development of cross-Straits relations." Whether it interprets the DPP victory in the elections as the work of "'Taiwan independence' separatist forces and activities" remains to be seen.

One option would be for China to "punish" the Taiwanese for making the "wrong" choice in the polls. Such a policy could take several shapes, from an economic embargo of Taiwan to the more coercive measures discussed in the previous chapter. Be that as it may, we need to be conscious of the fact that Beijing's rhetoric might not always be reflective of its official policy. Chinese officials probably know that an overly negative reaction to the outcome of the elections in Taiwan could backfire and further alienate the Taiwanese public. Slapping economic sanctions, freezing investment, or stopping the flow of Chinese tourists would be the surest way to ensure that Taiwan redoubles its efforts to diversify its economy and trade relationships, which would not serve Beijing's objectives. As the missile crisis in 1995–1996 demonstrated, direct Chinese coercion can backfire and instead of deterring the Taiwanese so that they make the decisions Beijing wants, it can convince them to dig in their heels, which in this case would imply the acceleration of Taiwanese nationalism and the redoubling of "anti-China" sentiments.

As such an outcome would threaten to quickly undo the years of rapprochement and growing interdependence that flourished under the Ma Ying-jeou administration, we cannot automatically assume that Beijing will take such risks and decide to punish Taiwan. There is a real possibility, therefore, that like Tsai, Beijing will initially seek continuity and stay the course on cross-strait dialogue, even though its ability to get what it wants through such traditional channels as the SEF-ARATS talks and MAC/TAO summits will be limited. In that regard, who President Tsai appoints to head those bodies will have a direct impact on the depth and quality of future cross-strait talks. On the other side, it is highly unlikely that President Tsai, who is committed to revitalizing Taiwan's struggling economy, would do anything that unduly alienates China, one of Taiwan's most important trade partners and the second-largest economy in the world. While China certainly was not the panacea that President Ma had promised, it nevertheless remains a crucial element of Taiwan's economic well-being and prosperity. Consequently, harming that relationship could prove damaging to Taiwan's economy and quickly turn into a nightmare for the DPP, which will have to perform well on the economic front if it wants to stay in office for more than a single four-year term.

Another possible strategy could be for the CCP and the KMT (plus the New Party and associated groups) to do everything in their power to discredit the DPP administration in order to engineer a return in force of the KMT in the 2018 municipal elections and the 2020 presidential elections. However, such efforts will be somewhat mitigated by the DPP's majority of seats in the legislature.

Beijing's third and most feasible option rests with unofficial actors. While official talks are expected to continue and, on the surface, relations between Taipei and Beijing will appear to be constructive, at the subterranean level, prounification forces will likely intensify their activities. As we saw in Chapter 5, substate actors, in cooperation with the GPD/LD and other prounification forces such as Chang An-le's party, will conceivably assume greater responsibilities and could be called upon to do their work to undermine Taiwan's institutions and democracy. This can be achieved through intimidation, violence, and money. China will also continue to use investments and allies in big business to weaken the institutions, such as the media, that form a firewall against authoritarianism. Given the years that prounification influences have had to establish their networks in Taiwan, the state apparatus is probably no longer in a position to monitor, let alone counter, all their activities. Elements from the deep blue and prounification civil society could also decide that they have "learned" the lessons from the Sunflower Movement and use civil disobedience to undermine the efforts of the DPP administration, which would contribute to social unrest.

As discussed earlier, the best prophylactic against those forces will be for Taiwan to further consolidate its democracy and for its constituents to work better together as part of a Taiwanese "united front."

The geopolitical context in which the DPP victory occurred will also have a substantial impact on Beijing's reaction. As we saw earlier, Washington and many of its allies in the Asia-Pacific have grown disillusioned with China, whose military buildup is at levels that are reminiscent of the Cold War. Beijing's bullying of its smaller neighbors, its militarization of the South China Sea, its unwillingness or inability to become the "responsible stakeholder" that the international community wanted, and the troubling developments within China that have marked a sharp shift toward a more restrictive and repressive form of authoritarianism have all contributed to shifting attitudes vis-à-vis engagement with China and the willingness to accommodate it.

Consequently, President Tsai will probably enjoy a more cordial relationship with her American counterparts than the more ideological President Chen did back in 2000 and even more so after the 11 September 2001 terrorist attacks and the launch of the U.S.'s wars in Afghanistan and Iraq. Even if the growing threat posed by ISIS or other crises in Europe or in the Middle East once again force Washington to shift its attention from Asia, it is unlikely that Tsai and her advisers will commit the same errors as those made by former president Chen and take actions that, as some critics have argued, "threaten to destabilize" the Taiwan Strait.

The outcome of the U.S. presidential elections in November 2016 will also have a direct impact on the levels of U.S. support for Taiwan, which in the current context will be largely predicated on the ideological stance of the new American administration vis-à-vis China. Although the Sinophobic rhetoric that will mark the election campaign will eventually be toned down after a new administration has settled in the White House, it is nevertheless possible that the future U.S. president will be less willing to give Beijing the benefit of the doubt that presidents Bush Jr. and Obama gave it. Consequently, the next U.S. administration will conceivably be more vocal in its support for Taiwan, which could lead to the extension of more robust security guarantees and more arms sales, among other things that would strengthen Taiwan's deterrent.

Note

1 Legislator Chi Kuo-tung (紀國棟), former legislator Chang Sho-wen (張碩文), former Taipei City Councilor Yang Shih-chiu (楊實秋), Central Committee member Lee Po-jung (李柏融), and Taipei City Councilor Lee Ching-yuan (李慶元). Chang had already resigned and joined the PFP.

PART 4
Why Taiwan matters

14

THE LAST FREE REFUGE

If we look at a regional map featuring all Chinese-speaking societies in Asia today, there is good reason to be discouraged.

After initial hopes of political reform in China, Beijing has successfully busted the myth that economic liberalization and the emergence of a middle class will eventually lead to the democratization of authoritarian states. Instead, the Chinese leadership embraced mercantilism to boost its national power, which it has accomplished with resounding success, but never for once considered abandoning one-party rule under the CCP. For all the hopes of reform, there never was the question of implementing *glasnost* and *perestroika* in China or of allowing the more liberal way of life that exists in HKSAR to influence developments in the Mainland.

Though undeniably richer and stronger, China's internal contradictions – a result of the immensity of its territory, the size of its heterogeneous population, and regional economic disparities – have nevertheless continued to intensify, prompting the CCP to increase its repression and to adopt new national security laws that have sounded alarm bells among China watchers and at the UN. Every aspect of Chinese society, from local activism to the Internet, the media to the education system, is now under stricter surveillance. Censorship has intensified, the party has increased its presence within businesses and organizations, and the CCP has reinforced an old Maoist ideology that many had believed had been buried by Deng Xiaoping.

Despite its impressive strength, China remains at the core highly uncertain of itself and the CCP fearful of what would happen (to the state and to itself) if it lost control. The intensely paranoid nature of the party, a trait that under President Xi appears to have reached levels unseen in decades, has also resulted in the strengthening of measures against perceived enemies both within China and those that presumably exist outside.

As a result of all this, China today is arguably a more repressive place than it was on the eve of the 2008 Beijing Olympics. In its *Freedom in the World 2015* report, the U.S.-based Freedom House described China as "not free." On a scale of 1 to 7 (1 representing the most free and 7 the least), China stood at 6.5, with 7 in political rights and six in civil liberties.

Meanwhile, the continued integration of HKSAR and the gradual mainlandization in its system so as to better align the former British colony with the CCP's preferred way of doing things has sparked a backlash among many residents of Hong Kong, who are realizing that the "one country, two systems" formula that was forced upon them is not living up to its promises. This reaction has in turn prompted Beijing to tighten its grip on the territory lest developments there influence groups of people in other parts of China to call for reform. Showing who is in charge in what constitutes China's most liberal territory therefore has become a priority for the CCP. While it showed a certain amount of restraint during the Umbrella occupation in late 2014, there is no doubt that Beijing would not allow such unrest to continue forever. Therefore, while the PLA stayed in its barracks, we can expect that the central government has nevertheless unleashed various forces that, working behind the scenes, will ensure that HKSAR does not drift away. The inclusion of Hong Kong in the new and highly restrictive national security measures is not a coincidence and opens the door to future human rights violations should its civil society continue to agitate and call for reform.

So in line with developments in China proper, HKSAR has also experienced an erosion of its freedoms. Freedom House ranked Hong Kong as "partly free," with a rating of 5 for political rights and 2 for civil liberties and 3.5 overall. The report also noted a downward trend for liberties in HKSAR.

Elsewhere in the Chinese-speaking world, Singapore also ranked "partly free" with a 4 in both political rights and civil liberties. The city-state has what is known as a "soft authoritarian" system of governance. The ruling People's Action Party (PAP, 人民行動黨) is *primus inter pares* in the ostensibly pluralistic political sphere and has used both its financial resources and the court system to ensure that its opponents remain marginal forces. State censorship of the press is common and assumed, while political dissent and criticism of the leadership are met with the heavy hand of the state, as the Amos Yee (余澎杉) case has made perfectly clear. Protests are illegal unless permission is obtained from the authorities, with severe restrictions as to where they can be held. Up until the shift in China under President Xi, it was believed that the Singapore model could serve as an example for the CCP worthy of emulation (with Chinese characteristics, of course).

Malaysia and Indonesia, two countries that have large Chinese ethic populations, also rank as "partly free" with aggregate scores of 4 and 3, respectively, with a downward trend for Malaysia.

Of all the countries with a large population of Chinese-speaking citizens, only Taiwan is "free" according to the Freedom House ranking, with a score of 1 for political rights and 2 for civil rights. Despite acquisitions by pro-Beijing conglomerates and tremendous pressure from China, Taiwan also continues to have the freest media environment in East Asia, ranking number 51 out of 180 in the Reporters Without Borders' 2015 report. By comparison, China was 176 (only Syria,

Turkmenistan, North Korea, and Eritrea did worse), Hong Kong 70, Singapore 153, Malaysia 147, and Indonesia 138.

Thus, in terms of its ability to demonstrate that even so-called Confucian societies can develop into vibrant democracies in which contention is arbitrated by non-coercive means, Taiwan stands as a rarity in Asia: It has what we could call "freedom value." Irrespective of one's position on whether Taiwan is part of China or not, free societies are something to be cherished, especially in an era where revisionist undemocratic forces seem to be staging a comeback.[1]

The preciousness of the freedoms that continue to exist in Taiwan is also felt in the book industry. In early 2015, the Liaison Office of the Central Government, Beijing's official presence in HKSAR, reportedly ordered Sino United Publishing (聯合出版(集團)有限公司) – a group that controls all the major bookstore chains in the SAR and accounts for an estimated 80 percent of the market – to remove all "inappropriate" books from their shelves, including texts about the Umbrella Movement. Industry insiders indicate that Sino United, which is also said to have a strong presence on university campuses in the city, is financially backed by Beijing. Travelers to Hong Kong observed recently that books deemed "controversial" by Beijing are no longer available at the airport bookstore.

With its directive and the unfair environment that is pushing smaller, independent bookstores toward bankruptcy, residents of what remains the freest part of China will likely find it increasingly difficult to purchase books on a variety of subjects that the CCP does not want people to know about, a list that can change over time and that includes but is not limited to human rights, Western-style democracy, the CCP's past mistakes, government corruption, the Tiananmen Square Massacre, Tibet, Xinjiang . . . and Taiwan. Books on such subjects are already hard to find in other Chinese-speaking countries like Singapore. Taiwan, which also faces pressure, is therefore the only country in the Chinese-speaking/reading world where books on subjects that Beijing deems sensitive remain available.

The interest that Chinese tourists have displayed for the great variety of books in Chinese that are on offer at Taiwan's best bookstores, including books on Chinese history and the CCP leadership, highlights a thirst for knowledge that is cause for hope and demonstrates why Beijing is cracking down on the industry. There is no doubt that if Taiwan fell under China's control, an entire universe of essential information and ideas in the Chinese language would disappear, which would be a loss not only to Taiwan itself but to all the other countries and regions in the Chinese-speaking world where people continue to hunger for information.

As the Hong Kong experience and (hopefully) this book have demonstrated, the annexation of Taiwan, whether by force of "peaceful" means, would inevitably have a corrosive impact on the freedoms and liberties that are currently enjoyed in Taiwan, thanks in large part to its status as a *de facto* country. Consequently and especially because of its geographical location, Taiwan plays an important role in the global balance of freedom.

How Beijing ultimately deals with the Taiwan "question" in light of the challenges that lie ahead will have a major impact on the kind of China that the international community will have to deal with for decades to come. If the rising power and presumptuous regional hegemon manages to deal with the dispute responsibly and in line with international law, then there might be hope that a great power confrontation involving the U.S. or a Third Sino-Japanese War can be averted. Although there is no indication at this point that Beijing has any intention to resolve the Taiwan issue in a genuinely peaceful way (as opposed to peaceful reunification on Beijing's terms), the international community has every advantage in encouraging future Chinese leaders to move in that direction, as all other options offer the promise of instability.

Conversely, should Beijing turn more hostile over Taiwan as its people continue to refuse unification or following a possible return of the DPP in the presidency, then the international community would have good reason to apprehend China's rise and to form an alliance to "contain" it, as seems to be occurring presently. As will be discussed in greater detail in the next chapter, the worst thing that the international community could do as the PRC emerges as a regional superpower would be to reward its belligerent tendencies by giving it what it wants. Instead, greater effort should be made to reach out and to support more moderate voices within the CCP.

This is something that Taiwan might actually be in a good position to attempt, although, because this would imply dealing with dissident voices in China, this would comport certain risks. But one thing is clear: "Negotiating" with CCP principals like President Xi and senior TAO officials is not the way to go if Taiwan is to guide the Chinese leadership in a direction of greater accommodation.

Lest this give the wrong impression, it is important to state that although Taiwan can have a positive influence on political developments in China, it is not its *responsibility* or *destiny* to do so, as some observers have argued. Contrary to what Yu argues, there is no Second Long March in which the "non-Communist Chinese have been embarking [. . .] for the sake of all the Chinese people at home and abroad." The Taiwanese people should not, as Yu claims, "work on the Chinese mainland, together with the non-Chinese Communists living over there to promote full-fledged and mature constitutional democracy." In fact, those who hold the view that Taiwan can or *should* help democratize China operate under the same fallacy that fueled hopes that a growing economy would lead to democratization or that the reunification of Hong Kong would have a liberalizing effect on the Mainland.

Moreover, the notion that Taiwan is somehow "destined" to change China implies that Taiwan is part of China, a view that contradicts both history and public opinion in Taiwan and that furthermore treats the Taiwanese as little more than means to an end rather than a people of intrinsic value.

The reality, *pace* Yu, is that Taiwan and China are two separate entities, and both have the ability and the responsibility to chart their own distinct courses. As such, whatever influence Taiwan can have on political developments in China is no greater and no less than the influence that, say, Canada has on developments within the somewhat less liberal U.S. It is not Ottawa's responsibility or that of the 34.8 million Canadians to influence the views of the American government on issues like gun control and the legalization of same-sex marriage, although if Canada's more progressive policies on those matters can inspire U.S. politicians to emulate them, then so be it.

As the recent histories of Iraq and Afghanistan have taught us, democracy is not something that can be exported. The decision to liberalize the political sphere and ultimately to democratize it was made by the Taiwanese alone, admittedly with a strong incentive to do so provided by the international context in which they occurred. The same holds for China, which has all the intellectual and moral resources it needs to do so provided that there is enough momentum within society to move in that direction and that the CCP either permits it or has lost its prerogative to exercise violence by the state. Of course, despite the Western belief that all human beings will eventually strive for the "universal value" of democracy, we should not discount the possibility that the Chinese would choose not to democratize, at least not in the sense that democracy is understood in the West and in Taiwan. If, as we saw in Chapter 5, Han and Chen correctly point out the lack of support among ordinary Chinese for Western-style democracy, then who are we and who are the Taiwanese to impose a system that they do not want for their own country?

If we operate on the assumption that Taiwan is a sovereign state and that it alone should therefore choose the political system that it wants, then it follows that similar leniency should in theory be granted to the Chinese. I say "in theory" because the great challenge is to determine whether the wishes of the 1.4 billion Chinese are indeed well represented by the CCP, something that will be difficult to determine as long as the party holds the population in a state of fear.

One can therefore *hope* that China will democratize, for, its imperfections notwithstanding, democracy has proven to be the "least bad" form of government and is probably the best way to negotiate contention. A quick comparison of the manner in which governments deal with, say, discontent over urban renewal and environment pollution in Taiwan and China should suffice to show the merits of adopting a more open and democratic system. But it is certainly not the *duty* of the Taiwanese to democratize China.

Critics of my argument so far could then counter that Taiwan does have a responsibility toward China because of the cultural and linguistic affinity between the two sides and that a free and democratic Taiwan is more likely to inspire liberals in democrats across China than other democracies. We have already dispensed with the notion that serving as a *source of emulation* and *duty* are the same thing. With regard to serving as an example, as something that can be emulated, there is no doubt that Taiwan has its appeal to those in China who seek greater political freedoms for their country. However, it is doubtful that a shared ethnicity, culture, and language are essential for a people to want to emulate another. Something more fundamental and essential appeals to democrats and freedom-seeking people that transcends ethnicity.

In other words, one does not need a cultural analog in order to learn from it or to want to emulate it. Democracy is still democracy if the people who practice it speak a different language or have a different skin color. If that were not the case, then who would the Taiwanese have turned to find an example to emulate, given that there was no other "Chinese" democracy at the time? Which example could the South Koreans have relied on to democratize their own country, given that the only other Korea was still mired in totalitarianism? The fact that after decades of contact with Western democracies China still hasn't democratized isn't because ordinary Chinese were unable to visit Taiwan, as many of them can now do since 2008. It remains authoritarian because the Chinese people – and this includes the CCP, which has its own reasons for maintaining the status quo – have yet to take the necessary steps to bring about democratization.

Therefore, Taiwan's democracy is of value not just to the Chinese as something to emulate but in fact to the entire international community, an equal in a community of nations that have embraced such values. And in an even more fundamental way, it is of value because this is the system that 23 million Taiwanese have chosen for themselves after decades of toiling under authoritarian and cultural rule by outside powers. It is of value because it is an expression of the desire of a people for *self-determination*, something that not so long ago was regarded as a universal right and something to be cherished. We need to ask ourselves why, in the context of cross-strait relations, has self-determination acquired such a reflexively negative connotation.

If, as the result of actions by the Chinese government and inaction on the part of the international community, Taiwan failed and was annexed by the PRC, it would have a grave psychological effect on other peoples – including the many across China and in HKSAR, Xinjiang, and Tibet – who are fighting for liberty. It would be a sign that the world has abdicated to tyrants and that, however valid or noble the cause may be, those who seek freedom are waging their battle alone. Therefore, besides its strategic value as a component of the "first island chain," Taiwan also has *symbolic* value in the ongoing ideological battle between "freedom" and "tyranny," which is no longer a mere confrontation between East and West. As Rigger argues, "Making sure Taiwan has a voice in deciding its own future is important to the United States and other democratic countries because democracy in Taiwan is an indicator and inspiration for democracy everywhere."

The disappearance of Taiwan as a sovereign entity – and the inevitable erosion of its freedoms after Beijing launched the mainlandization of its political system, as it has in HKSAR – would convince smaller powers that we have returned to the premodern state of Hobbes' Leviathan, in which the strong eat the weak, which is exactly the kind of language that senior CCP officials have used when smaller regional powers have defied Beijing over its territorial claims. And while Taiwan is, comparatively speaking, "small" in terms of its geography, the international community (since Taiwan would never agree to this unless it feels it has been completely abandoned) would have allowed a modern, peaceful, and highly successful country with the world's fifty-third largest population (about the same size as Australia) and twenty-first largest economy to simply vanish, an outcome that, quite understandably, would hardly inspire confidence among the many weaker nations that are also threatened by more powerful states.

It would also send the message that however much a nation plays by the rules and embraces accepted international norms – Taiwan has democratized, it has signed UN human rights covenants, it does not threaten its neighbors, it is a "responsible stakeholder," it has abandoned nuclear weapons and abides by nonproliferation regimes – such good behavior does not necessarily confer any protections against the voracity of more powerful neighbors, even when those have defied the international legal system or intend to supplant it.

And for what?

Enter the *uber*-realists, the subject of our next chapter.

Note

1 See, for example, the National Endowment for Democracy's Resurgent Dictatorship website at http://www.resurgentdictatorship.org, in which China is listed among the "big five."

Bibliography

Freedom House (2015) *Freedom in the World Report,* https://freedomhouse.org/report/freedom-world/freedom-world-2015#.VtftUoS9jzI

Lin, W-C (2015) "中聯辦掌控聯合出版集團擁三大書局兼壟斷發行　議員指涉違《基本法》," *Apple Daily*, 8 April, http://hk.apple.nextmedia.com/news/art/20150409/19106286

Reporters Without Borders (2015) *World Press Freedom Index*, http://index.rsf.org

Rigger, S (2011) *Why Taiwan Matters: Small Island, Global Powerhouse*, Lanham: Rowman and Littlefield: 189

Yu, K-H (2009) *The Second Long March: Struggling Against the Chinese Communists Under the Republic of China (Taiwan) Constitution*, London: Continuum: 169

15

THE FOLLY OF ABANDONMENT

Readers who have gotten this far should have an idea by now that for all its might, China still does not have the confidence that it can take Taiwan by force without paying a heavy price and that it has therefore adopted a multifaceted strategy to break the will of the Taiwanese while isolating Taipei internationally. Through a vast propaganda campaign, the CCP has attempted to discredit Taiwan's democracy and value, while fostering the idea that whatever the Taiwanese and their allies do, in the end the result will be the same: unification. Why, then, side with the losers when one can bandwagon with the winners and perhaps reap some benefits in the process?

Yet another aspect of Beijing's strategy has been to convince the international community that refusal to subscribe to its side of the story on the Taiwan issue will have costs, from the suspension of military-to-military contact to China's refusal to cooperate on other pressing issues such as other territorial disputes, the North Korean and Iranian nuclear programs, and global warming, to name just a few. The idea is that if Beijing is given what it wants – the complete abandonment of Taiwan and the removal of the security "guarantees" that have allowed the island to remain free and independent – it will be more willing to play ball on other issues. There is a word to describe this type of behavior, and that word is *blackmail*.

And yet a surprising number of "experts" have bought the idea, using books and publications in prestigious journals and magazines to convince the rest of us that a "grand bargain," in which Taiwan is ceded to China in return for guarantees and greater cooperation, is in our best interest.

Whether they know it or not, these experts – mostly academics – contribute to Beijing's propaganda campaign by regurgitating its menu of "scientific facts" and threats: China has become too powerful economically and militarily to resist; it could threaten nuclear war to defend its core interest; Taiwan "poisons" our relations with China by creating "distrust" in Beijing; and so on. It therefore uses sticks and carrots, the latter being little more than a promise, the expectation that the international community would get something in return – the "peaceful" resolution of the South China Sea territorial dispute or a more proactive effort on Beijing's part to pressure Pyongyang into abandoning its nuclear weapons program and being a better neighbor.

Above all, by abandoning Taiwan, some have argued that the U.S. would show its "goodwill" to China and thereby remove a major obstacle. "I assure you," writes a professor at China's National Defense University, "that a posture change of the U.S. policy on Taiwan will remove the major obstacle for ↔ military-to-military relations and also strengthen Sino-American cooperation by winning the hearts and minds of 1.3 billion Chinese people" (Xu and Twomey). Never mind that 23 million people are reduced to being a mere "obstacle," a type of dehumanization that is not uncommon among those who argue that Taiwan should be ceded to China.

For example, Glaser writes in *International Security* journal that as part of a strategy of geopolitical accommodation to China's rise, the U.S. should "negotiate a grand bargain that ends its commitment to defend Taiwan against Chinese aggression." In return, Glaser, who "draws heavily on international relations theory," argues, "China would peacefully resolve its maritime and land disputes in the South China and East China Seas, and officially accept the United States' long-term military security role in East Asia." By ending its security commitment to Taiwan, Washington would also "greatly moderate the intensifying military competition between the United States and China, which is adding to strains in their relationship."

For his part, White is among those who believe that China has simply become too powerful to oppose. "Back in 1996, when they [U.S. and China] last went toe-to-toe over Taiwan, the US could simply send a couple of aircraft carriers into the area to force China to back off," he writes. "But the stark reality is that these days, there is not much the US can realistically do to help Taipei stand up to serious pressure from Beijing."

Mearsheimer struck a similar note in a recent article, saying, "Given how dangerous it is for precipitating a war and given the fact that the United States will eventually reach the point where it cannot defend Taiwan, there is a reasonable chance that American policy makers will eventually conclude that it makes good strategic sense to abandon Taiwan and allow China to coerce it into accepting unification."

Although he rightly notes that most Taiwanese want to preserve their way of life, White strikes a pessimistic note. "The harsh reality is that no country is going to sacrifice its relations with China in order to help Taiwan preserve the status quo. China is simply too important economically, and too powerful militarily, for anyone to confront it on Taiwan's behalf, especially when everyone knows how determined China is to achieve reunification eventually."

In his book *The China Choice*, written before he had ever set foot in Taiwan, White also argued that the changing balance of power in Asia makes unification inevitable and that as long as it is "peaceful" and "consensual," the U.S. should not oppose such an outcome.

For his part, Goldstein proposes a step-by-step "cooperation spiral" *between the U.S. and China* on the "Taiwan issue," which, while less simplistic than outright abandonment, still forces Taiwan to make unacceptable choices under conditions in which it is a mere passive participant with little will or say of its own. Even more shocking is the fact that Goldstein writes that "Westerners claiming that 'unification' is an issue that should be decided by the Taiwanese alone lack an objective view of history, culture, and identity," a notion that would deservingly be derided by the 23 million people concerned.

In all the variations on the theme of a "grand bargain" over Taiwan, the wishes of the 23 million Taiwanese are simply ignored, as are the moral and ethical components of international relations. Taiwan is reduced to a commodity, a means to an end that can be traded if necessary. It goes without saying that the experts who make such claims tend to be individuals who have little, if any, understanding of or attachment to Taiwan and its people.

Not only are such views naïve, they're also historically blind, as the CCP has since its inception scored repeated successes in convincing others that supporting its ambitions would translate into better future relations, as U.S. State Department and intelligence officials discovered to their great chagrin during and after World War II (Bernstein). Moreover, such views operate on the assumption that the international community needs China more than China needs the international community, a proposition that is, at best, of questionable logic.

White's claim that unification can be "peaceful" and "consensual" bespeaks a lack of understanding of the dynamics in Taiwan. In his book *Middle Power, Middle Kingdom*, Bibliography has Mulroney, M a former Canadian ambassador to China and head of the Canadian Trade Office in Taipei (CTOT), demonstrates how important it is to have been on the ground and to get to know the people one writes about in books and academic journals. It also shows that no longer being in government probably gives one greater freedom to say things that hitherto had been impermissible. The retired diplomat observes that White is probably wrong: "[A]ny reading of Taiwanese public opinion over the last decade would argue that a consensual reunion is, if anything, improbable," he writes. Mulroney continues, "If reunification does happen in the near future, it would far more likely be the result of some form of military or economic coercion by China."

In fact, in light of the current trends, it is highly unlikely that peaceful unification can be achieved.

By claiming that Beijing could escalate to such a point that it would threaten to use its nuclear deterrent to seize Taiwan and prevent a U.S. intervention, those self-described offensive realists present as "unreasonable" the contention that Taiwan *can* and *should* be defended. Strangely, they do not seem to regard the idea that China would threaten nuclear war – and certain annihilation – as unreasonable. Their position assumes that the CCP leadership in Beijing is maniacal and suicidal and that it would risk everything to recapture Taiwan. And they would have no moral qualms in ceding a democracy and its 23 million people to an authoritarian regime that, in their view, would be willing to vaporize hundreds of thousands, if not millions, of people to achieve its expansionist aims.

Needless to say, if the community of nations yielded to such blackmail, the world would become a very unstable and dangerous place indeed. Not only would it encourage expansionist countries to increase their military capabilities and threatening posture, it would create an incentive for weaker states to boost their own military deterrent, to acquire nuclear weapons, or to create a web of alliances that would plunge us back into the pre–World War I era that led to catastrophe. Moreover, such a Hobbesian state would increase the risks of miscalculation, as it is impossible to know at which point a state has acquired enough comprehensive power that it can threaten and presumably take over a neighbor with impunity.

Consequently, far from being an isolated case, Taiwan in fact serves as an index case for the future of geopolitics, in which China is now, for better or worse, one of the principal actors. By succumbing to Beijing's blackmail, world leaders would ensure a future of high instability for all of us.

The impact of ceding Taiwan to an increasingly belligerent PRC in the Asia-Pacific region would also likely be substantial. Given Beijing's escalating territorial disputes with most of its neighbors, the abandonment of Taiwan would put U.S. security guarantees into serious doubt and make an arms race more rather than less likely, especially when Japan is concerned. In another misreading of history, Goldstein posits that this argument is "specious" and "built on crude and simplistic assumptions." According to him, "A clear view of history shows plainly that Beijing approaches the Taiwan issue quite differently than other issues, and so the expectation that China, following unification, would immediately seek to apply its hubris to other issues only stretches the imagination."

What stretches the imagination, in fact, is that analysts would not be aware that Beijing has a tendency to redefine what constitutes its core interests. But then again, as Neville-Hadley writes in his review of Goldstein's book for *The Wall Street Journal*, Goldstein's account "sometimes unquestioningly reproduces Chinese narratives of dubious accuracy." Neville-Hadley also rightly points out that Goldstein's book offers "an astonishing mix of heavy-handed realpolitik and fantastical wishful thinking in which both parties act in good faith." One wonders what Goldstein makes of the Tibet and Xinjiang "issues," two other "inseparable" territories that give China strategic depth or the South China Sea, for that matter, which is conceivably the next step in Beijing's outward expansion so as to add a buffer between the Mainland and potential external forces. It is very difficult to imagine that China would stop at Taiwan – even more so if it got what it wanted without having to fight (and pay a price) for it.

Once it gained control of Taiwan, China would finally be able to bust the first island chain and to expand its naval capabilities into the open West Pacific, a development that would cause apprehensions within the region while exposing U.S. forces stationed across Japan and in Guam to direct attack by PLA assets. It is difficult to imagine how such developments would not lead to a major arms buildup by Japan, which would suddenly find itself next door to its historical foe, and other countries within the region. It is equally difficult to imagine how such a development would benefit regional stability.

Of course, as Bernstein writes, "It's all well and good to wax eloquent about the struggle for freedom, but policymakers need to assess whether grand idealistic goals can be achieved." And here there is absolutely no doubt that the moral thing to do on Taiwan is also in the interest of the international community. In other words, the *moral* case for standing by Taiwan or for giving it enough room so that its people can make their own choices is also a *strategic* case that has implications for the region and possibly the whole world. Rather than reward an increasingly repressive regime with the fruits of blackmail by "ceding" Taiwan as part of a "grand bargain," the international community has every interest in making sure that blackmail and coercion do not become *en vogue* in the twenty-first century. Yielding to authoritarian regimes is not the best way to meet the challenges ahead and furthermore risks silencing the voices of moderation that exist in China by giving the CCP every incentive to silence them.

"When we cut corners in the defense of core values, we are often among the first casualties," Mulroney writes. "*We* are changed, even diminished when we fail to value the democratic rights of the people of Taiwan, or when financial concerns cause us to turn away from discussing unpleasant facts about China."

Moreover, meeting China halfway on the Taiwan issue should never come at the expense of the will of Taiwan's 23 million people. Forcing them to make concessions on their way of life – especially in light of recent developments in HKSAR and across China – is disingenuous to say the least. Ensuring that Taiwan does not find itself isolated to a point where its people feel they have no option but to cut a deal with Beijing (Beijing's favored strategy) does not mean threatening China with war or containing it to such an extent that it has no hope of developing to its full potential. It simply means drawing lines and making it clear that, if those lines are crossed, Taiwan and its allies in the international community will have the necessary tools to bring China back in line.

The best way ahead, therefore, isn't the abandonment of Taiwan for some vague promises by a party that has repeatedly demonstrated its ability to dissemble but rather a strengthening of Taiwan's deterrent capability. As Mulroney writes, "Up until now, Taiwan has been safeguarded within a fog of strategic ambiguity that depends at least as much on U.S. nerve and resolve as it does on Chinese pragmatism and caution." However, he cautions that military or economic coercion against Taiwan would be more likely if U.S. resolve weakens, "a change that would fatally undermine Taiwan's own self-confidence and deliver precisely the cost-free outcome that China seeks."

Lastly, as we have seen, even if a government in Taipei were completely abandoned and felt compelled to strike a deal with Beijing under its one-China principle, it is difficult to imagine that the Taiwanese public would stand by and allow their country and way of life to be taken from them. Consequently, the kind of "grand bargain" that academics write about in the comfort of their study back in the West also contains a huge moral responsibility if such recommendations were taken seriously: Most likely, abandonment and a takeover of Taiwan would spark opposition and necessitate a pacification campaign by the PLA or its proxies in Taiwan. Given the high opposition to being ruled by the CCP that exists across Taiwanese society, the ensuing crisis could result in a catastrophe on a scale that would make the 228 Massacre – perpetrated by an army of "liberators" that had actually been welcomed by the Taiwanese population – look like a mere paper cut.

Although the narrative of abandonment has enjoyed only partial support with decision makers, and it is nevertheless part of a chorus that reinforces Beijing's propaganda and political warfare campaigns against Taiwan and that could conceivably be taken more seriously if the U.S. decided to become more isolationist once it dispenses with its energy reliance, as Zeihan argues, or convinces itself that it no longer has the resources to continue its security guarantees in the Asia-Pacific. Such a prospect, though seemingly remote for the time being – especially in light of recent comments by U.S. officials, who are now talking about a "transformed and redefined" way that the U.S. thinks about Taiwan (Lowther) – makes it essential that Taiwan bolster its own deterrent and develop closer security ties with regional partners, chief among them Japan, which has the most to fear from the PLA's gaining control of the Taiwan "unsinkable carrier."

While it is probably true that within a decade or so, as Mearsheimer claims, China will have the ability to launch a successful invasion of Taiwan, we should note that capability alone is insufficient as a determinant of the use of force. Of equal importance in the equation is *intent* (otherwise, every state that is more powerful than its neighbor would logically feel compelled to attack it). As such, even if it becomes more difficult to counter the PLA as its capabilities expand, there will always be more room to counter the *intent* of the Chinese leadership. One way to do so is to guarantee that, even if an invasion of Taiwan were "successful," the price of doing so (materially, economically, and politically) would be overwhelmingly prohibitive.

The key for Taiwan and its allies is to increase the cost of Beijing's refusal to play by the international rules. For better or worse, modern Taiwan has adopted a Western-style nationhood that simply cannot work within the civilizational nationalism that exists in China. Abandoning Taiwan would be one step further in Beijing's efforts to change the system of international relations with which most of us have become accustomed to, the outcome of which raises the prospect of global disorder.

Consequently, the community of nations would benefit tremendously from a better understanding of the situation in Taiwan and how Beijing's one-China claim has a lot more in common with expansionism – illegal under international law – than with a moral case for the reunification of a divided family versus "separatism" or "irredentism," as the propaganda wants us to believe. Once more people understand that the Taiwan issue is one of outright *annexation*, and once they realize that the matter is hugely complex because politicians in Beijing have made it so through a web of illusions and propaganda (forcing the Taiwanese side to engage in similar rhetorical summersaults), then the notion of "abandoning" Taiwan will lose much of its appeal and logic.

Crimea and Taiwan both have in common a powerful neighbor seeking to seize territory for strategic purposes. Where Moscow's justification for taking action was crude, Beijing's has been much more refined but no less specious. The international community would be committing a grave mistake if it gave the CCP what it needs to bolster what amounts to a false legitimacy.

The CCP should stand or fall not on territorial conquests and the subjugation of other peoples but rather on its ability to improve the lives of the Chinese and to give them the rights and freedoms that they deserve as citizens of a great nation.

Bibliography

Bernstein, R (2014) *China 1945: Mao's Revolution and America's Fateful Choice*, New York: Alfred A. Knopf

Cole, M (2015) "Don't Let China Swallow Taiwan," *The National Interest*, 23 April, http://nationalinterest.org/feature/dont-let-china-swallow-taiwan-12708

——— (2015) "If the Unthinkable Occurred: America Should Stand Up to China over Taiwan," *The National Interest*, 7 May, http://nationalinterest.org/feature/if-the-unthinkable-occured-america-should-stand-china-over-12825

——— (2015) "The Question That Is Never Asked," *The Diplomat*, 13 May, http://thedip lomat.com/2015/05/the-question-that-is-never-asked-what-do-the-taiwanese-want/

Glaser, C (2015) "A U.S.-China Grand Bargain? The Hard Choice Between Military Competition and Accommodation," *International Security*, Vol. 39 No. 4 (Spring 2015): 49–90

Goldstein, L (2015) *Meeting China Halfway: How to Defuse the Emerging US-China Rivalry*, Washington: Georgetown University Press: 46–78

Lowther, W (2015) "Taiwan Important to US: Burghardt," *Taipei Times*, 15 July, http://www.taipeitimes.com/News/front/archives/2015/07/15/2003623054

Mearsheimer, J (2015) "Say Goodbye to Taiwan," *The National Interest*, March–April 2014, http://nationalinterest.org/article/say-goodbye-taiwan-9931

Mulroney, D. (2015) *Middle Power, Middle Kingdom: What Canadians Need to Know About China in the 21st Century*, Toronto: Allen Lane: 244–5

Neville-Hadley, P (2015) "Peace at All Costs: A Blueprint for U.S.-China Relations that Abandons America's Allies," *Wall Street Journal*, 2 July, http://www.wsj.com/articles/peace-at-all-costs-1435849728

White, H (2015) "The Harsh Reality That Taiwan Faces," *Straits Time*, 15 April, http://www.straitstimes.com/opinion/the-harsh-reality-that-taiwan-faces

Xu, H and Twomey, P (2014) "Military Developments," in *Debating China: The U.S. –China Relationship in Ten Conversations*, Hachigian, Nina, ed, Oxford University Press: 162

Zeihan, P (2014) *The Accidental Superpower: The Next Generation of American Preeminence and the Coming Global Disorder*, New York: Twelve

16

WHAT CAN TAIWAN DO?

Our journey has almost come to an end. We have seen how Taiwan's history and democracy have contributed to the deepening of an idiosyncratic nationalism that sets Taiwan apart from China, regardless of the shared culture, language, and DNA. We have also seen how Beijing, whose concept of nationalism can neither accept the idea that Taiwan exists as a sovereign state nor accommodate the existence of genuine autonomy within the PRC under one China, has sought to isolate Taiwan internationally while using various means to undermine Taiwan's democratic institutions. The clashing ideologies – on one side a desire for self-determination, on the other a mixture of feverish nationalism and expansionism – portend future tensions and occur at a time when China's economic and military power has given it the ability to throw its weight around to get what it wants.

So what can Taiwan do? Can anything be done, or have the forces of history taken Taiwan to the brink of inevitable extinction?

Echoing Beijing's propaganda, the pessimists would argue that resistance is futile and that Taipei should cut as good a deal as it can with Beijing while it can, lest future developments lead to less favorable alternatives (e.g., unification by force). As we saw in the previous chapter, the pessimists also counsel the abandonment of Taiwan in order to simultaneously remove an irritant that undermines relations with China and to secure Beijing's goodwill on other pressing issues. However, such a strategy is based on little more than wishful thinking and stems from a myopic reading of the CCP's past history. By "giving" Taiwan to China, the community of nations would reward intimidation, cause regional instability, and strengthen the CCP when the party should instead be striving for legitimization by promoting and implementing political reforms in China.

For the optimists (and I consider myself to be part of that group), Taiwan's situation is not as dire as it seems. Though extraordinary challenges do exist that it would be pure folly to ignore, Taiwan has several things going for it, including a geography that would make an amphibious assault by the PLA a hugely costly and potentially disastrous enterprise.

However, Taiwan's greatest asset is its people and the resilience that stems from its democratic institutions and a consolidating nationalism that, once and for all, could close the gap of "ethnicity" and party-color-affiliation that have hitherto kept the nation in a state of division against itself. Recent developments in China and HKSAR, as well as the greater contact between Taiwan and China since the election of Ma Ying-jeou in 2008, have also reinforced the distinctiveness of Taiwanese identity and the desire to maintain the way of life that makes Taiwan both unique and an example to the world. Although President Ma's policy of détente with Beijing has engendered much needed normalization, for which he should be commended, this rapprochement has also brought into greater contrast the fundamental differences that explain why Taiwan and China simply cannot work as one China and why the imposition of such an outcome on the Taiwanese people would be both terribly unfair and a source of future tensions. The Taiwanese have had the advantage of seeing what has happened to HKSAR and how "one country, two systems" will ultimately lead to the *mainlandization* of more liberal societies, regardless of Beijing's promise to grant them autonomy – and that is not something that they want for themselves, not the blues and certainly not the greens.

To improve its chances of survival, Taiwan can and *must* do several things. The strategy that I propose rests on three pillars: *counterpropaganda*, *consolidation*, and *deterrence*.

The term "propaganda" tends to have a negative connotation, but in reality it is nothing more than a sustained public relations strategy meant to shape the perceptions of an "other" who needs convincing. Both facts *and* lies can be part of a propaganda campaign, and usually both are components of the narrative. There is absolutely no doubt that China has had a much more effective propaganda campaign than Taiwan and that its successes have led to a weakening of Taipei's position internationally. Even though historical facts are not on its side, Beijing has nevertheless managed to convince almost everybody – including governments – that Taiwan was, is, and always will be part of the PRC and that those who refuse to recognize that claim constitute a minority of individuals who, for one reason or another, want to keep China divided and weak. Now that it has passed its new National Security Law, Beijing's next step in its propaganda efforts will conceivably be to convince the rest of the world that those who favor independence for Taiwan are actual criminals.

In reality, as we saw earlier, a substantial majority of the people in Taiwan support the existence of Taiwan as a separate state, a group that includes both those who seek *de jure* independence and those who want the status quo. The energy that was unleashed by the Sunflower Movement in the spring of 2014 – in fact, the very dynamics that led to its rise – derives from the knowledge that Beijing has been trying to change the status quo in its favor through incentives, economic pressure, and the actions of substate actors. Despite what the critics have said, wanting the status quo for Taiwan doesn't mean that one is naïve about the dynamics that exist in the Taiwan Strait. But one thing is certain: As an ideological concept, it is very much equal to a desire for independence.

Part of Taiwan's *counterpropaganda* effort should therefore be focused on better explaining the complexities of Taiwanese society and countering Beijing's narrative that the desire for independence (as well as opposition to unification) is much higher than is usually believed. It should also try to debunk the myth that Taiwanese and Chinese are one and the same or that one's ethnic origins should serve as a determinant of his or her identity. Ironically, such a concept shouldn't be too difficult to explain to the West, where multiculturalism is very much part of the national fabric. And yet when it comes to Taiwan, the "Chinese-ness" of the Taiwanese people seems to close the door on any possibility of self-determination.

To counter this, the Taiwanese should explain how Taiwan has adopted a Western-style definition of the nation that is in sharp contrast to that espoused by China, which regards the matter from the perspective of civilization. This doesn't mean that one definition is better or more valid than the other, but it nevertheless makes it clear why the conflict of identities that exists in the Taiwan Strait will not go away anytime soon and why unification would be an undesirable outcome pregnant with the seeds of instability. The message coming out of the Presidential Office in Taipei and the Ma administration's emphasis on the ROC and the "Chinese-ness" of the Taiwanese have both contributed to the confusion abroad and supported Beijing's official rhetoric. Clearer signaling on the part of future administrations would help dispel some of that confusion, though pressures will continue to exist to calibrate the message so as not to create the impression that Taipei is once again a "troublemaker."

Another component of Taiwan's propaganda efforts should dispel the notion that refusal to be part of China stems from a hatred for the country, lingering pro-Japan sentiment, or other, more self-interested considerations (e.g., profiting from arms sales, working with Western intelligence to keep China divided, etc.). The truth of the matter is, like the rest of the international community, most Taiwanese are perfectly fine with the existence of China and have no problem conducting business with it, even though they may have issues with the manner in which the CCP runs things in the country. Most Taiwanese do not "hate" China, and given that many of them have a stake in its success through investments and business relations, they do not want it to fail. However, what most of them want is a normalized relationship, one in which doing business with China does not come at the risk of their country being taken over by a regime that would inevitably change the fabric of their society, and probably not for the better, as we've seen in HKSAR.

Taiwanese could do a much better job telling the world – and by this I mean more than just the U.S., which often seems to be the only foreign country that the Taiwanese care about or regard as relevant to their cause – that they are not politically apathetic or unwilling to defend their country or that they can simply be "bought" by the Chinese. In other words, they need to show the world that they are resilient and proud of their accomplishments as a nation. While those issues may have been resolved among the people of Taiwan, they are not necessarily evident to people overseas, who know very little about the place and its history and who rely on media and academics that more often than not are providing information reflecting Beijing's propaganda on the subject.

Ultimately, what the Taiwanese could do much better is to show that opposing Beijing's efforts to annex their country is not irrational but is rather legitimate. Their communications strategy should also seek to demonstrate why the continued existence of Taiwan as a sovereign state matters to the international community. Simply stating the fact that it is a democracy, without explaining what democracy means and why it matters, is not enough: Linking Taiwan's fate with future Chinese behavior both domestically and in a geopolitical context – now *that* should grab people's attention.

Luckily, the recent actions of the Chinese government, from its belligerent stance on territorial disputes to the intensifying crackdown on civil society across China, should make it easier for the Taiwanese to explain the contrast to an international audience. The fact that nearly half of all wealthy Chinese (with a net worth of more than US$1.5 million) are actively considering leaving China within the next five years – usually to start a new life in a Western democracy, where they won't risk losing everything if they somehow anger the CCP, as the Ai Weiwei (艾未未) case made all too clear – speaks volumes about the state of the rule of law in China and should help explain why the Taiwanese have no intention of allowing their country to be absorbed by China. However, in order to do so effectively, the Taiwanese themselves will need to better understand the connection that exists between the two societies, which in turn requires that the Taiwanese pay closer attention to political developments in China.

Of course, to do any of these things, Taiwan will have to find ways to break through the intellectual firewall that has been erected against it. The reason why Beijing's propaganda campaign on the Taiwan issue has been so successful is that ignorance about Taiwan has remained high, in large part due to the self-censorship that has occurred in academia and the inattention of a global media that has left Taiwan and transplanted itself in China. As this chapter was being written, *The Wall Street Journal* had just announced that it is closing its bureau in Taipei, joining a long list of media that, as we saw earlier, have left the country amid restructuring and cost-saving measures. That the *Journal* decided to pull out of Taiwan six months before a presidential election that had every likelihood of having serious ramifications on the future of cross-strait relations and that from then on its reporting on Taiwan would be carried out of China spoke volumes about the importance that the managers of global media empires give to political developments in Taiwan. However good and well-intentioned are the *WSJ* reporters who will report on Taiwan in future, they will be doing so from afar and cannot possibly get the pulse of Taiwanese society, let alone translate its complexity to an inattentive audience overseas. As a result, the homogenization of news and knowledge about Taiwan will continue and will do so with a strong Beijing flavor to it.

The Taiwanese cannot simply blame institutionalized censorship and biases in the system for their isolation. New media and the creative industry offer ways to circumvent the wall that has been built around Taiwan, but for the Taiwanese to use this new tool effectively, they will have to do a much better job at reaching a global audience by making Taiwan interesting and relevant to *them*. In order to be able to tell a foreign audience why Taiwan matters, the Taiwanese themselves will have to become more worldly and aware of the other issues that keep peoples and governments busy. For many Taiwanese, the Taiwan Strait might seem like the most important thing in the world, but in reality, developments here – especially when the situation is relatively "stable" as it has been in recent years – tend to get lost in the noise of world affairs. A visit to the halls of power in Washington or other major capitals will quickly bring Taiwan enthusiasts back to earth.

The challenge, therefore, is to find out what will make world leaders tick and to repeat it often enough and loudly enough that they will pay attention. What is certain is that the traditional protests by a few dozen Taiwanese Americans waving the same placards they have been waving for the past two decades across from the White House in Washington, D.C., have outlived their utility.

Another step that needs to be taken is for the Taiwanese to greatly improve their communication skills and to understand the necessity of speaking to an international audience in a language that is intelligible to them. More often than not, this involves being able to speak English, a skill that is inexplicably lacking among most Taiwanese. The Sunflower Movement's international media campaign was a successful example of how this can be done. However, this *ad hoc* effort needs to be institutionalized.

At the same time, Taiwan needs to continue the *consolidation* of its society, democracy, and political system, a process that civil society has made clear is both needed and desirable. The anger that was directed at both the KMT and the DPP in the months prior to and during the Sunflower Movement occupation of the Legislative Yuan is indicative of a growing disillusionment with politics as usual. Taiwanese have grown fatigued with scorched-earth politics, the zero-sum approach adopted by legislators and party representatives, and the short-term view of politicians whose sole aim seems to be to ensure their reelection. Although such problems are certainly present in other democracies, Taiwan is in a situation where it cannot afford the kind of politicking that often has brought the nation to a standstill and that has led politicians to make decisions that, while maximizing their chances at the polls, have betrayed the nation's ideals and undermined its safety. The bitterness of politics has become such that candidates will sometimes take steps that they know are detrimental to the country but that will nevertheless give them an advantage over their opponent, a strategy that has worked wonders for Beijing, which has stepped in and played one side against the other, much as it did in Tibet by exploiting the mutual antagonism that existed between the Shika-tsé faction and Lhasa prior to the 1959 uprising and invasion by the PLA.

Even though the influence of the "third force" in the 2016 elections was somewhat limited, their ascendance is nevertheless a sign of change and is part of the institutionalization of new voices that also want the old system to be reformed to benefit Taiwanese society.[1] They still have a lot to learn about life in politics, but if they stay the course, there is a chance that they will eventually have an impact on the political scene by forcing the main parties to consider greater cooperation. The recent crisis within the KMT over the Hung candidacy for the presidency also points to the "middle ground" that both sides should be striving for, one that better reflects the wishes of the majority of Taiwanese. By appealing to those rather than to the extremists on both sides who would turn back the clock, politicians will realize that they have a lot more in common with their adversaries than the deeply divisive nature of Taiwanese politics often leads us to believe. Taiwan needs much more bipartisan decisions, especially on matters that pertain to national defense and the maintenance of the mores, values, and practices that define contemporary Taiwan. The more the parties learn to work together, the greater the challenge for the CCP and its allies. By their nature, political parties will always oppose one another. But on the fundamental issues, it is preferable that they cooperate, as parties in other embattled societies have demonstrated (e.g., Israel, the U.S. after the 11 September 2011 attacks, etc.).

Society also has a lot of work to do. The green–blue divide continues to poison the relationship between groups and exacerbates "ethic" tensions that should have been put to rest a long time ago. Although the damage caused by the KMT after its arrival in Taiwan – the 228 Massacre and subsequent White Terror – was as traumatic as it was undeniable, it is high time that the people of Taiwan, regardless of their "ethnicity," engage in genuine reconciliation. While this means admitting the atrocities perpetrated against the native population from 1947, it also means acknowledging the immense contributions that "Mainlanders" have made to this land, which is now as much of a home to them as it is to those who came before them. In other words, what it means to be Taiwanese needs to be redefined using inclusive measures rather than the exclusivism of old, which has tended to make people feel as though they are not welcome here, that they are not full participants in Taiwan's democratic experiment.

Thankfully, that process appears to have been launched by Taiwan's youth; the healing needs to be institutionalized and to be reflected among politicians.

The heterogeneous composition of the Sunflower Movement and of the many movements that came before it was a perfect representation of such an inclusive future, transcending gender, ethnicity, levels of education, social status, and political affiliation. Gradually, those dynamics should be reflected by the political parties both in their member composition and in the rhetoric that they use. A more united front would also help Taiwan's propaganda abroad by removing some of the contradictions in language and action that have befuddled foreign audiences.

This coming together of the various groups within Taiwanese society and of the main political parties is no wishful thinking. Rather, it is the logical outcome of a process of consolidation that began a long time ago and that has accelerated as a result of greater contact with China. Although this may not be what President Ma intended when he extended an olive branch to China, his cross-strait policies were instrumental to the rapprochement that has occurred within Taiwanese society.

The next step is to remove the dinosaurs in the main parties who oppose change whatever the cost, even if this is detrimental to Taiwan.

Lastly, Taiwan must think of the ways by which it can increase its *deterrence*, a strategy that has but is not limited to a military component. This strategy, which has a propaganda arm, is to be targeted directly at decision makers in Beijing in a way that convinces them that the costs of military adventurism would be such that they would overshadow the benefits, even if, in the end, the PLA did succeed in putting boots on Taiwanese soil. Working with allies overseas (secured using the first two legs of our strategy), Taipei could dispel some of the ambiguity that has surrounded a possible intervention by the U.S. and Japan during hostilities in the Taiwan Strait. In fact, part of Taiwan's propaganda efforts should aim at convincing Washington that this ambiguity, though it worked well for decades, has outlived its utility and now risks inviting adventurism and miscalculation by Beijing, which could convince itself that the U.S. will never intervene and that it can achieve its objectives quickly and "cleanly." Red lines and clearly signaled trip wires would contribute to Taiwan's deterrent against China, much more so than an ambiguous posture that risks being interpreted as weakness.

As important as the military aspects of deterrence are the political and economic elements, which can also be brought to bear against Beijing, especially as the decades of extraordinary economic growth in China show signs of deceleration. For all its attraction, China needs the rest of the world just as much as, if not more than the rest of the world needs China, something that is unlikely to change for decades to come. It needs the natural resources (energy, minerals, timber) that only countries like Russia, Australia, Canada, as well as parts of Africa, Central Asia, the Middle East, and South America can provide. Consequently, a concerted effort by the international community to prevent China from breaking international law over Taiwan or to punish it should it act on its threat would make the leadership in Beijing pay attention.

There should therefore be little doubt as to the severity of the costs in political and economic terms of a transgression that, as we saw, would very likely contribute to regional instability. In other words, rather than being regarded as a domestic affair, the Taiwan issue should be placed in its proper context, as both a matter of regional stability *and* a dispute that inevitably will have repercussions globally. Since the manner in which Beijing deals with Taiwan will serve as an indication of its future behavior on other matters, capitals around the world have every incentive to encourage Beijing to make decisions that are aligned with international law. Taiwan serves as a barometer of China's "rise," which gives it a powerful asymmetrical tool against its opponent. One wrong step, and China's international reputation could suffer a serious blow that will determine the course of its future relations with the region and the rest of the world. What needs to be drilled into the minds of the leaders in Beijing is that annexing Taiwan through force or coercion is not worth the price.

This takes care of the military aspects of the Taiwan Strait. What about other matters? Through the consolidation of its society and democracy, Taiwan could also promise that annexation – even by "peaceful" means – would result in serious unrest requiring the kind of pacification that, like war, would seriously endanger China's reputation abroad. In other words, Taiwan should turn itself into a kind of poison pill, one whose bitter taste overshadows whatever medicinal value it might have. By promising that the absorption of Taiwan would result in a major headache for the Chinese security apparatus – one that furthermore could spill over into other parts of China – Taiwan could make itself much less appealing to Beijing. As long as Taiwanese society is divided, it will be difficult to convince the CCP that such pain is possible. But a more united society, one that is in agreement on the need to avert unification, would present a much more credible threat.

Of course, none of those measures are a guarantee of success, but at the very least they make it less likely that Taiwan will lose. For the time being, maintaining its current independent status, however tenuous it might appear, should be the principal objective of all Taiwanese, as this buys them time to further consolidate their nation and to increase the costs of annexation by China. Hopefully over time, political change will occur in China where a leadership is willing to recognize that coexistence in the Taiwan Strait would be much more beneficial than persistent conflict or annexation against the wishes of millions of people. What form such coexistence would take is anyone's guess. But what is certain is that it would look nothing like what the current leadership in Beijing insists is the only solution to the Taiwan issue.

And whatever happens, the *sine qua non* is that the Taiwanese should *always* have a choice.

Note

1 The New Power Party won five seats in the 16 January 2016 legislative elections and displaced the Taiwan Solidarity Union as the third largest party in parliament.

Bibliography

Khétsun, T (2014) *Memories of Life in Lhasa Under Chinese Rule*, Matthew Akester, translator, New York: Columbia University Press
Roberts, D (2014) "Almost Half of China's Rich Want to Emigrate," *Bloomberg Businessweek*, 15 September, http://www.bloomberg.com/news/articles/2014-09-15/almost-half-of-chinas-rich-want-to-emigrate

ACKNOWLEDGMENTS

I will not even attempt to name all the individuals who played a role, directly or indirectly, in the creation of this book. Lest I commit some dreadful omissions, I will limit myself to generalizations. The people responsible know who they are.

This effort would not have come to fruition without the many people in Taiwan and overseas – from the local merchant to the senior government official – who generously gave time, advice, and ideas as I tried to make sense of the highly complex political scene in Taiwan and the equally daunting (albeit always fascinating) relationship in the Taiwan Strait. Literally hundreds of activists, officials, academics, journalists, and ordinary citizens opened their homes and hearts so that I could inch closer to the "truth" about Taiwan and, to the best of my abilities, attempt to translate all of this for an audience that may have only a passing interest in those issues. I thank each and every one of them. I would also like to thank the two anonymous reviewers whose excellent recommendations made this a better book. All errors in omission, commission, and inference are mine alone.

Still there are individuals whose role must be mentioned in other than general terms. Special thanks go to Yang Ju-yu, Hsia Chun-pei, and Lin Hong-tau at Business Weekly Publications for proposing this book project and encouraging me throughout its completion as I strove to meet the very strict deadlines imposed by the January 2016 elections. The Chinese version of this book was initially published in Taiwan under the title 島嶼無戰事：不願面對的和平假象. Nearly a decade ago, when I moved to Taiwan, I would never have imagined that one of the largest publishers in Taiwan would approach me to write a book about politics in Taiwan, let alone one that would be published in Chinese first. Thanks also go to Martin Williams, for offering me a job at the *Taipei Times* and helping launch my career in journalism. Martin has been a mentor, friend, and critic who never hesitated to pull me back down to earth when I erred or to pat me on the back when I hit the occasional home run. And to Mark Stokes of the Project 2049 Institute, who over the years has been a steady friend and a ceaseless source of ideas and inspiration and much guidance on a wide range of topics, from China's Second Artillery Corps to the GPD/LD's political warfare strategy.

To the editorial staff at *The Diplomat, The National Interest, The Wall Street Journal, China Brief, Asia Today International,* IHS Jane's, the *Taipei Times,* and the *Ottawa Citizen* for giving me the space I needed to connect with readers worldwide. To the members of the China Policy forum (C-POL) for the extraordinarily helpful and lively discussions on all things China, which have kept me abreast of the latest developments in China while I focused primarily on Taiwan. To the China Policy Institute at the University of Nottingham (Steve Tsang, Jon Sullivan) for making me a senior fellow *in absentia*, the French Center for Research on Contemporary China (Stéphane Corcuff) and the Thinking Taiwan Foundation. The views expressed here are entirely my own and do not necessarily reflect those of the institutions just mentioned.

To Antonio Chiang (江春男) for the wisdom and support, and to Tsai Ing-wen for convincing me to stay in Taiwan in early 2014. Not only did she make an offer that I could not refuse, she also gave me the complete latitude to do what needed to be done. She provided the home (temporarily, as it turns out) I needed so that I could continue my work on Taiwan.

To my parents, Réjane and Craig, for believing in me and for understanding why I do what I do. I should have been a better son and visited them more often in Canada. And to my parents-in-law, who welcomed me into their family and shared with me so much of their experiences, both as Taiwanese and as immigrants to the U.S. To Stephanie Lin, who brought me to Taiwan in the first place, where I found not only my calling but myself as well. And to our neighborhood's motorcycle repairman, whose simplicity and kindness kept us grounded and served as a constant reminder that our work on behalf of Taiwan isn't for the politicians, who far too often lose sight of the reason they entered politics in the first place, but for its people, who dream of a day when external powers will no longer seek to decide their future for them.

To the great George Orwell, for showing us how it's done.

Last but certainly not least, to Dr. Ketty W. Chen, my wife and intellectual partner, who never ceases to amaze me with her overabundance of talents. Her love and passion have sustained me through it all. She is my muse.

INDEX